FAULT LINES

FAULT

LINES

Fractured Families and
How to Mend Them

DR KARL PILLEMER

First published in the USA in 2020 by Avery
An imprint of Penguin Random House LLC

First published in Great Britain in 2020 by Yellow Kite
An imprint of Hodder & Stoughton
An Hachette UK company

1

A CIP catalogue record for this title is available from the British Library

Trade Paperback ISBN 978 1 529 34999 3
eBook ISBN 978 1 529 35148 4

Printed and bound in Great Britain by Clays Ltd, Elcograf S.p.A.

Hodder & Stoughton policy is to use papers that are natural, renewable and recyclable
products and made from wood grown in sustainable forests. The logging and manufacturing
processes are expected to conform to the environmental regulations of the country of origin.

Yellow Kite
Hodder & Stoughton Ltd
Carmelite House
50 Victoria Embankment
London EC4Y 0DZ

www.yellowkitebooks.co.uk

For my family, and families everywhere

Note to Readers

All names in this book are pseudonyms created by a random-names generator. Any resemblance to those of actual persons, living or dead, is entirely coincidental. Indeed, if you find your name in this book, you can be certain that it's *not* you. Please also note that the information in this book is not intended as psychological advice, nor is it a substitute for professional expertise or treatment. Readers should seek the advice of a qualified mental health provider with questions regarding specific family issues they are experiencing.

CONTENTS

INTRODUCTION

Once there was a boy named Christopher Robin. His greatest joy was to wander in the Hundred Acre Wood with his friends: the little bear named Winnie-the-Pooh, Piglet, Rabbit, Kanga, Roo, Eeyore, and other quirky, lovable animals. Christopher Robin participated in their many adventures and misadventures, living an enchanted childhood in a secure, benign world. My guess is that you read and loved these stories as a child (and watched the many movies based on them). If you are of a certain age, you have read them to your children and grandchildren.

You probably know that the stories are based on a real person: Christopher Robin Milne. The real Christopher Robin's father, the author A. A. Milne, wrote the stories for his son's enjoyment, based on Christopher Robin's menagerie of stuffed animals. The setting was a lovely forest near the family's summer house where father and son wandered and played together. We see these stories as testimony to the love of a father for his son, bringing his childhood fantasies to life. We imagine the warm, loving relationship that Milne and the real Christopher Robin must have had.

What you may not know about Christopher Robin Milne is this: He became estranged from his father, and they remained alienated throughout their lives. Milne believed that his father had stolen his childhood. By early adulthood, he felt that his father had never approved of him because he was not living up to the family name. From the vantage point of midlife, the younger Milne leveled the accusation that his father "had got where he was by climbing on my infant shoulders, that he had filched from me my good name and had left me with nothing but the empty fame of being his son." The estrangement extended to his mother, whom he did not see for the last decade of her life. The feeling was apparently mutual, as his mother pointedly refused a last visit from Christopher when she was on her deathbed.

Given this family's fame, why aren't these facts well known? For the same reasons that you do not know about your friends, neighbors, and co-workers who are in precisely the same situation right now. Shame, isolation, and embarrassment pervade family estrangements. In a society in which few topics are taboo, most people in a family rift feel so alone that they avoid speaking about it even to their intimate friends. Estrangement is hidden within the confines of the family and, when revealed, implies failure, poor judgment, and suspicious family secrets. As reported by many people in this book, revealing an estrangement from a parent, a child, or another close relative leads other people to silently wonder, *What's wrong with you?*

When I began my interviews with estranged people, I was not aware that they experienced such an acute sense of shame and isolation. One of my first interviews revealed the stigma attached to estrangement and gave me a powerful goal for this book.

Dominic Guerra has never given up trying to maintain a relationship with his parents, despite periods of estrangement that have lasted years. His story is complex, involving a difficult childhood, rejection of his wife by his family, and dueling views of past events. I was struck by the degree to which Dominic felt deeply alone. He told me:

> There's been many times where I have felt like I have the worst family situation ever. I know that's not true, but when I've had some irrational moments, I think that my situation is the most bizarre, the weirdest that could ever happen. If I could hear from other people who have had family complexities like this, it would help to know that I'm not alone, that every family has issues. And I would certainly be able to let them know that they're not alone if they heard my story.

The goal of this book is to bring the topic of estrangement out of the shadows and into the clear light of awareness and discussion. By mining the wisdom of hundreds of people who have experienced this problem, I will offer new insights, data, strategies, and practical tips for coping with and healing family rifts. Not all these ideas will apply to everyone, and some readers may fail to find solutions or will disagree with the advice offered here. However, I will feel that my years of work on this project and book are justified if I am successful in this one goal: creating an environment where people can freely acknowledge the problem and open up about solutions in productive and positive ways. If I accomplish nothing else, I want to reassure you that your family's situation is not the worst or the weirdest in the world, and that you are not alone.

HOW THIS BOOK CAME ABOUT

Like many important choices we human beings make, my decision to write this book emerged from disparate sources. Let me get the first one out of the way, because I can hear the questions in readers' minds: Yes, there have been estrangements in my extended family, and no, I'm not going to tell you much about them (as tempting as it may be). As to the first point, I have observed processes of estrangement and reconciliation up close and therefore have a personal understanding of family rifts and how they can be resolved. Regarding the second point, this book is not a first-person account of estrangement. One reason is that I cannot offer my relatives the anonymity I provided to my respondents, and I do not wish to cause new family rifts by revealing stories that are not mine to tell.

More important, however, is the scientific basis for this book. I conducted a series of studies over the past five years in what I named the Cornell Family Reconciliation Project. The research includes the most extensive in-depth interview study ever conducted on family estrangement and reconciliation. To gain an even broader perspective, I conducted a national survey of 1,340 individuals and interviews with marriage and family therapists. My goal is not to provide you with my own, necessarily limited, personal experience, but rather to offer concrete guidance using the "wisdom of crowds" on how to understand, cope with, and resolve family estrangements.

So, where did this book come from? It emerged in part from my career-long research interests. For over thirty years, I have studied family problems, such as conflict, domestic violence, and parental favoritism. I have helped pioneer the study of ambivalence in families, recognizing that our idealized expectations of the perfect family are never met. Everyone, to some degree, experiences a complex interplay of positive and negative thoughts and emotions about their families. We want closeness, but we simultaneously seek independence. We feel obliged to assist our family members, but we also resent their demands. When it comes to our typically untidy family lives, most people nod in agreement with the fully ambivalent old expression "Can't live with 'em, can't live without 'em!"

Thus, I was primed by years of research to look at family complexity, closely attuned not just to the cheerful outward appearances that make up social media posts but also to the darker sides of family life in which people feel unfulfilled, abandoned, or abused. But it took one particular event to make me decide to spend years studying family rifts and how to overcome them. I owe this book in part to a very special older person. Here's what happened.

In 2012, I published my book *30 Lessons for Living: Tried and True Advice from the Wisest Americans*. I had spent a decade interviewing people in their seventies, eighties, nineties, and beyond, focusing on members of the Great Depression and World War II generation. In long and detailed conversations, these elders openly discussed many emotionally charged issues, including bereavement, divorce, failure, and their fears about illness, dependency, and death. I traveled the country to talk with the "oldest and wisest" people among us, learning about their struggles and gathering their practical wisdom for living.

Fault Lines really began on an afternoon in Texas when I sat with one such elder, eighty-three-year-old Susan. Petite, feisty, and funny, she regaled me with stories of a "pretty darn good life," her travels, her two husbands, and her love to this day of a glass of fine bourbon. We spent a lot of the interview laughing together.

But when I asked about her relationships with her children, a storm cloud descended. Susan's face fell, she drew in a long breath, and then she exploded: "I don't know! I don't know what happened! I never hear from them, and it hurts like crazy!" She pounded her fists on the arms of her chair, and tears began to stream down her cheeks. Susan told me that she slowly grew apart from her two sons after divorcing their father. For many years, she ignored the gradual estrangement, but now her sons were not there at the end of her life, when she needed them the most. Birthdays and Christmases went unnoticed unless she reached out. Susan is not alone. Of all the regrets older people have, a family estrangement is often the most painful.

That meeting with Susan was a turning point in which I realized that people who are cut off from family members desperately need help. To test this idea, I wrote an article for my blog based on Susan's story. The response to this post on family members "who break your heart" was overwhelming. Over five thousand individuals continue to access that single post every month, and more than six hundred people provided heartbreaking accounts of their own experiences. Many comments contained the plea: "Isn't there any good advice for this problem?"

To my great surprise, and after an exhaustive search, I realized that the answer to this question is largely no. From a research standpoint, only about a dozen studies have been published in academic journals on the topic of family estrangement. There is also hardly any clinical literature on the topic (with the notable exception of the Bowen family systems theory, discussed in later chapters). The monumental *Handbook of Family Therapy* does not have an entry on "estrangement" in its index. Even the self-help literature on family estrangement is scarce, with only a handful of books published in recent years that offer guidance for dealing with family rifts.

I found myself sitting at my desk in the famously confused state of the

Grinch, who "puzzled and puzzled 'til his puzzler was sore." I opened up a file on my computer and wrote down the following statements:

- Estrangement touches millions of people and causes distress so profound that it can last a lifetime.

- Estrangement attracts hundreds of thousands of people to websites on the topic, surfaces regularly in highly publicized celebrity cases, and is a perennial staple of media coverage and advice columns.

- No reliable professional guidance exists for family estrangement, so most people who suffer from it are on their own in finding solutions.

- In what world does this make sense?

While I was pondering this state of affairs, something happened that has occurred only two or three times in my professional life. I was suddenly filled with an overwhelming desire to find out, a thirst to understand, a drive to bring a problem into the light and point the way to solutions. I realized in that moment that I was about to embark on an adventure. It would be a journey that would take me into some of the darkest recesses of family life, but that would also open up vistas for hope, reconciliation, and personal growth. In this book, I invite you to join me in exploring a problem that is hiding in plain sight in our society and around the world. Along the way, we will meet some extraordinary individuals who found new ways to rebuild broken relationships.

FROM ESTRANGEMENT TO RECONCILIATION

During the years after I decided to explore the world of family estrangement, my path took a number of interesting turns. But one such "course correction" was by far the most important. Take a look at the subtitle of this book and you will see that I set myself an ambitious goal, but I found myself stuck. I had learned an enormous amount about the "fractured families" in the subtitle. I was pretty much lost, however, on the topic of "how to mend them." What happened next transformed the project.

This book began as a volume on *estrangement*. I used a variety of methods (described in the Appendix) to locate a broad and diverse group of individuals who were cut off from other family members. My advertisements about the study reflected this goal: to speak with individuals who had no contact with one or more family members. Hundreds of people in that situation opened their hearts and minds to me, sharing their views on what had caused the estrangement, how it affected them, and how they coped. Some people had initiated the cutoff, whereas others were the involuntary recipients of the demand "Do not contact me anymore." They introduced me to a world of suffering that I had barely imagined.

For several years, I gathered and immersed myself in their stories. As I describe in Chapter 3, estrangement is an unimaginably painful experience for some individuals, one that dominates many of their waking hours. I sat with people who wept uncontrollably about their loss. I listened to the barely contained rage of parents or children who felt they had been abandoned, shunned, or cut off without warning. I heard stories of grandparents who conspired with friends to sneak a look on Facebook at a teenage grandchild they had never met.

I encountered over and over people who were stunned by the loss of the relationship, most of whom said, "I never imagined this could happen in our family!" I learned of mothers whose dying wish was simply that their children would reconcile and learn to love one another. Dozens of college students told of their struggles to find an identity and a mature sense of self without ties to one or both of their parents. Young mothers and fathers lamented the absence of loving grandparents in their offspring's lives, while elders longed for a lost relationship with grandchildren. Siblings of all ages mourned the lack of that lifelong kinship connection. I learned that the loss of contact with more-distant but once-beloved relatives—uncles, aunts, cousins, nephews, nieces—was also painful. Sometimes whole extended families were cleaved in two, as siblings, their children, and grandchildren took sides against one another.

As I was completing these interviews, I admit that I began to internalize some of their despair. I even found myself asking whether a book on this topic was possible. My original goal was to ask people experiencing estrangement about their advice for others. However, when I asked individuals in the throes of a family rift what counsel they would offer, I most often received the answer: "Well, if I knew what to do about estrangement, I would have already done it myself!" These interviewees did provide invaluable advice on the causes of long-term estrangement and ideas for what might prevent others from falling into that situation. Solutions, however, escaped them.

Thinking of the landscape of estrangement, I was haunted by the image of a vast canyon with crowds of people on either side, standing paralyzed at the edges. I understood why the geological term "rift"—meaning a fissure or crack in the ground like that resulting from an earthquake—feels so appropriate. Then I met Tricia Stewart, who showed me that building a bridge over a rift is possible, even in unlikely circumstances. Here's her story, as she told it to me while we sat together one spring afternoon.

Tricia's mother married a man with a criminal history and gave birth to Tricia as a teenager. Her parents were divorced when Tricia was very young, and she has few memories of the family being together. Tricia went to stay with her father when her parents divorced, visiting her mother on the weekends. Her mother lived on life's margins, becoming involved with a number of men. When Tricia was ten years old, her mother remarried and disappeared. Tricia told me:

> She moved without telling anyone. I came for my weekend visit and she was gone. She left whatever was in my room behind and moved. She dropped off the face of the earth. She just stopped communicating with me. I didn't speak to her again until near the end of high school, when her husband died. She called us the next day. She had been imprisoned by him, he beat her—it had been a bad situation.

Naive interviewer that I was, I made the initial mistake of assuming that Tricia's father had stepped in during the intervening years to be the supportive parent. Nothing could have been further from the truth. Tricia laughed at that suggestion and explained why: "At that time, my dad was not a good person. So, not only did my mom bail, but she left me with someone like my father. I was abused, both physical abuse from my dad and sexual abuse from people coming in and out of my life as a child. My dad was crazy; he couldn't really function well."

The story of Tricia's childhood went from bad to worse:

> So, my father was always a drug dealer my whole childhood. And I was made to sell drugs to people by the time I was ten. Someone would come by, and my dad wouldn't be there, and it'd be somebody that came regularly that I knew, and I would give it to them. That's just how my life was—I didn't know anything different. He never came to any of my sports or activities. Then he got busted for drugs, and it was in the newspapers. My friends were no longer allowed to come to my house, so I was suddenly disconnected from the friends that I had.

This tenuous arrangement lasted until Tricia was sixteen years old, when a crisis occurred. Her father had agreed to counseling with Tricia through a family services agency. On the day of an appointment, he hit Tricia and assumed that she would not mention it to the counselor. Tricia decided, for once, to stand up for herself and revealed the incident. The counselor, as a mandatory reporter, informed the authorities. "I fought back for the first time in my life. I was like, 'Never again. I will never let you touch me again. It's just not going to ever, ever happen again.'"

Tricia was allowed to become an emancipated minor, living on her own with state assistance. As she moved away from her troubled family relationships, her life improved dramatically. Now living on her own, she did well in school, worked part-time to help support herself, and excelled in sports. She obtained fulfilling work after high school, found a partner, and had a son, Brian, now in college. Brian's father was not long in the picture, but Tricia devoted herself to her son and to being the best parent she could be.

Tricia told her story in a way that had me in suspense regarding the current state of affairs. When I asked, "Where do the relationships with your parents stand now?" I assumed that I would hear the by-now-expected tale of separation, stonewalling, and avoidance that characterized the family relationships of many people with far less troubling histories. So the last thing I expected was to hear this survivor of abandonment, abuse, and deprivation tell me that she is in regular and largely positive contact with both parents. Through persistence, counseling, self-examination, and acceptance, Tricia has achieved a hard-won reconciliation with both her mother and, even more surprisingly, her father.

It was not until she reached her twenties that she allowed her mother and father to enter her life again. I asked Tricia why she would choose to reconcile with her parents in the face of such an adverse past. Over time, both parents had settled into new, healthier marriages and their lives had stabilized. More important, Tricia believed that her son should have a relationship with his grandparents. This reflects Tricia's values that give family life a central place. She told me:

> I have this idea of what a family should look like, and so to not have my parents be part of that, I just can't see that. I could see a million other people being in my shoes and never speaking to them again. It's not that I depend on them. I haven't depended on them since I was a teenager. But the idea of not having any contact or any relationship with them doesn't cross my mind—it really doesn't. I'd have to change my self-image, to be somebody else, in order to abandon them.

Reflecting on decades of stormy family drama, she told me that working to move through estrangement to reconciliation was worth the cost. Achieving the reconciliation taught her critically important lessons about how to meet her own needs while accepting differences and showing compassion to others. She explained: "My dad's not capable of saying he's sorry, because he doesn't really understand the ramifications of his actions. I can still be in a relationship with them and not own whatever they have going on. The biggest thing is being comfortable with who I am and the choices that I've made."

At the end of this intensely emotional interview, I felt like a lost traveler who was suddenly handed a road map. The landscape of estrangement, as I was conceptualizing it, was scarred by fault lines and vast rifts. Yet Tricia and, as it turned out, many other people managed to build a bridge.

After absorbing Tricia's story, my research goal shifted. I refocused my efforts on identifying people who had been fully estranged from one or more family members but had reconciled. You can imagine the challenge; there is no database or national organization of the "formerly estranged." Groups exist on various internet platforms, but I quickly learned that such sites attract only those who are currently estranged (indeed, a few even promote cutting oneself off from family).

I used "snowball sampling" techniques, in which a large group of people are contacted and then asked to contact others in turn to help find interviewees. I was greatly helped by my friend Amy Dickinson, the well-known "Ask Amy" syndicated advice columnist, who informed her readers about the project in her column. In the end, I was able to assemble a sample of one hundred reconciled individuals from across the country and all walks of life.

Of course, the themes of estrangement and reconciliation are closely intertwined in this book. I learned an immense amount both from people who remained estranged from a family member for decades and from those who reconciled. My respondents who have not reconnected taught me about the causes and consequences of a family rift and how some people move from anger and despair to acceptance. But because this book is for them and millions of people like them, it necessarily focuses to a greater degree on people who have sunk down into the depths of a rift and managed to find their way out. I expected them to be a powerful, rich source of practical wisdom and guidance for overcoming estrangement, and I was not disappointed. This book is built on their experiences, stories, and advice.

WHAT YOU WILL FIND IN THIS BOOK

The main goal of this book is to provide readers with a range of ideas that they can apply to their own situations. These ideas derive from two sources. First and foremost, the data were collected from individuals who have experienced estrangement. To mine the insights from these personal experts on family rifts, I went beyond all previous research to gather the richest possible detail. My efforts included following up with some of the estranged respondents over time to determine whether their situations had changed and interviewing more than one person in a number of families. I sought out unique opportunities, such as accompanying a son on his first meeting with his mother in twenty-five years.

In addition to the treasure trove of insights available from people who have deep personal experiences of family estrangement and reconciliation, I also bring in relevant psychological and sociological research. Scientific findings can help us step out of our own immediate situations and see how larger social and psychological forces push and pull our emotional responses to relationships. We will learn, for example, how estrangement is shaped by attachment and rejection, which can help us understand its negative effects. We will see that psychological research on self-esteem and defensiveness sheds light on how people become stuck in family rifts. My goal is both to provide the big picture of estrangement and to offer concrete tips, ideas, and strategies for resolving or coping with it.

Taken together, the information presented here is geared to help estranged people (and those who love them) step back and understand their relationships. Individuals in family rifts become so fixed in their own narratives that it becomes impossible to assess the facts of the situation or to adopt new perspectives in light of changed circumstances. The stories, examples, and science included in this book will help you get a new perspective, shake up what you are taking for granted, and thereby open up new possibilities for action. No one will find all the suggestions useful. But if some of the people are helped some of the time, the book will have achieved its purpose.

Fault Lines begins, in Part One, by exploring the "landscape of estrangement." In Chapter 1, I present data from the first national survey of estrangement ever conducted, showing how pervasive family rifts are in our society. These facts can help dispel the sense of isolation many people experience, demonstrating that if you are cut off from family members, you are definitely not alone. Next, in Chapter 2, I examine pathways to estrangement, profiling six common routes to a rift.

I then turn to the question of why estrangements are so painful and difficult. I show that even in our rapidly changing society, family relationships matter. Connections among parents, children, and siblings are "hardwired" into us, such that complete separation is among the most painful experiences in adulthood. In Chapter 3, I identify the "four threats of estrangement"—factors that threaten mental, social, and physical well-being. I show that estrangement can be best understood as a form of chronic stress, in which people experience common and sometimes devastating outcomes. Other threats come from broken attachment, rejection, and prolonged uncertainty.

In Chapter 4, I examine the aftershocks of a family rift for other relatives, which often force them to take sides. This "collateral damage" can separate grandparents from grandchildren and cousins from one another, who had no part in causing the rift. I also document the stress experienced by bystanders as they attempt to mediate among other family members or to support spouses as they negotiate estrangement.

Part Two, titled "The Road to Reconciliation," shifts the focus to creating a different future for estranged relationships. I begin by asking the question in Chapter 5, "Why reconcile?" It turns out that there are both obvious reasons to attempt a reconciliation and ones you may not have considered. In the chapters that follow, I share the suggestions of reconciled family members. In each chapter, I provide a section called "The Tool Kit," which contains specific advice for overcoming estrangement.

In Chapter 6, I look at a feature of many rifts: an outsize, single event that appears to have been the cause. I term these incidents "volcanic events," and I offer guidance for understanding them and using that knowledge as a step toward reconnecting. In Chapter 7, I examine a major barrier to reconciliation: forcing a relative to accept one's view of past events. In Chapter 8, I look at the importance of exploring one's own responsibility for the rift.

The following two chapters highlight critical steps for bridging the rift: changing our expectations for the relationship (Chapter 9) and setting boundaries (Chapter 10). I also delve into the important role of counseling in helping overcome or deal with an estrangement. In the final chapter, I show the value of offering "one more chance" to end a rift and provide suggestions for how to make that last chance work. The chapter concludes with a surprising insight from my research: how the process of overcoming an estrangement can be an engine for personal growth.

The advice in this book comes directly from hundreds of individuals who have experienced almost every conceivable aspect of estrangement and reconciliation. The premise is that real people who have been through a challenging experience are extraordinary sources of advice. I firmly believe that when scientists have the answers, we should consult them. But I am also convinced that we can learn invaluable lessons about how to overcome family problems from people who have walked the path themselves. You don't have the time and resources to survey hundreds of people for their group wisdom about family rifts. I've done that work for you, summarizing and synthesizing what they told me so that you can put it to use.

I want to alert you to some things you will not find in this book, or which I treat in only a limited way. First, every reader must be clear that *nothing in this book should be seen as clinical or psychological advice*. I am a research sociologist and have no clinical credentials of any kind. Estrangement can be a traumatic, disturbing, anxious, and depressing experience. Nothing in *Fault Lines* replaces the assistance you can receive from a psychotherapist or other counseling professional.

You will note that I have devoted limited attention to the prevention of estrangement. I do so for two reasons: First, there is a lack research on what leads to family rifts and there have been no studies, to my knowledge, of how they may be prevented. Second, I went to my respondents to learn their prevention advice, but in most cases I received answers like, "If I knew how to prevent an estrangement, I wouldn't be where I am now."

I examine different reasons for family estrangement in Part One, and selected causes are discussed further in Part Two. But my belief is that readers of this book are most interested in what they can do to overcome an estrangement, rather than ruminating about how they got there. Further, I do not treat in depth the issue of how to adapt to and cope with an ongoing estrangement. Again, my respondents generated only limited ideas on that topic, and the possible solutions and treatments, such as counseling, are similar to those for other family problems.

In this book, you will find stories of tragedy, conflict, strength, joy, and sometimes even humor. Together, they shed light on what happens when people are cut off from family members and what they can do to get back into their lives. For individuals experiencing estrangement, and people who care about them, I use my interviews to offer new ideas, practical tips, and possible techniques for reestablishing connections to relatives. However, this book has a larger goal as well: to shed light on the complex world of family life in the twenty-first century.

We are living through one of the most extraordinary demographic changes in history: the dramatic increase in the human life span. This means that the amount of time children spend in the home with their parents is only a fraction of the shared lifetime they will have together. Indeed, after our offspring reach age eighteen, we are likely to have thirty, forty, or even fifty more years to go in the relationship. Our sibling ties may now last ninety or more years. The huge "longevity bonus" means that our family relationships can affect us—positively or negatively—for many decades.

We live in a time in which pundits and opinion-makers frequently downgrade the importance of family life. We hear that families are fading in importance and that people are becoming unmoored as a result. These stereotypical views, however, are misleading. Surveys show that for most people around the world, the family is still the strongest and most reliable source of support. It is where they turn in times of trouble and where they go to celebrate life's milestones and successes. By examining situations in which family bonds break down completely and exploring how they can be rebuilt, I hope to capture the critical importance of family as a key resource in a challenging and rapidly changing world, and show how the fabric of family life can stay intact for a lifetime.

PART ONE

THE LANDSCAPE OF ESTRANGEMENT

CHAPTER 1:

YOU ARE NOT ALONE

Five years ago, my husband and I were cut off completely from our daughter, and nothing we do has made any difference in getting back together with her. When we meet people, it's devastating to tell the truth, but we deal with it by being straightforward: "Oh, there are problems," or "We don't see each other." It is not a question that they will ask more about. It is such an intimate topic—it's almost like talking about hemorrhoids or other things that people just don't want to hear. I've been approached by former neighbors and they say, "Well, you seem like such nice people. How come it's like this?" We're labeled with this black cloud.

The big thing that I would recommend is that estranged people should not feel they are isolated in corners, because it's not just happening to them, and they should share it. It's letting the news out that you are not alone. This is happening in many families, and when someone hears our story, they may then say, "We have it too."

—SKYE FERRARO

We live in a world where personal problems are made public, from struggles with mental illness to histories of abuse and intimate details of sex lives. Reality television, although heavily scripted, has encouraged an "anything goes" attitude toward sharing information about ourselves. The "private" has become so public that some people document much of their lives on social media. Therefore, it is striking when one comes upon a topic that is *not* freely exposed to others. Estranged people do not feel part of a community that can share its pain in public. Across hundreds of interviews, I heard one particular phrase over and over: "I thought I was the only one." Among the estranged, there is a pervasive feeling of being all alone in a world that doesn't understand this problem.

Kristine Freeman was by all appearances a vibrant, successful career woman. A business executive, she led a large work team and was considered to be an exceptional communicator and an empathetic boss. Her second marriage was warm and loving, and she relished the role of mother to her young son. To others, her life seemed full and balanced. But Kristine suffered in silence with a shameful secret: Her parents had rejected her and driven her from their lives.

The estrangement began when Kristine decided to divorce her first husband after years of increasing unhappiness. She avoided informing her parents for months that the marriage was ending. She told me: "I never wanted to detail what was going on in my private life, so nobody really knew what awful stuff I was dealing with in my marriage. All they saw were the beautiful white picket fences, and everything was great. But I wasn't great." Her mother's reaction when told about the divorce was angry and punitive:

> My mother completely rejected me. She said some harsh things to me and told me that I had made a vow to God and I had disobeyed my marriage vows. I would hear from people I knew that she was talking about me and praying for me that I would see things the way that she wanted me to see things. I had made a decision to better myself and to become happy, and my mother could not understand that and didn't want to understand it. So we were estranged for over five years.

There was much that pained Kristine about the estrangement. Her prior relationship with her parents had been close, and she deeply felt the loss of contact. She stayed away from family gatherings to avoid interacting with her mother. Her holidays were lonely, and she felt unmoored in her life without connections to her family. But above all, she felt *alone*. She told me:

> It was very difficult—I had no one. You feel as if you are being looked at like you're in the spotlight on a stage and you're being judged by everyone. All I knew was my parents didn't want me. I was on my own in dealing with it. That's where a lot of the fear of judgment and embarrassment came from, because I didn't know how prevalent estrangement was. I didn't know there were other people out there that were dealing with this same problem.

Society's expectations for family life compound the feelings of aloneness. We still hold to the cultural ideal that the family should be, in the famous words of Christopher Lasch, "a haven in a heartless world." Family means unbreakable bonds, loyalty in even the most trying circumstances. We present our family lives in idealized ways on social media. On Facebook, there are many photos of happy family events, but few of relatives sulking and weeping after a fight. Celebrities like Angelina Jolie and Meghan Markle are excoriated in the press because of their family estrangements. Estrangement is a stigma, a social identity that makes other people value them less. Individuals who perceive themselves as stigmatized often feel alone in an unsympathetic world.

But are estranged people really so alone? Or are they, in fact, in the company of many others? I set out to answer that question using scientific survey methodology. My goal was to understand the landscape of estrangement by providing hard data about how many people's lives are touched by the problem. First, however, we need to spend a little time on what we mean by "estrangement."

DEFINING "ESTRANGEMENT"

There is a famous statement that has been used in many contexts: "I don't know how to define _____, but I know it when I see it." That blank can be filled in with anything from "modern art" to "pornography." The same holds true for the subject of this book; writers on the topic have created varying definitions of "estrangement." I won't be able to solve the definitional problem here (and you would probably stop reading at this point if I tried to), but it's important to describe what "estrangement" means for our purposes.

The consensus is that estrangement involves cutting off regular contact between two or more family members. After that, however, things get tricky. Some researchers believe that estrangement must always involve experiencing the cutoff as negative, resulting from conflict, disagreement, or other difficult or disturbing interactions. Other writers on the topic discuss "emotional estrangement," in which contact of some kind continues but in an atmosphere of emotional distance and detachment. Another distinction is whether estrangement means that all contact of any kind has ended, or whether people can have marginal interaction (e.g., being copied on a family email or allowed to be a "friend" on Facebook) but still be considered estranged.

I am now going to let you in on a trick we social scientists use. As you can imagine, we conduct research on many topics that are hard to define, and on which reasonable people disagree mightily about the definition. For example, a term like "child abuse" has many definitional controversies: How does it differ from socially accepted punishment of children, for example, and how do we account for cultural differences in what people consider abusive? Nowadays, what used to be considered simple categories, like race and gender, also create definitional struggles. What's a poor sociologist to do?

When in doubt, we *operationalize*. That is, we take a concept like "estrangement" and tell you how we defined it and measured it for a particular purpose. My goal in organizing the interviews for this book was to cast a wide net and avoid artificial restrictions that would exclude people who might see themselves as estranged. At the same time, I needed to set some boundaries so readers would know what I am talking about. Therefore, when I asked people to be interviewed for this book, I told them, "By 'family estrangement,' we mean situations in which a family member has cut off contact from one or more of their relatives." I did not restrict participation based on why contact stopped, allowing the reasons to include conflict, disagreements, distance, and other factors.

However, I went a step beyond this definition in two ways. First, I asked people not only if they were *currently* cut off from family members, but also if they had *ever* been estranged. I expected that people would move in and out of estrangements over their lives, and I was interested in people who were once estranged but now reconciled. Second, I sought to include people who were estranged themselves as well as some individuals who were affected by a rift that did not directly involve them. Later in this book, you will see how useful these interviews were in understanding a rift's "collateral damage" and the way other family members can help or hinder reconciliation.

The people who appear in this book perceive themselves as having experienced—temporarily or permanently—a complete cutoff from one or more relatives. There was, in fact, little ambiguity about whether an estrangement was present or not in these families; simply by using the word "estranged" in introducing my interviews, people understood exactly what I was looking for. I did not nitpick over minor issues; for example, if someone attended a family gathering where the estranged relative was present, he or she was still considered estranged.

This book is premised on the idea that estrangement is *different*. It is different from family feuds, from high-conflict situations, and from relationships that are emotionally distant but still include contact. As later chapters in this book make clear, the declaration of "I am done" with a family member is a powerful and distinct phenomenon, one that affects people in different ways from a conflictual relationship. In this book, we will spend our time with people who experienced as complete a relationship cutoff as is possible in our connected society, some of whom later resumed contact and others who did not.

ARE YOU ALONE OR NOT?

On any given day, how many people would answer yes to the question, Are you estranged from one or more relatives? Before I give you an answer, take a minute for a thought exercise. Think about what you have heard about estrangement from your friends, relatives, co-workers, and acquaintances. Consider also what you have seen in the media. Approximately how many people are estranged from someone? According to popular culture, estrangement is a "silent epidemic." Is that the case?

When I began exploring the topic, I was surprised to learn that no one had an answer to those questions. As a survey researcher, I knew what I needed to do next: Conduct a survey! Over the course of my career, I've surveyed thousands of people about very sensitive topics, and I knew from experience that we could get solid information on an issue like this by asking directly.

The survey methods are described in detail in the book's Appendix. In brief, I obtained a nationally representative sample of 1,340 Americans ages eighteen and older. Everyone was asked this question: "Do you have any family members (i.e., parents, grandparents, siblings, children, uncles, aunts, cousins, or other relatives) from whom you are currently estranged, meaning you have no contact with the family member(s) at the present time?" You will see that this question is broader than just estrangement between parents and children, which has been the topic of most research. It also doesn't mince words; I clearly asked about a complete end to contact.

How much estrangement is there? Over one-quarter of Americans surveyed—27 percent—reported currently being estranged from a relative. Extrapolated to the U.S. adult population, that's around 67 million people. By any standard, that is a very impressive number. However, the actual prevalence of estrangement is likely higher, as some survey respondents may have not wished to admit the problem. Therefore, the 27 percent figure should be considered a low estimate of the scope of family rifts.

With whom are people estranged? Around 10 percent of the total sample were estranged from a parent or a child. Translated to the United States population, approximately 25 million people are cut off from a parent or a child. Overall, 8 percent of the total sample was estranged from a sibling, which translates in the U.S. population to around 20 million individuals. The remainder of the estrangements (9 percent of the sample) involved, in order of prevalence, cousins, aunts and uncles, grandparents, nieces and nephews, and other relatives. This percentage translates to 22 million Americans.

For those of you currently involved in a family rift, you are indeed not alone. You are in the company of over a quarter of the U.S. population. However, here's a question you may be asking: Does my survey overstate the amount of estrangement? After all, people might have no contact because they have simply lost touch or haven't gotten around to calling each other in a while. To look at that issue, I asked how people felt about the rift and how long it had gone on.

I asked everyone who reported being estranged, "How upsetting is it to you to be estranged from your relative?" When I removed those who said they were not upset at all about the rift, the percentage of estranged people dropped from 27 percent to 22 percent—not a major reduction. That's still around 55 million Americans who have at least one estrangement in their families that bothers them to some degree. Everyone was also asked how long the estrangement had gone on. The vast majority (85 percent) had been estranged for a year or more, and fully half of the respondents had not had contact with the relative for four years or more. Thus, even under more restrictive definitions of "estrangement," a large number of Americans are facing long-standing and upsetting family rifts.

A PROBLEM FOR EVERYONE

Some problems concentrate more heavily in certain groups. Malnutrition, for example, is much more likely to occur among poor people. Both genders experience depression, but women tend to be more affected than men. Other life challenges are more evenly distributed throughout the population. To examine the assertion that estranged people are not alone, I used the national survey data to answer the question: Are certain groups more likely to report estrangement than others? That is, do family rifts primarily occur in a small subset of the population? I learned that the answer to that question is clearly no.

The data allowed me to look at whether there were differences in estrangement according to the following factors: race, marital status, gender, educational level, age, and geographical region. Social scientists look for what are termed "statistically significant" differences—that is, differences that are large enough that they are unlikely to have occurred by chance. There was only one way in which estranged people differed from other individuals: their age group. People were somewhat less likely to be estranged if they were under age thirty-five or over age sixty-four. However, this finding is easily explained: People in their middle years are likely to have both living parents and adult children (and to still have living siblings and grandparents). Thus, middle-aged people are more likely to report being estranged because they have a larger potential pool of relatives with whom rifts might occur.

For all the other variables I was able to measure, family rifts appear to know no bounds. They are equally prevalent whether one identifies as White, Black, Latino, or Asian American; across social classes (as measured by educational level); between men and women; and throughout all regions of the United States. These findings support the idea that you are not alone in an estrangement, but rather are in the company of people from all walks of life and social situations.

As compelling as these findings are, the numbers do not entirely speak for themselves. What do these unique data tell us? By any standards, estrangement is a big issue. Anything that affects up to one-quarter of American adults deserves serious attention. Even if we look only at immediate families (parents, children, and siblings), nearly one-fifth of American adults (or over 44 million people) consider themselves estranged. I will admit that I was astonished by these numbers, and they confirm many people's belief that estrangement is widespread.

Paradoxically, there is some good news here. The media and social networking sites for estranged parents and children may overestimate just how often that specific type of estrangement occurs. I found in the survey that around one in ten parents and children are experiencing a rift between them. Put another way, in 90 percent of families, parent-child contact still goes on. This finding is consistent with the general research literature on parent-child relations throughout the life course, which shows that the majority of both older parents and adult children report good-quality relationships.

You may be feeling like former president Harry Truman, who was so tired of economists saying "on the one hand . . . on the other hand" that he asked for a one-handed economist. In fact, we can have it both ways. Most parents and children make it through life without becoming estranged. But lots of people experience just such a fracture and suffer greatly as a result.

The data also show that estrangement goes well beyond just the parent-child relationship and is widespread among other relatives as well. That's why this book takes a unique perspective, including all kinds of family rifts. For many people, losing the relationship with a beloved cousin, uncle, aunt, or grandparent can be a terrible thing. I want to assure all of you in those situations that you, too, are not alone.

In the Introduction, I invited you to accompany me on a journey to explore the landscape of estrangement in families. In this first chapter, we have looked carefully at the terrain, gaining an overview of the extent of family rifts. We learned that the estranged are absolutely not alone. Instead the problem is extensive; most Americans have either experienced it or have a close relative or friend who has. We found out that many people feel isolated and stigmatized by the estrangement, such that they hide the problem from all but their closest associates.

The playwright Anton Chekhov described the common belief that everyone else's life is better than our own, writing: "Think of all the people who go to the market to buy food, who eat in the daytime and sleep at night, who prattle away, merry . . . But we neither hear nor see those who suffer, and the terrible things in life are played out behind the scenes." Psychologists have shown that we overestimate our own emotional problems in comparison with others', because most of us suppress our negative emotions when we are out in public. We are, as the psychologist Alexander Jordan has pointed out, "embarrassed by our own sadness." He explains: "With everyone reluctant to express their genuine attitudes lest they be embarrassed or rejected by peers, people end up feeling more alone in their private attitudes than is warranted."

Being able to compare difficult emotional experiences helps us to become more realistic about problems like estrangement, to get new ideas for how to cope, and to make us feel less isolated or—as some of my respondents put it—less "weird." In the next chapter, we will look at common routes to estrangement. We then will explore the damaging effects of life in the rift, both for those involved in estrangements and for others who are unwillingly pulled into them.

CHAPTER 2:

PATHWAYS TO ESTRANGEMENT

I made some life choices that conflicted with my mother's beliefs, and she completely rejected me. She said harsh things to me, and I decided that I could no longer be in contact with her. The more she tried to get me to see things her way or believe her beliefs, the further it pushed me away. I want to understand what led us here. You're always thinking of what has transpired and how you were treated. I reached a point where I was continually saying, "Why me, why me, why me?"

I have uncovered some reasons. I looked at our past history, and I realized that my family is cold. I really, truly don't remember being told "I love you" at all. Another reason is how much our values differed. I made my choices to be happy. In my eyes, I think God would want me to be happy. But my mother was not open and didn't want to hear what was going on with me. I've learned that each estrangement is unique, because we all have our own personalities and our own outlooks. Everyone wants to be given a road map to understand this situation, but we eventually have to create our own story.

—LYDIA PETERSON

"I am done."

That phrase sealed many of the estrangements described in this book. When one family member says it to another, the meaning varies: The person is done trying, done working to make the relationship better, done accommodating demands, done overlooking intolerable behavior, done apologizing for a lifestyle to someone who does not approve, or done with disrespect for a spouse or partner. Whatever the context, the words have a stark finality, and most people who utter them to a family member mean them that way. It is the end of the line, and there is no way forward.

The person who declares—sometimes for good reason—that he or she is "done" often sees the rift as inevitable. Frieda Greenwood, who is estranged from her emotionally abusive mother, felt all other possibilities were exhausted: "I don't have the time and the emotional space. I'm not going to drain myself. I feel like I've wasted far, far too much of my inner and outer life wrestling with family-of-origin issues. I just don't want to waste any more of it. I don't want to give that emotional energy away anymore."

Jeanette Vogel suffered a challenging relationship with her son Joey for two decades. She and her husband struggled to support Joey in the face of his insults, criticism, erratic behavior, and dishonesty. In her mid-sixties and with positive relationships with her other offspring, Jeanette was *done*. She told me:

> When I think of what he's done that was so unfair and how disrespectful he is, I think, "I don't want you in my life. If you were a stranger, I would never let you treat me that way." I don't want to live without him, but I certainly am going to live without him. I have other children and grandchildren, and they're enough. With Joey, I'm done.

Over and over, I heard this finality in statements from people who decided that no contact was better than enduring the stress of the relationship. Long-term bonds of attachment and cultural norms of family solidarity exert powerful influences. They lead us to remain in contact with difficult family members, even in the face of conflict and disappointment. Some individuals, however, overcome these pressures and declare the relationship to be over. In a rift, the age-old relationship question—"Should I stay or should I go?"—is resolved by saying: "I'm gone." The question remains: How does a family reach this point of no return?

From my studies, I discovered that there is no easy answer to this question. The decision to terminate a family relationship follows a path that twists and turns its way to that bleak destination. I learned that each situation is unique; of my 270 interviews, there are 270 individual routes to standing on the edge of the rift with a relative on the other side. No two families are alike; history, personalities, and traumatic events combine in infinitely diverse ways.

Given this complexity, what can we say about how some families wind up in rifts whereas others do not? Through careful analysis of my in-depth interviews, it was possible to identify pathways to estrangement. By "pathways," I mean identifying diverse trajectories that unfold across people's lives, leading to the same outcome. My interviews provided an "up close and personal" view of many individual stories, offering insight into how and why family issues led to estrangement. Qualitative research like mine allows us to look at the typical journeys traveled by these families, why a particular journey is undertaken, and what factors shape the journey. If it is not possible to pinpoint a single cause of family rifts (and a Nobel Prize awaits whoever does), we can do the next best thing: Identify what some journeys to estrangement have in common.

Based on my large and diverse sample, I was able to identify six common routes to the destination "I'm done." In later chapters, we will delve further into specific causes, but here I would like to orient you to the landscape of estrangement by describing six pathways that lead from family connection to estrangement:

- **The Long Arm of the Past.** The groundwork for an estrangement can be established early in a person's life, through disruptions and difficulties that occur while growing up in the family. A history of harsh parenting, emotional or physical abuse and neglect, parental favoritism, or sibling conflict can shape relationships decades into the future.

- **The Legacy of Divorce.** One frequent scenario for estrangement involves the long-term effects of divorce on adult children. Loss of contact with one parent and hostility between the former spouses can weaken parent-child bonds.

- **The Problematic In-Law.** In-law relations cause strains in many families. They can reach a breaking point, however, when the struggle between the family of origin and the family of marriage becomes intolerable.

- **Money and Inheritance.** Money may not be the root of all evil, but it is the origin of a striking number of estrangements. Conflicts over wills and inheritance emerged as a major source of family rifts.

- **Unmet Expectations.** Family relationships are built on expectations. We expect our parents, children, siblings, and other relatives to step up in times of crisis and to involve us meaningfully in family events like weddings and funerals. When our relatives violate norms for what we believe is proper behavior, people can become estranged.

- **Value and Lifestyle Differences.** Disapproval of a relative's core values can turn into outright rejection. Estrangements result from conflicts over issues like same-sex relationships, religious differences, or adopting alternative lifestyles.

I will profile each of these pathways, introducing a family in each one who traveled this route to estrangement. Then we will explore some possible causes of estrangement that cut across the individual pathways.

THE LONG ARM OF THE PAST

Some estrangements have deep roots in the past. Early experiences such as harsh parenting, substance abuse, and obvious parental favoritism have lasting effects. The desire to escape from one's family can form early in life, and a legacy of negative interactions (including teasing, jealousy, and sibling aggression) can make cutting a relative off seem like a justifiable choice.

Dani Bartlett grew up in a small picture-perfect Midwestern suburb, with stately homes, manicured lawns, and driveways strewn with tricycles, soccer goals, and basketball hoops. As Hollywood loves to show us, however, calm and pleasant exteriors sometimes mask complex and painful family dramas. Dani was raised in one such home.

Her father was born in this suburb, and his parents still reside there, a half mile away. Dani's father's success as a financial manager allowed him to purchase his own comfortable house and her mother to stay home full-time with Dani and three younger siblings. Dani is now twenty-one and an undergraduate at a university. Her childhood memories reflect the troubled interior of suburban family life:

> I was the first child, and my mother was abusive toward me. She wanted me to do really well in school, but there were things that I was struggling with, and I couldn't keep up with what she wanted. When I couldn't do that, it ended up with me being locked in the basement. She would punish me by not giving me food. It is the same with my younger siblings. Every time she gets mad, she breaks one of their toys or something else absurd, and no one knows how to deal with it. She isn't really fit to be a mother. She was also very abusive toward my father. She would call him terrible things, and she'd slap him, which led to police getting involved and my mother just getting angrier.

The last straw in the relationship with her mother occurred when Dani was in high school:

After a school event, she was driving in the car with me. She kicked me out of the car because I made a crude joke. Then she started speeding after me and almost hit me with the car. I had to call 911 and the police came. I went to my grandparents' house, and I just said, "I can't do this anymore." My grandparents took me in. I haven't talked to my mother in five years.

Her nurturing grandparents allowed her, despite her age, to separate completely from her mother:

I have no contact with her, although I am still in touch with my father. There's been a time or two where I've driven by her in town, and we'll make eye contact, but I'll just turn away. The only exception is I'll call home asking for a sibling, and she always asks, "Who is this?" I'll say my name, and she'll give them the phone. When I moved out, my mother really started getting worried, because she didn't think that anything would happen as a result of her abuse. She now understands that I'm not making any contact and she doesn't push it.

Dani has accepted the estrangement and is not optimistic that it will ever change. She told me:

I've grown to a point where I'll be fine. I worry about my siblings and will until they are old enough to move out of the house. Maybe when that happens, my mother will come to her senses a little bit more. Will I ever speak to her again? I haven't made up my mind completely. But as of now, she's in an emotional or mental health state where it's not beneficial for me to let her in.

THE LEGACY OF DIVORCE

Divorce can have negative effects on children's relationships with parents that reach into adulthood. Although the legacy of divorce can affect the tie to either parent, research tells us that it tends to weaken the father-child bond in particular. Of course, this effect varies greatly, and some fathers remain close and influential figures in their children's lives. But other divorced fathers move, find new partners, and become invested in a new family. They may feel that their former spouse is an obstacle to involvement with children, and they also can experience problems in their own lives that hinder contact. It is not surprising, therefore, that a number of estrangements in my studies involved the offspring of divorced parents.

The challenges of maintaining a relationship with her father, Luis, after her parents' divorce have affected Elena Fuentes from the time she entered college to the present, fourteen years later. Her family immigrated from Venezuela to Miami shortly before Elena was born. Elena told me that describing her childhood relationship to her father is not easy, as it involves both strongly negative and positive memories:

> When I was a kid, he would do things that were odd and uncomfortable behavior for me. My dad had a drinking issue. On his day off, he would drink all day and become a little incoherent and too emotional. I remember my dad being flirtatious with other women, being inappropriate in front of strangers. It turned out he had relationships with a number of other women. My mom seemed to live in a bubble, as if she didn't see it—she was a little blind to things.

But as in many parent-child relationships, good times were mingled with the bad for Elena. Reflecting on why she tried to maintain the relationship, Elena looked back to her childhood:

> Fortunately or unfortunately, however you want to look at it, I do have love for him. Growing up with him, I have some fond memories. He was a very playful guy. He would take us out, he would tell us that he loved us all the time. He would speak to us in English, even though he didn't speak it very well, because he wanted to assimilate and he saw it

as a fun opportunity to bond with us. Things were sometimes bad, but they were definitely not all bad.

Problems between her parents increased when Elena was in high school. She told me: "He would do a lot of suspicious things that didn't add up until he finally left the family for another woman. He told my mom, 'I don't want to be with you anymore.'" Luis wanted his children to accept his new partner and welcome her into their lives, and he refused to take any blame for the divorce. Elena's mother felt humiliated by his behavior and his treatment of her.

Despite the difficult history and the divorce, Elena initially did not give up on her father. She explained: "I wanted to continue a relationship with my dad, and I tried for many years. Although there had been a lot of tension over the years, I got past it and tried my best with him. Once I had a child, he wanted to be involved with our family and to be part of his granddaughter's life." However, Elena continued to struggle with Luis's self-centeredness; he ostensibly wanted a relationship with Elena and her family, but only when it was convenient for him. Arguments intensified over issues like when and where they would meet, and Luis's unreliability. As in many estrangements, a key event occurred that proved to be the last straw.

Elena described what happened:

There was a pivotal moment when I felt like he wanted to have a relationship with us only on his terms. He would cancel or not show up for something all the time, but if I canceled on him or if I was too busy, he was deeply offended. He would yell at me and insult me. The last time, he was yelling at me on the phone, and I reached a point where I said to him, "I'm going to hang up the phone, because if you can't speak to me like an adult, then I don't want to speak to you. When you're ready to speak to me like an adult, then call me back." And he never did. And here we are.

Elena came to the conclusion that contact with her father was more painful than estrangement:

> I decided I didn't want to put my children through periods of them being happy with their grandpa and then they don't see him for ages. The up-and-down relationship was too much of the same stuff I went through. So I cut the tie, at least until I see a change in his behavior and an apology for everything I went through emotionally, because there was a lot of emotional damage.

It was difficult, but Elena resolved her ambivalence—at least temporarily—by giving up on her father. A businesswoman, Elena took a long, hard look at what the relationship was costing her and her family. She used a metaphor from economics:

> I reached the point of giving up by asking, "What is the rate of return on this?" You know what "ROI" is? "Return on investment." Sometimes, you have to do an ROI on relationships. I felt that at this moment, this is the best way it can be. Family gatherings are easier to handle without him. I don't have to deal with constant arguments and me feeling disrespected. I don't worry about finding out new information about him that's going to bother me and make me overanalyze things. I looked at the return on investment. "What am I getting out of a relationship with him?" It was really not much. There's a part of the heart that always wants to explore getting back in touch with him. But my heart is also with what is best for my children and for me.

THE PROBLEMATIC IN-LAW

It's no coincidence that popular culture focuses so heavily on in-law relationships. I grew up with comic strips like *The Born Loser* and *Andy*

Capp, in which mothers-in-law were portrayed as large, aggressive, and threatening characters to be avoided at all costs by hapless husbands. More recent television shows and movies maintain the stereotypes—witness the meddling mom and dad in *Everybody Loves Raymond* and movies like *Meet the Parents*. These images reflect deep-seated worries about balancing loyalty to one's spouse with lifelong bonds of attachment and obligation to parents, siblings, and other kin. This worry is not an irrational one; research also shows that in-law relations are a key determinant of marital happiness.

The risk of estrangement increases because of the structural differences between family and in-law relations. Whereas we grow up with loyalty toward our family of origin and an almost intuitive understanding of their motivations and behaviors, in-laws can be seen as interlopers who disturb the family's equilibrium. Cindy Barber summed up this fact succinctly:

> I figured out a long time ago that the only trouble with in-laws is that *they are not you*. They don't have the history you have. That's what makes your family easier to deal with, because you know what to expect. But your in-laws' biggest sin is they're not you and they're not your family.

In some families I studied, the balancing act proved to be impossible, and an estrangement resulted. A common pattern occurred when a new spouse deliberately attempted to isolate the partner from his or her family. The tie to the spouse typically wins out, sometimes resulting in not only emotional distance but also a physical move away from the extended family. In other situations, the new spouse was perceived as demanding, difficult, or hostile, which repelled in-laws from interacting with the couple. A further scenario involves the family's rejection of a new partner because of differences in personality characteristics, values, or religious views. Over time, the rift deepens and the pair further removes themselves from relatives, who may also lose contact with the couple's children.

Roy Shaw found his true love—and lost his family. Of course, nothing is that simple, but the seeds of Roy's years-long estrangement were planted when he met Camille in college. The couple shared many interests, but most important, they shared a set of basic values. Both admit they are "save the world" types, choosing careers in the human services field because of their desire to improve the lives of disadvantaged people. Their relationship was not always smooth; Roy concedes that he had lots of growing up to do and that he sometimes had difficulty controlling his emotions. But Roy and Camille knew they were right for each other, and they worked hard at building a strong relationship.

Like many young couples, they talked about what the future would be like, sharing their dreams and aligning their plans. But they did not anticipate what would become the major impediment to their budding relationship: Roy's family. His parents disliked Camille and disapproved of the relationship. Roy's brother, Bob, was particularly vehement in his hostile reaction to Camille, repeatedly urging Roy to break off the relationship. Bob's opposition influenced his parents, who became hardened in their view that the relationship was unhealthy and should be ended.

Roy believes that the rejection occurred in part because he and Camille were too honest with their opinions about social justice, which conflicted with his parents' conservative and materialistic values. They believed Camille had unduly influenced Roy in this countercultural direction. The family was close when Roy was growing up; indeed, so close that there was little respect for necessary boundaries. Roy's parents, therefore, felt free to invade the couple's developing relationship, seeking to stop it before it really got started. Bob's and Camille's values and personalities also clashed. Roy told me:

> Camille was my fiancée at the time, and my brother was against her. Bob gave me an ultimatum: Either you choose Camille or you choose us, the family. I tried to understand, but I said, "I'm not going to call off my engagement just because you guys have concerns about Camille." That really set things off.

The relationship with his parents had improved somewhat by the time Roy and Camille married a few years later. Roy's mother and father attended; his brother did not. However, the honeymoon was barely over when arguments began again. The family persisted in their attempts to convince Roy that he was in a bad relationship, and his brother adamantly refused to have anything to do with Camille.

After several years of trying to win her in-laws' acceptance, Camille withdrew. Roy explained: "From Camille's perspective, she was like, 'These are not my issues; it's not my fault.' From then on, I was trying to find a balance between my wife and my biological family." Unable to force acceptance of Camille and obtain a sincere apology from his parents and brother, Roy began the process of cutting off contact with them.

Blame has remained a sticking point. Roy told me:

> What we were looking for was my parents to just apologize; in particular, to apologize to Camille and acknowledge that their concerns were false. And my parents took the stance of "No, it's just her, this was all Camille, and we're not going to apologize for it." It's clear to me that when Camille came into the picture, it shined the light on a lot of dysfunction that my family had, but they couldn't see that. I was very much a scapegoat in my family, and Camille shook the family system.

Over the past several years, Roy and Camille have given up the attempt to reconcile with his family. Roy tries to put the family situation out of his mind. He is working hard to change the focus to what he is able to control: "I'm going to worry about myself. My wife and I have a young child, and I'm just trying to focus on being a good father and being a good husband and not really worrying about my family of origin."

Despite his resolve to go forward with his life, Roy's sadness about the loss of his family resonated throughout our interview. He longs for his son to have a family connection:

I emailed my brother and said, "You and I have struggled, but your kids have had nothing to do with this, and I want that relationship with your kids." He hasn't allowed that at all. I've also pushed for his kids to have a relationship with our son, and he's refused to have any of that. My parents haven't had any contact with my son. I would like my son to know them. I've gotten to the point where it's, "Well, this is the way it is." But it takes a long time to really let it go.

MONEY AND INHERITANCE

Money may not be the root of all evil, but it is at the heart of many estrangements. Conflicts over money that contribute to estrangements include failing to pay back a loan, deceiving a family member out of his or her funds, and not providing financial support when a relative believes it is necessary. One financial theme in particular stood out as a pathway to estrangement, however: conflicts over wills and inheritance.

Even though many people leave equal amounts of money to their offspring, a parent may punish one of the children by excluding him or her—sometimes to that person's dismayed surprise. Even when the distribution of the financial portion of the estate is equal, some possessions cannot be divided. A family heirloom, a piece of fine jewelry, a work of art can go to only one person. In addition, an estate can be equal without being perceived as fair. For example, a daughter who gave up work to care for her frail parents may expect to receive a greater portion of the estate than her brother who never even visited.

Research has shown that inheritance exerts a powerful symbolic force that transcends the financial impact. As the sociologist Jacqueline Angel points out, wills can convey favoritism or disapproval in a way that is legally irrevocable and eternal. Everyday objects that take on intangible worth are fought over. The chipped platter that has no financial value is cherished because it served the Thanksgiving turkey for a half century. Further, a will may specify that everything should be "equally divided," but difficulty ensues when it comes to dividing a nonfinancial asset. In the case of Rayna Bergstrom, her mother, and her aunt and uncle, the catalyst was the legacy of a business and a house.

Rayna grew up in a close-knit extended family, in which she had warm relationships with her mother's two siblings and her cousins. She told me: "The estrangement took place between my mother and her brother and sister. It was an argument among the three of them, but it turned into an entire family debacle."

The siblings were very close, as were their children. Rayna describes the extended family as a warm, secure environment: "It was amazing. It was so close. They lived close to us, and I remember holidays and birthdays and time spent at my aunt's house with my cousins as such happy times." It was not to last, however. Things began to fall apart when Rayna's grandparents died. They owned a business, a house, and a summer home in Vermont that was much loved by the family.

An intense battle began over how to handle the estate that split the family for the next thirty years. From her viewpoint as a teenager, emblazoned in Rayna's memory is the anger:

> I remember them fighting all the time. I remember a lot of tears and a
> lot of angry phone calls and not seeing my cousins. Finally, there was a
> point where they were just *done*. As I understand it, my mother's
> brother and his wife wanted to take over the family business and
> manage it themselves. His sisters and their husbands objected. They
> ended up selling the business and splitting everything three ways. That
> was the final straw, because around that time everything got cut off.

Fighting between the siblings and their spouses went on for many years. According to Rayna:

> They were fighting over who would get the china, who would get the
> contents of the house, and whether they needed to sell the house or
> not. My grandparents had left a will that said divide everything equally

among the three siblings. But that would work only if everyone agreed to sell everything and split the profits. The uncle who ended up cutting himself off felt that he was being ganged up on by the sisters and their husbands. I'm not saying my parents were blameless, either. But my uncle never explained or discussed with me what my mother actually did to him.

The rift that began thirty years ago still permeates the life of this family, creating both sadness and persistent anger among those involved. Rayna would feel better knowing why her uncle, aunt, and cousins behaved the way they did, but she has no way to satisfy her curiosity. She stated sadly:

> The whole family was affected. My dad and my uncle were friends, and that ended. I had several cousins I was very close with, and they suddenly didn't ever talk to us. They were my idols and they cut off ties with me. I want to know, "What in the name of God did you all do this for?" I still want things to be cleared up for the record, or at least for there to be some closure of what it was that happened. I feel like I was punished. I wish someone had thought beyond themselves in this whole matter.

UNMET EXPECTATIONS

It is difficult to imagine a relationship without expectations. The expectations we have for the behavior of others emerge from the personal relationship history, but also from powerful social norms of how people should behave toward one another. These standards for behavior are often taken for granted—until they are broken. In fact, the existence of the family depends on a feeling of group membership based on shared norms. They embody joint expectations for the amount, type, and timing of support we will receive from our relatives.

When it comes to the behavior of family members, our expectations are affected by the norm of solidarity; that is, that our kin should help us out when we need it. In this pathway to estrangement, expectations are repeatedly violated, leading the parties involved to become hostile and resentful. Family relations are also influenced by the norm of reciprocity; if we help family members, we feel angry and cheated if we are not helped in return. I discovered that perceived violation of norms was particularly likely to occur among siblings who struggled with differing understandings of the norms for mutual support and assistance.

The sibling bond is unique. We share half our genes with our brothers and sisters, and we experience the same family growing up. By the time we reach middle age, few people have known us as long as our siblings, especially after the death of our parents. For many people, simply knowing that one's siblings are present in the world and available in time of need is a comforting thought. In some families, however, sibling contact is contentious and difficult. When expectations are severely violated, some people break the sibling bond.

Grace Brock tried again and again with her sister, Marlene—until she finally gave up. Grace recounted the history:

> I'm from a family with just us two sisters. Marlene is four years younger than me. It was not an easy childhood. We grew up in a home with a depressed father and a very codependent mother, so we didn't really have a lot of experience with conflict resolution. Pretty much everything was swept under the rug, and we were never given those tools. We just went forward despite my dad's issues, and we somehow managed to get through childhood and grow up. I got married and moved out when Marlene was in high school, but we were very close.

The two sisters began to distance themselves as they reached their late twenties. From Grace's point of view, Marlene was not living up to expectations for a daughter or sibling, as she seemed to be withdrawing from the family:

As time went on, we began to live different lives. Also, she wasn't very interested in coming to family events, maybe because she didn't have a family yet and I did. So birthdays, holidays, she would come sporadically, at the last minute, and leave early. But she was part of our lives, and I was still pretty close to her.

This holding pattern continued for a number of years. It was not a fulfilling relationship for Grace, but she had her own family, and both she and Marlene were absorbed in their careers. Grace was primarily responsible for taking care of her parents, in addition to being a single parent. Her anger grew because Grace believed her sister was avoiding responsibility. Grace told me: "Children should help their parents. But she left me with all the responsibility. I was incredibly disappointed that she wouldn't live up to her obligations."

Conflicts over unmet caregiving expectations set the stage for the estrangement. The pressure and emotion surrounding her mother's death led to a conflict that became the trigger for a lasting rift. Grace battled tears as she told me:

> When my mother died, we were going through an incredibly difficult time. It was just overwhelming. So it came time to decide what to do with my father, because he had Alzheimer's and was unable to live on his own. We had to make a decision to sell the home that they had lived in their entire lives. I expected Marlene to be reasonable and to see my side of the story. I also felt that she should give me more say since I had been the one who did all the caregiving work with our parents.
>
> But it didn't work out that way. Marlene wanted to keep the house. She thought we could rent it, and then maybe she would live in it someday. I wasn't happy with that. I said, "I really need the money from the sale of the house." That was the really big blowup. I said some things, and she said some things, and I felt I really didn't ever want to

talk to her again. I was like, "I'm so done." And I think I even said that to her: "It is too much, I'm done."

The sisters solved the immediate problem, but the damage was done:

We sold the house. We took care of my father for another few years, and we were very aloof with each other at that point. We were visiting my father on different days, so we were never there together. When my father was dying, we didn't go together. We went in shifts to sit with him in hospice, and we were never in the room together with him. We actually were both there when he died, but not talking to each other.

As the estrangement took hold, Grace came to regret it. As she explained to me:

I'd love to have our relationship be the way it was, but I don't know that it could ever be that way. We both expected things from the other one that just didn't happen. Now we're holding on to all the disappointment, and we can't let things go. If you hold on to things, it's hard to go back to how it used to be. When my father died, I was tearful, I cried and apologized. I even said to Marlene, "I don't want to lose you too. I already lost my parents." But it just wasn't enough. I said: "Can't we work it out? What can we do?" And she wouldn't even look at me, she wouldn't talk to me. She turned away, and I left in tears that day.

VALUE AND LIFESTYLE DIFFERENCES

In some ways, family relationships are different from those we have with our friends and co-workers. There is one basic principle, however, that applies to all close relationships: the importance of similarity. Over a half century of research has shown that we are more likely to develop friendships with people who are similar to us in important characteristics. For instance, we tend to associate with others who resemble us in marital status, whether we have children, and level of education. Even more important is the degree to which two individuals perceive their attitudes and values as similar. People who share this kind of common orientation toward what is important in life can comfortably express their views to one another and thus have more rewarding interactions. When it comes to choosing friends, "birds of a feather" is much more accurate than "opposites attract."

What promotes friendship and attraction also applies to members of our families. Studies have shown that family members who see themselves as similar tend to have closer relationships, and they are more likely to spend time together and confide in one another. In a series of studies that I have conducted over the past two decades with Jill Suitor, we found that of all kinds of similarity, sharing the same basic values is especially important in promoting higher-quality family relationships.

For example, our studies show that children and parents report closer relationships when they share religious values and when they agree on their general outlook on life. The same dynamic applies to siblings and other relatives. In general, when family members have common values, they tend to more strongly identify with one another, have similar goals, and agree on how those goals should be reached. We specifically studied estrangement between parents and their adult children with our colleague Megan Gilligan, and again we found that sharing values helped prevent family rifts.

It is, therefore, no surprise that unresolvable conflicts in basic values and lifestyle choices can set family members on the path to estrangement. Over and over, I heard from respondents that their relative had "crossed a line" in his or her actions, engaging in decisions and behaviors that represented a fundamental violation of their basic values. Indeed, some estrangements that appeared to result from other issues could, in fact, be reduced to value differences and conflicts.

Some of the most damaging rifts I encountered involved the wholesale rejection of family members because of how they decided to lead their lives. In such cases, it is not a matter of straightforward arguments or disagreements. Instead, the person's very worth as a human being, deserving of respect and autonomy, is called into question. The relative comes to embody the rejection of values another holds sacred, and any sense of tolerance is lost. Resolution is extremely difficult, because the "ask" is not trivial; it is essentially a request to become a different person.

Marian Russo's story was painful to hear, involving traumatic rejection by her parents that has reverberated throughout her family for almost a decade. Marian was a mother with four young children when her marriage to her troubled husband dissolved. She struggled to hold the family together as a single parent while coming to terms with her own relationship life. At a time when she most needed the support of her extended family, they abandoned her because of a clash in values. Marian told me:

> I became estranged from my mother, and because my mother is the matriarch of the family, I also lost contact with my father. The extended family is pretty much ruled by my mother, so then I lost contact with uncles and aunts and cousins. I was excluded from all family gatherings at my mom's house. I truly became a stranger in my own family, at a time when I was most vulnerable. It's been eight years with no contact.

Even after such a long time, Marian's sense of shock over her mother's sudden, hostile, and seemingly irreparable behavior is evident. The memory of the incident that started the estrangement has not faded over the years:

> It all began about eight years ago. I was divorced from my husband and I was raising my kids by myself. After a lot of self-exploration, I came out and started dating a woman. My mom absolutely flipped out. A few weeks after I began dating this woman, my mom came over to the house one night when I had all the kids there. It was a

school night, and homework needed to be done, and kids needed to be fed.

My mom was out of control, screaming that I don't take care of my kids anymore, and that she was going to take the kids away from me. My kids were all very upset and crying, and I kept asking her to leave, and she would not leave. She was always argumentative, but this was extreme behavior. Then, as we were arguing in front of my kids, she started hitting me and kicking me. I said, "You need to stop." And she didn't stop. My kids were witnessing this. They were crying and they were asking their grandmother to stop.

So I said, "Look, if you don't stop, I'm going to call 911." And she didn't stop, so I called 911. I said, "I have my mother in my house, this is the situation, my children are very upset and they're crying." They sent two state troopers over to the house, and she still wouldn't leave the house. They had to go into the house and remove my mom. They asked me if I wanted her arrested, and I said, "No, she just needs to go home."

From that point on, I have not spoken to my mom basically at all. She has such a strong conviction that gay people are all going to hell and that we shouldn't be on the face of the earth. I've been living with that for eight years.

Her mother's intolerance disrupted the entire family, interfering with Marian's relationship with her own children. Despite the estrangement, Marian allowed her children to stay in contact with their grandparents. She told me: "I've never interfered with my children's relationship with their grandparents, and they still attend the family functions there. I was the one kicked out of the family." She went on:

I think it was really important for them to know their mom wasn't going to take them away from anybody. They can love their grandparents, even though their grandmother is crazy. I was not going to interfere with that; they still have their relationship with their grandmother and their grandfather and their aunts and uncles. They know that "Mom didn't really do anything; it's Grandma that kicked her out of everybody's lives."

Although she still believes that the children should interact with their grandparents, Marian regrets the loss and damage her mother's actions caused them:

> My children needed a family. After the divorce from their father, they needed a solid family, and it got torn apart when my mother decided to disown me. I feel bad for my kids. I probably should've done better at communicating with my mom, but I was fighting for my life and to be a gay person. That's what my kids have grown up with. They know that it hurt me and that they suffered too, because their mom isn't with them at family functions. It's heartbreaking to me.

BREAKING THE TIES THAT BIND

We began this chapter with a common destination: the end of contact with a close family member. To be sure, there are minor differences; for example, the relative might be seen across the room at a family gathering, or tense emails might be exchanged. But in an interconnected world where it feels challenging to avoid anyone for a long period of time, the silence is stunningly complete. The psychologist John Gottman has identified the phenomenon of "stonewalling" in relationships, in which one person shuts down, withdraws from interaction, and closes himself or herself off from the other person. Gottman selected the perfect term: In estrangements, it is as if a stone wall has been erected to keep the other person out.

The six pathways appear to be different, but as you read them, you may have detected overarching themes that link these narratives. Despite the varying details, in my studies I found that these and many rifts share certain characteristics. Cutting across the individual stories are five common points, which we will revisit in later chapters.

- **The Power of a Single Event.** Many narratives of people in family rifts focus on a signature incident (what I call "volcanic events" in Chapter 6). In the stories I have shared with you, volcanic events can take many forms: It may be a single phone call that ended all future conversation, a screaming fight in front of frightened children, or an argument over a family business. These occurrences are seen as "last straw" events that serve as critical turning points in the relationship.

- **Diverging Views of the Past.** Each party in an estrangement has his or her unique view of past events. A son's belief that his parents are hostile and unkind to his wife is countered by the father's view that he is protecting his child from an obviously bad marriage. In cases of inheritance or unfilled expectations, each person involved can cite incidents (and sometimes the same incident) to support his or her point of view. Many arguments prior to estrangement involve attempts to get other people to "see the light" and admit that their past behavior was wrong.

- **Unclear Boundaries.** When family members interact with one another as adults, a degree of detachment and differentiation is needed for a mature relationship. In this chapter, we have seen that the theme of blurred boundaries is very prominent. When is it appropriate for a divorced father to make demands on his daughter? How much should a young couple share about their relationship with their parents, and when must parents acknowledge that they cannot change their child's choice of a life partner? How much can one sibling ask of another before requests become invasive?

- **The Role of Others.** We have known for nearly a century that families form a system, as all the interacting members affect, and are affected by, the others in turn. In this chapter, we have seen that children may try to promote peace between parents, uncles, and aunts. The possibility of reconciling with parents can be disrupted by a sibling who continues to provoke the estrangement. A safe haven with grandparents makes possible a daughter's rift with her mother. Estrangement does not end with the family members immediately involved but ripples out across the kinship network.

- **Breakdown in Communication.** In all the family stories in this chapter, the inability to have reasonable dialogue led to a breaking point. Repeated interactions become increasingly hostile; feelings are hurt; the pain increases through ruminating about negative incidents; arguments become bitter and contemptuous. The accumulation of unpleasant contacts becomes highly aversive, creating difficulty making decisions about hot-button issues like the distribution of an inheritance or the care of an older parent. Establishing new ground rules for communication is a key component of trying out a reconciliation.

EXPLORE YOUR NARRATIVE

Because you are reading this book, my guess is that you may be struggling with an estrangement of your own. While you read the family stories in this chapter, some aspects probably felt very familiar and you could identify with them. At other points, you may have disagreed with statements or disapproved of actions you read about. I would expect this reaction, because your story is uniquely your own and no one else's. Before you continue reading this book, I have a suggestion for you: Take an hour or two to craft your own narrative.

Researchers have shown the importance of our narratives about major events in our lives, and in particular, traumatic ones. The psychologist Robyn Fivush has studied extensively the importance of narratives about our families. This research shows that narratives do not just recount the facts from a personal memory. Instead, they transform the many details into stories about important experiences. Our narratives, in turn, help guide our behavior in the future and how we connect with others.

So, what is your narrative? For my interviews, I devised a set of questions that helped hundreds of people to tell their stories, creating a narrative from their painful experiences. Whether you choose to write down your narrative or just think through it, the insights in this book will be more useful if you take some time to consider your own story. You can ask yourself these questions:

- What is the history of your estrangement? How did it start, what happened next, and where do things stand today? It can help to think of your experience as if it were a book: What are the main chapters, from the beginning to the present day?

- What do you think caused the estrangement? What do you think is your relative's view of what caused the estrangement?

- Was there a specific event that began the estrangement? If so, what happened?

- Do you believe anything could have been done to prevent the estrangement? Is there anything you or someone else could have done differently?

- If you were talking to someone in a similar situation, what kind of advice would you give him or her about coping with an estrangement?

- Where do you think the relationship with your relative will be this time next year? In five years?

In the next two chapters, we will delve more deeply into the experience of family rifts, focusing on how they affect the people involved and others in the family. We will then move to the advice provided by many people who overcame estrangement and reconciled with their relatives. You will hear many more stories in the chapters to come. Taking some time now to tell your own story will help you to appreciate the experiences of others and to determine what suggestions are most useful to you. As you will see, your story may appear to have reached an end, with the finality of "I'm done." But many stories of estrangement have alternative, and unexpected, endings.

CHAPTER 3:

"IT NEVER STOPS HURTING": LIVING IN A RIFT

I am 100 percent confident that being estranged from my daughter
has knocked ten or twenty years off my life. I would tell people going
through this that they should not underestimate how much stress
they're under. It's really, really difficult. Emotionally, I'm a wreck.
There is hardly a day that goes by that I don't cry. I continue to go to
work, I continue to try to do what I have to do, but it's very hard. The
holidays are lonely, birthdays are lonely. I find I don't particularly want
to be around other families. When I see other people my age and their
daughters doing things together, I avoid being there. I haven't really
found a way to cope yet. And I don't see an end in sight. I don't
know how there would be. I continue to reach out, but I don't know
what to do.

—BRAD FINNEY

Why does family estrangement even matter?

Yes, I mean that as a serious question. Given that I have written, and
you are currently reading, a book about estrangement, asking it may
seem odd or absurd. But the question is worth considering because the
media have lowered our expectations for family life in recent years.
We hear reports that traditional family bonds have broken down, that
the extended family is a thing of the past, and that we have entered a

"post-family" era. In fact, there is some truth to the assertion that family life has changed over the past one hundred or even fifty years.

Unlike in previous eras, in ours most people do not live in large, extended families. Indeed, because of our society's high geographic mobility, many people do not even live in close proximity to family members. The divorce rate, although it has dropped in recent years, still hovers at around 40 percent. New forms of relationships have expanded our notion of what constitutes "family," including increases in nonmarital cohabitation, out-of-wedlock births, same-sex marriages, blended families, and couples remaining childless. Researchers at the respected Pew Research Center tell us that "there is no longer one dominant family form in the United States. Parents today are raising their children against a backdrop of increasingly diverse and, for many, constantly evolving family forms."

Along with these societal changes are cultural ones as well. In comparison with those of earlier generations, norms about how family relationships should be carried out today are not as clear. Throughout much of history, relations between the generations and with extended family members were conducted under rigid social rules about proper conduct. Nowadays, people struggle to reconcile different value systems regarding what family members ought to do for one another and feel at a loss for rules to guide their behavior.

Given this state of affairs, does estrangement still matter in our more fluid and less structured society? The answer, based on my research and the work of social scientists and clinicians, is a resounding *yes*. It profoundly matters. I learned that people who are estranged from a family member feel deep sadness, long for reconnection, and wish that they could turn back the clock and act differently to prevent the rift. It's the kind of pain expressed by Felice Hoskins over her estrangement from her daughter:

> I have a scar on my chest from heart surgery. Okay, it's healed—it's a scar. But the estrangement is an open wound. Every day I have to wrap myself and insulate myself and protect myself, because it's an open

wound. You can't fix it; you can't change it. It's still there every day. You can't recover from it. I will tell you: I went through divorce; I went through heart surgery—piece of cake compared with losing a child like this.

Why, in our rapidly changing culture, does estrangement have such a strong effect on human happiness? If you are not in a family rift, you may have asked yourself, "What's the big deal anyway? Why can't people just get over it and move on?" And if you are in the midst of an estrangement, your question is probably, "Why does this bother me so much, even after years?" When confronted with the powerful negative emotions that result from an estrangement, people wonder, "What's wrong with me?"

My interviews shed light on why estrangement matters so much. By combining my data with research findings on family and other close relationships, I identified four factors that lead people like Brad Finney to say, "Emotionally, I'm a wreck." It is not abnormal or even unusual to experience estrangement as a crushing blow. As I will show in this chapter, humans are hardwired for these effects. I call them the "four threats of estrangement," because individually and cumulatively, they threaten mental, social, and physical well-being.

One core principle underlies the four threats: *Human nature is such that our happiness depends on reliable, secure, and predictable social relationships, and without them we feel lost.* As we will see in this chapter, we naturally become attached to family members, and disruptions in our ties to them create a devastating form of chronic stress. We have evolved to be this way. As the neuroscientist Matthew Lieberman puts it, "To the extent that we can characterize evolution as designing our modern brains, this is what our brains were wired for: reaching out to and interacting with others."

Here are the four ways that estrangement threatens human health and happiness. First, I discovered that estrangement meets the criteria for what researchers term "chronic stress," a set of challenging circumstances that persist over a long period of time. Second, estrangement disrupts biologically based patterns of attachment, causing anxiety and insecurity. Third, family rifts involve social rejection, which research shows is extraordinarily damaging. Fourth, estrangement violates a basic psychological need for certainty, instead creating a situation that is disturbingly ambiguous. Estrangement disrupts what are still the most reliable ties available in our society: family relationships. If you are feeling the effects even after many years, once again: *You are not alone.*

THE FIRST THREAT: LIVING WITH CHRONIC STRESS

When we think of stress and how to cope with it, major stressful events most often come to mind. These events can be entirely negative, such as a disease diagnosis or losing a job. It is also the case that positive events, such as the birth of a child or buying a house, raise our levels of stress. Research even has shown that the proverbial positive event—winning the lottery—stresses out the lucky individual.

Scientists say these events produce "acute stress," and that's a problem for which we humans are actually pretty well equipped. Your car gets in a fender-bender; your child runs into the street and you grab her just in time; your purse gets stolen—in these cases, most people are resilient and quickly bounce back to a steady state. Your heart rate rises, your muscles get tense, and you breathe quickly for a while. This doesn't last long, however, and soon you are back to whatever the normal level is for you.

Another form of stress, however, has very damaging consequences: what scientists refer to as "chronic stress." Acute stress is time-limited and may even be caused by an exciting event, such as performing a song in public or running your first 5K race. In contrast, there is nothing good to say about chronic stress. Chronic stress depletes your physical and mental resources, grinding you down on a day-to-day basis. It occurs in situations where demands are unrelenting and we do not see a way to break free from the causes of the stress.

People describe estrangement in precisely these terms: a form of chronic stress that never goes away. It may be punctuated at times by a burst of contact from the estranged relative, followed by silence. It is characterized by attempts to reach out that become highly stressful sources of disappointment. As a stigmatized condition, it involves the stress of concealment and of explaining oneself to people who may not understand. The effects of chronic stress are very serious; it lowers your resistance to other life problems, worsens your daily mood, and impairs your physical health. So it is for many individuals living in a family rift.

Scientists have shown us another fact about chronic stress that helps explain the unending distress of estrangement. It's not just the actual events that stress us; additionally, simply thinking about the situation has almost identical negative effects. Psychologists call this source of stress "perseverative cognitions," or what we laypeople might call rumination. Even if the stressor is not actually present—say, for example, the big argument with a child or parent occurred months ago—we re-create the event in our minds. We play the scene over and over in our imagination, ruminating about it long afterward. This kind of thinking has the same psychological and physical effects as the event itself, so we suffer by keeping the stress alive in our thoughts. Indeed, that's why it's called "chronic."

My interviews convinced me that people in estrangements often suffer from chronic stress because of the negative emotional state that results from a difficult, unfixable family situation. Kim Padilla speaks for many who have had this experience. Kim is estranged from her daughter, Sandy. The initial break occurred around ten years ago when Kim was in her late fifties. Kim went through a difficult time emotionally after her husband's illness and death, becoming anxious and behaving erratically. She acted toward her children in ways she now regrets, causing them to label her as selfish and "toxic." There were also conflicts over her husband's care at the end of life that left bad feelings on both their parts.

Sandy responded to the difficulties by cutting off the relationship and refusing most contact with her mother. Kim told me:

I have seen her maybe three or four times in the past six years, and she will not respond to any emails. Well, sometimes she responds to emails, but her responses are unpleasant. She won't respond to texts, she won't return any phone calls. I just quit trying to reach her because she would never respond. However, I do still send her birthday cards. Whether she throws them in the garbage or not, I don't know.

For Kim the stress of the estrangement has been reactivated continually over the years. Kim acknowledges that her own attempts at contact are distressing. For example, after reaching out repeatedly to Sandy to better understand the causes of the conflict, Kim found the response brought stress rather than relief:

In one email she sent me, she told me that I was selfish because of something I did thirty years ago. This was something she had never mentioned before, so it hit me out of the blue. I tried to get more information. I asked her in an email: "Sandy, what have I done? I don't know. I certainly didn't do anything intentional. What have I done?" Her response to me was, "You shouldn't have to ask me about it; you should know," and that was it.

Kim's stress is exacerbated by keenly missing closer ties with her grandchildren. Although other estranged parents might consider her lucky to have minimal contact with them, the interactions are intermittent, unpredictable, and exclusively via the internet. Sandy prevented her children from contacting Kim for several years, but as they have gotten older, some contact was allowed. However, Kim lives in fear of overstepping the uncertain boundaries, as happened recently:

I commented on one of my grandson's Facebook posts. Then a couple of days later, I went on Facebook, and he had unfriended me. His mother had found out and told him it was not appropriate for me to comment on his posts. I was feeling like I can't catch a break here no matter what I do. And my grandson and I used to be so close.

Although she has tried to move on by engaging in other activities and relationships, Kim cannot help reliving the arguments and unpleasant episodes, which produce stress during the long periods in which no contact is taking place. Kim summed up the effects:

Let me tell you, it took its toll on me. It is very difficult emotionally. I had the anger, and the bitterness, and the "why, why, why?" Physically, there were a few issues. I started having some problems with my digestive system. I went to a specialist, and he could not find anything. I truly believe it was the stress of not having my daughter and my grandson in my life, and missing them so much, and not being able to do anything about it. There's a sadness in me that just will not go away.

Seeing estrangement as a form of chronic stress helps us understand its long-term effects. As with some chronic illnesses, flare-ups are followed by periods of relative calm but colored by worry that things could easily take a turn for the worse. Persistent rumination and "awfulizing"— imagining that the situation is the worst it can possibly be—thus add to the chronic stress. This is the experience of people like Lily Heath, who in her initial interview was depressed over the estrangement from her daughter. In a second interview a year later, the stress persisted unabated:

My feelings haven't changed. I love her. I'm in a state of bewilderment. I don't know what to do. It shouldn't matter, but it does. It matters to me. I'm just in the same pathetic place I was last year, basically. I make a conscious effort to accept it, but I know I haven't, because even if I manage to shove it out of my mind during the day, I dream about it at night. It's like I'm sabotaging myself. The longer time goes on, the less hope I have, so the sadder I feel.

Understanding estrangement as chronic stress helps explain why it leads to problems like depression, anxiety, insomnia, low self-esteem, and feelings of helplessness. It's why people don't "just get over it" when they are estranged. As we will see from the remaining threats, several factors keep the painful experiences alive and hinder coping and acceptance.

THE SECOND THREAT: BROKEN ATTACHMENT

One of the most powerful ideas about how humans develop is attachment theory. Research into understanding bonding between parents and children has shown that attachment plays a major role in relationships at every stage of our lives. When children feel frightened or stressed, they seek out an attachment figure, usually a parent. They find in the attachment figure a sense of security and a "safe haven" they can turn to for comfort when they are anxious. I happen to be the grandfather of twins. When they were around a year and a half old, I would watch them playing happily with their toys—until their mother or father left the room. They would begin quickly to seek them out, display anxiety, and rejoice when their parent returned.

This process of seeking out an adult who offers care and protection is built into children. Indeed, it helped ensure human survival because our offspring cannot fend for themselves for many years. When people to whom they are attached are easily accessible and responsive, children feel secure; if not, children respond with anxiety. Growing up in a family, we develop attachments to parents and other members naturally; it becomes part of our mental makeup.

This biologically based process of bonding has enormous effects over the entire life course. We never cease to need the benefits that attachment relationships provide. People to whom we have lifelong attachments serve as a secure base when we are in trouble, protecting us when needed physically or psychologically. The presence of these attached figures helps us get through life's difficulties and, more important, gives us a feeling of being at home in a secure and reliable social world. Attachment figures who play these roles are often our parents, but as parents grow older, adult offspring become attachment figures for their elders in turn. We also experience attachment to our siblings and other relatives to whom we are close.

When these bonds break, we can experience profound emotional reactions. Losing someone—in this case through estrangement—activates what psychologists call the "attachment system." Based on the old bonds, the person's absence leads to grief at the loss. Because family members are specific, irreplaceable individuals, our attachment leads to feelings of separation anxiety, yearning for the relationship, and disruptions in our other social relationships. The human bonding that occurred over years of childhood makes us feel deeply insecure about the loss. It's one main reason why estrangement matters so much to so many people.

Frieda Greenwood's parents went through a messy divorce when she was a teenager, after which her mother engaged in a series of relationships with a number of men. The relationship between mother and daughter was always difficult. Although she was able to keep the household together, Frieda's mother was emotionally withholding and unsupportive. As Frieda put it, "She was too tangled up in her own stuff to focus on the needs of her children. She was incredibly demanding. She demands, demands, demands, and what you do isn't right. And then it's a thank-you with a hook in it."

For these reasons, Frieda felt compelled to cut off contact with her mother. A sense of resolution is not possible, however, because she cannot escape the pull of attachment. She began to cry as she told me:

> I think of the mother-daughter relationship as primal. I guess that's why I'm crying, because I miss that. Some people really have lovely, powerful, strong relationships with their mom, and they're internalizing that secure bond. I think every human being yearns for a secure bond with at least one parent. I just think we're mammals, that's how we're made, and we need that secure bond. And when we don't get that secure bond, it impacts our internal core stability. Do I still wish it

could have been different? Yes, because when someone doesn't have a secure, stable bond with a parent, it has major implications for that person. It does for me.

Kip Proctor also struggles with unfulfilled attachment needs. He tried for many years to maintain a relationship with his parents. Both are alcoholics who were neglectful of their children and raised them in a chaotic household. Despite numerous attempts to intervene, Kip has been unable to help his parents change their behavior and finally gave up the effort. He told me: "I was just angry. I was really angry at them for not taking better care of me as a child and for exposing me to kind of awful things. I've later come to understand that they're both addicted and they're both sick, and obviously, I can't do anything about that."

Kip continues to feel a longing for the broken attachment relationship. Normally reserved, he could not conceal his emotions as he described the sense of loss:

> I miss having a family relationship that is really solid. The hardest one for me is my mother, because I still yearn for some kind of maternal connection. I used to call my mother every day, and we'd talk for a half an hour about whatever. That wanting a relationship especially is stronger now as I enter a time when I'm thinking about starting my own family. I would love to be able to talk to my mom. It's always there in the background. I'm supposed to be doing something that I'm not. I think that for these reasons, I struggle with relationships in general.

Understanding the importance of attachment helped me answer a perplexing issue I'd struggled to understand. I discovered in my interviews that even when a relative was difficult and unrewarding, a desire for contact and connection persisted. Some people expressed bewilderment that they still longed for the relationship despite a history of problems. The fundamental attachment bond, reinforced by even a few positive memories, made acceptance of a permanent break difficult or impossible.

Cecily Gunderson shows how attachment makes estrangement emotionally complex. After her parents divorced when she was in high school, her father became an unreliable figure. He occasionally visited during her college years, but she found that if she disagreed with him or asked for support, he would become angry and disappear. Her contact with him as an adult has been sporadic; he pops into her life for a time, followed by periods of estrangement. She poignantly described how the desire to have a father still exerts a strong pull:

> There's a lot of reasons on paper that it doesn't make sense for me to continue to reach out and to continue to put energy into a relationship with him. However, when we are cut off, it always bothers me that I don't have a relationship with him. I feel bad about the idea of my dad not being at a wedding in the future, or not being in my kids' lives when I have them. So I still want a relationship with my dad. There were some things that were really good about my childhood. When I was little, he was really fun. It took me a long time to come to terms with the fact that I don't know why I want a relationship with him, but I do.

John Bowlby, the English psychiatrist who created attachment theory, became deeply interested in loss because it is when we lose someone that we truly see the power of attachment. I heard many estranged people describe the symptoms Bowlby identified when people lose an attached figure. There is initial shock when they try to process what occurred and deal with grief, followed by a yearning for the relationship that was broken. An estrangement brings out longing for the comfort a relative provided and makes reminders of him or her very painful. Hopelessness then becomes an eventual result as the estrangement progresses. Here we have an explanation for why estrangement still matters in contemporary society: The biologically based process of attachment persists and influences our emotions for as long as we live.

THE THIRD THREAT: THE PAIN OF REJECTION

Why is estrangement so acutely distressing? Losing someone we love is clearly a factor. Since the earliest analyses of the causes of depression, interpersonal loss has played a central role. But research shows that losses involving social rejection have especially damaging effects. The psychologist George Slavich has studied what he terms "targeted rejection," which involves "the exclusive, active, and intentional rejection of an individual by others." Slavich found that people who experience targeted rejection are three times more likely to become depressed, compared with people who experience other types of severe life events.

Rejection is especially stressful because human beings have a fundamental drive toward social inclusion and belonging. Being rejected threatens our evaluations of ourselves, causing us to feel worthless and lowering our self-esteem. Slavich discovered that the stress caused by the shame and insecurity of targeted rejection has more than psychological effects; it also leads to potentially damaging biological processes such as inflammation. In fact, research shows that the same regions in the brain that respond to physical pain are activated by social rejection. The double whammy of a threat to self-esteem and a lack of ability to control the situation makes social rejection one of life's most harmful experiences.

Estrangement embodies all these features, giving it a high potential to cause chronic stress. It is no surprise, therefore, that individuals struggling with a family rift often report depression, anxiety, and reduced physical health. The intentional, active severing of personal ties differs from other kinds of loss, involving humiliation and the uncertainty brought on by the purposeful actions of another person. In estrangement, the other person does not disappear, remaining potentially available but deliberately inaccessible.

In Chapter 1, we met Kristine Freeman, who became estranged from her mother because of Kristine's decision to divorce. For Kristine, the loss of the relationship was secondary to the devastating impact of sudden and complete rejection. Instead of receiving support, Kristine told me: "I made that decision, and I told my parents, and at that point my mother completely rejected me. Her message to me was, 'Your actions do not align with what I believe you should have done, so I cannot accept that, I cannot accept you.'"

Kristine eloquently summed up the pain of family rejection and how it is reactivated over time:

> When rejection happens from your family, it's ultimate. When rejection happens, you tend to lose everything—you lose your self-esteem, your confidence. You question who you are, you doubt everything, and you are the lowest of the low. I wanted to try to move forward with my life, but I couldn't because this had such a hold on me. So with each letter from her I would receive in my mailbox, I'd think, "Ah, here we go again." I'd open it up, I'd look at it, I'd get angry, feel rejected again.

The impact of rejection, according to my interviewees, exceeds that of other losses. Tanya Page's relationship with her son began to deteriorate after his marriage. Tanya and her son's wife were unable to get along, and over time her daughter-in-law came to control all access to the family. After many attempts at contact, including unannounced visits that were rebuffed, Tanya was totally cut off. The experience of rejection has been the most painful of her life: "It feels like every time I reach out, I get rejected again. That's very painful to get rejected again and again and again. I've just about had my fill of that after all these years."

Rejection from such a close tie has colored Tanya's other relationships, making her feel deeply insecure:

> I feel like it just ripped the rug right out from under me, and everything I believed in, and everything I thought I knew. Everything I

worked for my entire life was taken away. I try to accept it or get over it, but it's a huge part of me every day. I don't understand a person being in a position in life where you could say, "I don't want someone who loves me to come close to me." How can you say, "I have enough love in my life, so I don't need you and I hate you"?

The rejection also has affected Tanya's approach to life in general:

I used to be out there; I was involved in lots of organizations. Now I've retreated. I lost faith and trust in myself and my ability to perform and make decisions and be around people. If anybody does reject me out there, because I'm already coming from such a higher load of rejections, it has a huge impact on me. Before this happened, I would have brushed it off, but now I don't have room for one more rejection.

My interviewees taught me that not all losses are the same. Estrangement almost always involves personal rejection, which keeps the pain from abating. The psychologist Guy Winch points out that mentally reliving a painful rejection floods us with the same emotions we had when it happened, and our brain is activated in much the same way. By violating our need to belong, rejection highlights our isolation and lack of vital connections. Because experiences of rejection are not something most people enjoy talking about, they are likely to hold their feelings inside rather than share them with others. Taken together, these factors make estrangement a key threat to well-being.

THE FOURTH THREAT: THE PERILS OF UNCERTAINTY

If there is one thing we humans like, it's certainty. Research shows that we are made uncomfortable when we have to weigh two relatively equal choices with limited information to guide us. We like to place people and relationships into clear categories, which allows us to understand and predict them. When in a difficult or upsetting situation, we seek resolution, trying to avoid an open-ended, insecure state of being. Sometimes we even prefer a negative but certain outcome to being kept in limbo for a long period of time. However, for most people estrangement brings a prolonged state of *ambiguity*.

Every once in a while, someone comes up with a concept that is so brilliant I wish I'd thought of it. Pauline Boss combines the training of a family therapist and a social scientist. In the 1970s, she began to work with family members of military personnel who had gone missing in action in Southeast Asia during the Vietnam War. In other studies, Boss examined families of people missing in disasters or of people who were kidnapped. These families suffered from much more than the loss itself. They found themselves in a situation Boss famously described as having a family member who is *physically absent but psychologically present*. So it is with estrangement.

Boss termed this phenomenon "ambiguous loss." Decades of research show us that this kind of ambiguity is traumatizing. The lack of clarity freezes the process of grieving, blocks coping, and hinders decision-making. In her words, the stress of ambiguous loss occurs because "family members have no choice but to live with the paradox of absence and presence." The distressing and traumatic aspect of ambiguous loss results from the core human need for clarity and closure. Beyond the individual, concerned others find it hard to be supportive. They are often uncertain as to how to help someone suffering from ambiguous loss.

This perspective helped me understand a frequent statement that initially shocked me: Some estranged people would find it easier if their relative had died. Felice Hoskins told me that she could have coped better with the death of a child:

> It is like a death, but it's the death of a relationship with no funeral and no closure. You're not prepared for this. There are no family stories of how to deal with this. You know how to cope when a child or

another person dies. There's no story to help you cope with this. There's nothing in the Bible; there's nothing anywhere.

Don Valentine contrasts grieving over a death with the ambiguity of being estranged from his son:

> I'm going through the usual grieving process. But this is the thing: It is not like what you would have with a normal death of a child. It's like living in this situation where you don't know how he is, you don't know how he's doing. I'm not getting any feedback, no matter how hard I try, to see what his well-being is. It's different when a child dies versus being estranged. This never goes away. It's constantly like a ball and chain. You can't get rid of it—it's there all the time.

The stress of ambiguity and lack of closure is exacerbated in estrangements in which contact with a relative is intermittently broken and restored. I learned a great deal about living under the threat of ambiguous loss from Crystal Buchanan, who for over a decade has struggled to maintain contact with her daughter Betsy. It began when Betsy was in graduate school and suddenly refused to take part in what had been a long tradition of regular phone calls. "One day, we had our normal weekly conversation, and then we never had another one. That was it. I have no idea what happened. She didn't call me."

Crystal went from shock to frenetic activity as she tried to understand the reasons and to restore the relationship. She told me:

> There was no event that happened—nothing transpired. There was no argument, there was no bad scene—there was nothing at all. I wanted to visit her, but she refused to see me. I made a lot of effort. I wrote her letters. I said I was willing to talk about anything or do anything. It was brutal. The thing is, she's a really great person. She's a nurse, she loves helping people, she has a lot of friends. She's actually a lot like me. We're fun people. So I never understood it.

Crystal sought the help of a psychotherapist. Working with him and talking with other family members, she tried to uncover possible reasons for the estrangement. She recalled that there had been conflicts when Betsy was in high school, but those seemed resolved after she graduated. A relative suggested that Betsy felt she "needed space." There was no way to communicate with Betsy about these new insights, but it helped Crystal to identify possible causes, and she worked to accept the estrangement.

No sooner had acceptance begun to set in when things took an unexpected turn. She told me:

> And then a weird thing happened. One year on Valentine's Day, I got a box of candy from Betsy. Just chocolates at the front door; it was kind of strange. And then a couple of times during these ensuing years, she'd call me on a holiday. Then I had a couple of holidays where I stayed by my phone all day and she didn't call. So I thought, "Well, that's not very useful."

The mix of hope and disappointment, relief and anxiety, was very stressful for Crystal. The ambiguity tormented her, as she longed to know whether she was "in" or "out." After another long spell of estrangement, her daughter inexplicably began to reach out again:

> Starting around five years ago, I'd go to visit my other daughter, who lived near her. And she would come and have dinner with her sister and me. And it was really awkward at first, and she'd be pretty nasty to me, and I tried to stay calm and quiet. But then it happened a couple of times where she and I would get together for lunch and that would be much better. I still didn't hear from her much, but she would always call on Valentine's Day.

Crystal allowed herself to hope that the relationship could be restored. Then came Betsy's announcement that she was taking a job across the country. Initially, Betsy stayed in touch. Crystal told me: "She went off, and about once a month or so she'd include me in a group email—an update about what she'd been doing. But now I haven't heard anything from her in months."

The renewed cutoff has plunged Crystal back into uncertainty and ambiguity. She is afraid of remaining in the vague on-again, off-again relationship because of its impact on her mental health:

> I don't know what the situation is right now. She told me she doesn't want me to mail her anything. I want to ask her if it would be okay if I come visit her at her new place in Florida, but I would rather the invitation came from her. I am hesitant because her response could be nothing, and then I'd never hear from her again. Her response could be no, and I don't know if I can handle that response either. It makes life pretty difficult.

During our interview, I asked Crystal if she ever felt it would be easier emotionally to give up on the relationship. She didn't hesitate with her one-word answer: "Definitely!" But her feelings of attachment to Betsy keep her hanging on to the relationship, despite the consequences for her mental health. In summing up her sense of ambiguous loss, she spoke for many of the people I interviewed:

> I don't know where it's going to go. I haven't heard from her again for a while, and I think, "Maybe I'll never hear from her again. Maybe I will." I don't know. To stand this, you have to be pretty resilient. You have to put up with the good times and the bad times, and sometimes you survive and sometimes you don't.

For individuals on the receiving end of an estrangement, ambiguous loss compounds the other threats, making the stressful effects chronic and risking repeated rejection. The uncertainty of estrangement and the denial of closure combine with warring emotions to keep the stress alive.

These themes were eloquently summed up by Trevor Dean, who has cut off and reconciled with his difficult brother several times. Unable to let go entirely, he vacillates between connection and distance:

> There are times when I see him and I have brotherly affection for him. I see him from a distance, and think, "There's my brother, who feels like an ex-brother; but still, there's my brother." Because I've oscillated back and forth between accepting who he is and just saying, "Okay, that's the way he's going to be. I'll just cope with it." But then he does something that just really irritates me or saddens me or whatever. Then I say, "No, it's better off that I don't have anything to do with him."

Like many others dealing with a family rift, Trevor threw up his hands and sighed, saying, "It's complicated."

Most of us are puzzled when we are conflicted about a person or a relationship. Why, we ask ourselves, can't we just resolve our feelings in one direction or another? When confronted with an irreconcilable dilemma, we struggle to resolve it, explain it away, or pretend it doesn't exist. Similarly, persons experiencing a rift are often troubled by the complexity of their interior lives. My interviews revealed a web of positive and negative feelings toward the relative that rocks back and forth like a light craft on the ocean, temporarily righting itself, then nearly tipping over. The unfulfilled striving for certainty and closure forms a key part of this chronically stressful experience.

THE SILENCE OF ABSENCE

The suffering from loss is unique to each individual and is almost impossible to describe fully to others. Sometimes it takes the skills of a gifted poet to transform raw experience into words. The underlying sense of the painful stories I have shared is captured in these lines from the poem "For Grief" by John O'Donohue:

When you lose someone you love,
Your life becomes strange,
The ground beneath you becomes fragile,
Your thoughts make your eyes unsure;
And some dead echo drags your voice down
Where words have no confidence.

Your heart has grown heavy with loss;
And though this loss has wounded others too,
No one knows what has been taken from you
When the silence of absence deepens.

In this chapter, I have conveyed what has been taken from people who are estranged from relatives and the resulting sense of alienation, insecurity, and fragility. Because of the ambiguity of the loss, the heaviness of heart can persist for years. One source of the pain comes from silence: silence in response to requests for forgiveness and for a second chance, silence in response to expressions of anger and disappointment. Unlike in the aftermath of a death, one's awareness that the silence could be broken never goes away. For many estranged people, however, moving from silence to dialogue is an overwhelming obstacle.

What can be learned from our in-depth look at the effects of a family rift? The four threats make one point crystal clear: If you are deeply affected, even over years, by a family estrangement, *you are not alone.* I have shown that estrangement from family members triggers responses that are built into us as human beings. We long to belong, we crave stable attachment relationships, and we desire certainty in the face of loss. We are ill-equipped to cope with the chronic stress that results from these assaults to our sense of security and our self-esteem. To use the terms of my interviewees: You are not "strange," "weird," "weak," or "losing your mind," nor are you expected to "just get over it." Because of how we have evolved, experiences of rejection, shunning, and ostracism make us feel miserable, even if we played a role in making them happen.

For people not in a rift, this information on the negative consequences of estrangement can serve as a cautionary tale. The best way to deal with a rift is not to enter it in the first place. I learned from my interviewees how important it is to carefully weigh the costs and benefits of our actions *prior* to an estrangement. Cutting someone off in anger because of a perceived slight or breaking off contact because of a relative's lifestyle choice may seem satisfying in the moment. However, the long-term consequences for those involved should make us cautious about taking irrevocable steps in family relationships.

Finally, a keen awareness of the effects of estrangement can be a motive to reconcile. One reason to consider reconciliation is the desire to relieve another person's suffering from the four threats. If you have initiated an estrangement, it is likely that your relative is experiencing at least some of these devastating effects on his or her well-being. But no one is unscathed by estrangement, including the person who initiated the cutoff and maintains it. In Part Two of this book, we will look at how some people have managed to move from the "silence of absence" to restored, if not necessarily perfect, contact and communication. Unlike for some other stressful and painful conditions, there are "cures" for estrangement. I will share ideas for how to build a bridge over the rift and find freedom from the chronic stress of family rifts.

CHAPTER 4:

COLLATERAL DAMAGE

I have a very large family on both sides that was really fun and warm growing up. We always hung out with grandparents, cousins, and uncles, and it was exciting. That was the life I was born into. Then one day there was an argument, and my dad got me and said, "We're going home." Apparently, it had been building for a long time—something happened that caused them all to not get along anymore. It was never ever the same. I remember feeling there was no choice. My parents told us, "No, we can't go there anymore." We just accepted it for what it was.

I have two children, and I'm starting to become aware that their perspective is different because they didn't grow up seeing this harmonious family. They're left with wondering why their grandfather doesn't get along with any of his siblings or any of his big family. They're missing out right now on what could be warm and loving, like what I got to experience growing up. Our kids are strangers to a lot of the family, and they don't really engage much with them. It's missing from their life. You have to figure out a way to fix those things, or the innocent get hurt for generations.

—ROSS MACK

In recent years, my wife and I have been adding family. Both my daughters found their true loves, and we have welcomed their husbands, Michael and Richard. We are lucky that these sons-in-law are delightful individuals who enhance our lives. But in addition to the two of them, the marriages have brought into our orbit an array of other family members. In both cases, we have gained access to a cadre of interesting, and also useful, new relatives.

What do I mean by "useful"? Well, Michael's mother happens to be one of the world's leading experts on sensory testing. When it comes time to select wines for a big event, we can count on her to tell us what tastes good and what doesn't. When Michael needs medical advice, he calls my brother, the doctor. If someone in our family wants to buy a car, Richard's brother-in-law runs a major dealership and can advise us. If I need a place to stay in New Jersey, Rhode Island, California, Georgia, or anywhere else these extended in-law families live, I can save on a hotel bill. Thus, through my daughters' husbands, I have inherited a large network of individuals whom I may not know well but can access through the family linkages.

Such a reservoir of potential social support is extremely valuable. It even has a name: "social capital." That term refers to networks of trusted individuals who can be called upon in times of need. These social ties provide a safety net, available for information and advice if and when it is needed. Possessing social capital, in the form of people we see as friendly, supportive, and there for us if required—even if we are not in touch often—makes us feel more at home in the world. For example, I know that if I ever doubted that the Yankees are far superior to the Red Sox, I could call Michael's father, Frank, and he would convince me in a few minutes.

By adding family, I have gained access to resources that I never would have had otherwise. These benefits are precisely what is *lost* in a family rift. Suddenly or over time, an array of close and distant (and potentially useful) ties are broken. Thus, it is not only those who create the estrangement who suffer the loss. In many families, other people are forced to take sides. Just as we can add networks of relatives, we can also lose them—sometimes an entire side of the family—through no fault of our own. The split extends into the future, cutting off children and grand-children from a side of family life they will never know.

I usually am not one to inject military language into discussions of family dynamics, because juxtaposing images of love, intimacy, and sup-port with concepts like combat, attack, and surrender feels incompatible. But as I immersed myself in hundreds of accounts of estrangement, one military term entered my thoughts again and again: "collateral damage." Used to describe the effects of war, the term means injury inflicted on something other than an intended target. Substitute "someone" for "something," and it is difficult to come up with a better description of the far-reaching ripple effects of a family rift.

When scholars and therapists refer to a "family system," this is precisely what they mean. A family is not simply a bunch of individuals who act independently, but instead is a system in which change in one person or relationship profoundly affects the others. Tension among family mem-bers proliferates, rippling out as when you toss a stone into a pond. The ripple effects wash over innocent bystanders, particularly children and grandchildren. Entire sides of the family may cleave from each other. The shock waves of an estrangement do not simply go away, but rather they carry on through generations.

Jody Alessi is a busy working mother of three who is content with her hectic and fulfilling life. But, as I found with many victims of an es-trangement over which they had no control, there is an underlying sad-ness that emerges as she recounts the rift in the family. While Jody and other relatives stood helplessly by, a warm and nurturing family was disrupted. The collateral damage extended across individuals and genera-tions.

Jody's childhood was of a kind we more closely associate with earlier times or different cultures: She was embedded in a large extended family. Her parents divorced when she was an infant, and she and her mother moved in with her maternal grandparents. Her mother's siblings lived nearby and often took care of her while her mother was working. Jody told me:

I have seven cousins between these two families. They were like siblings. I would go to the elementary school in their neighborhood, walk home with them after school, and stay at my aunt and uncle's house until my mom finished working. It was a tight-knit family. I'm an only child, and my dad was in and out as a part of my life. I was really close to my cousins, especially one who was near my age. She was like a sister to me. And one of my uncles was like a second father to me when my dad wasn't around; he would take me to father-daughter events.

This story of estrangement has numerous twists and turns, but it revolved around one basic issue: the family business. Jody's grandfather had started a successful company, and her uncle Jack worked with him there. Her aunt's husband, Uncle Fred, also worked in the business. Over time, some of the older grandchildren began to work there as well.

As a child, Jody was aware that there was conflict regarding the business. She told me: "I don't really know what the business disagreements were about. But I know that it was bumpy, rocky. And that was the beginning of the end of my family." The rift began when her uncle by marriage, Uncle Fred, quit the business. Fred felt that he was treated like a second-class citizen in the business because he was a son-in-law rather than a son. He resented being paid less and saw the arrangement as unfair.

When Fred departed the business, it did not simply cause an estrangement with those directly involved. Instead there was a dramatic impact on the entire family. Jody summed it up in a single sentence: "So, he left the business and got a different job—and those two sets of relatives stopped talking to each other." The initial rift deepened as a result of conflicts over who would inherit the business after Jody's grandparents died, leaving a trail of resentment and hurt feelings among Jack, Fred, their wives, and Jody's mother. A key problem was a lack of communication. According to Jody, "They were never open enough just to sit down and have a conversation about it; it was more making snide comments under your breath, that sort of thing—a simmering resentment."

As a teenager, Jody experienced the tragic ripple effects of this fracture:

> We stopped having family holidays together. It was tough being stuck in the middle. I could go see one side of the family or the other side of the family, but we didn't all get together anymore. It got worse after I went to college and I wasn't there to help repair the situation. Now I have no contact with my aunt or my uncle or any of their children. One cousin was like a sister to me. Before the blowup, we would email and I would see her when I came to town. After all this happened, I felt really awkward because I knew she was really angry, even though I didn't have anything to do with it.

Jody's attempts at bridging the rift were rebuffed:

> I tried to patch things up. I finally plucked up the courage and wrote my cousin an email. I said: "I'm really sorry for how things happened. I want to let you know that I wasn't a part of it, I'm not involved." She wrote back a short email saying: "I understand, but it's going to be hard for us to be in contact. I can't be in touch with you anymore." And that was devastating. She was such an important person in my life. Then I was in town a couple of years ago, and I wanted to stop by and visit. Her family said: "No, you can't. We know that you weren't the person involved, but we just can't deal with you, we can't have contact with you."

The effects on Jody have been profound. She feels pulled apart from relatives she considered as close as her own nuclear family. The rift caught up innocent bystanders who became collateral damage from their elders' conflict. Her sadness mingles with confusion regarding how such a situation could have occurred:

> I feel badly because my cousins have a family unit that gets together. They're going to have all these family experiences that my kids aren't

going to have because I'm cut off from my extended family. People get so entrenched, and they're not really willing to waver from that. I don't know what to do about it. We didn't do anything to each other; it all happened above us.

When two people split the family, they are often thinking only of themselves. Caught up in a vortex of anger, blame, and conflict, they focus on their own hurts and bruised egos. They may take extreme stands, believing that they have been wronged, and are consumed by a desire to retaliate. Their own issues become of paramount importance, leading to what we identified in Chapter 2 as "perseverative cognitions." Hurtful events are played out over and over in the imagination. As the spiral of negative interactions mounts, a complete cutoff becomes more and more attractive. Each side seeks out supporters for their position, and opinions toward the other side become hardened.

At that point, my interviewees told me, people should stop and ask the question: *What are the long-term consequences of a rift for the well-being of the rest of the family, extending over generations?* What example is being set for children and grandchildren regarding the value of family solidarity versus self-interest? Do we want them to learn the lesson of outright rejection of those with whom we disagree? Is an estrangement worth an end to family gatherings, friendship among cousins, ties to uncles and aunts? These are critically important questions, because once broken, the connections are very difficult to repair.

THE WRONG KIND OF FAMILY TRADITION

I love family traditions. For example, I learned how to celebrate Christmas from my Pennsylvania Dutch grandmother, whom we called Nan. The Germans know how to celebrate Christmas, having invented a number of traditions like the Christmas tree and the carol "Silent Night." Every year, my daughters and I made Christmas cookies using Nan's recipe (inherited from her own grandmother). I now use this time-honored recipe with my grandchildren. Our method of opening gifts (slowly, one at a time) was carried over from my childhood, and my daughter continues the ritual with her own family. Family traditions are a source of security, allowing us to connect the past with the future over the course of generations.

There is a dark side to family traditions, however, and estrangement is one of them. As my interviews progressed, I became aware of an insidious pattern: A surprising number of people in a family rift pointed to a history of estrangement, sometimes stretching back generations. They were aware that cutting off relatives was a family theme that had been passed down. Some described it as a learned behavior, in which cutoff was seen as a viable option when conflict becomes too intense.

For this reason, people on the verge of an estrangement should carefully consider whether they are starting the wrong kind of tradition, one of exclusion and isolation. Rather than helping their offspring develop a benevolent family narrative that they can use in their own relationships, those who enter into an estrangement can provide a negative example for their descendants to follow.

Jody Alessi is an example. As my conversation with her drew to a close, she paused for a moment, deep in thought. Then she told me:

> You know, this is a legacy on my mom's side of the family. My grandpa and his brother had a big estrangement—I have no idea what it was about, because I was a small child. They didn't talk for years. We had family members whom I sort of knew they existed but had never met. Even before that, on my grandma's side of the family, there was a great-aunt I didn't know existed. She got into an argument with them and was cut out of the family. Mine was not a family where if you have a problem with someone, you talk it out. Instead they go without talking for decades.

Addie Eaton was cut off from her siblings for thirty years after a series of seemingly trivial incidents. Asked to explain why it happened, Addie pointed to a family tradition spanning more than a century of cutting off relatives as a solution to interpersonal difficulties:

> The family as a whole, even going back generations, was like that. My mom got mad at her brother in the 1950s and never spoke to him again. It goes even further back. My great-grandfather died at the turn of the last century and left behind a wife and two children. She just disappeared with the two kids and cut off contact with his family. In my dad's family, too, people cut one another off. He was one of nine kids, and he was having problems of some kind. Well, his whole family cut him off except for a couple of his siblings.

Family themes can develop over time that have enduring consequences for future generations. Research shows that positive family outcomes, such as marital quality and warm parenting styles, are transmitted across generations. Studies have also found that negative themes persist over generations, such as marital instability, harsh parenting, and aggression. When a family theme of estrangement as a solution for conflict emerges, it can be hard to halt the trajectory.

YOU DON'T KNOW WHAT YOU'VE GOT 'TIL IT'S GONE

What do bystanders lose when an estrangement occurs? I claimed in the Introduction that I wasn't planning to share much about my own experiences, but here's the exception. I feel comfortable telling this story because the main characters are long departed and will not read about themselves. It's a rift that occurred in my family, and which I recently came to understand had profound implications for me as I was growing up. I learned that I, too, experienced the collateral damage of estrangement. I am cut off from dozens of relatives with whom I might have shared family history, celebrated events, and support because siblings disagreed seventy years ago.

How did I come to this realization? After embarking on my research, I was exposed to an approach to understanding the family called Bowen theory. This perspective is unique in the attention it pays to what Bowen theory practitioners call "cutoff," a concept that, although broader in its meaning, encompasses the family estrangements that form the subject matter of this book. Murray Bowen, a psychiatrist, conducted pioneering work on what came to be known as family-systems theory. He founded the Bowen Center in Washington, D.C., which, after his death in 1990, continues to foster clinical practice and research on his key concepts, several of which you will hear about in this book.

If you decide to see a therapist with expertise in Bowen theory, on your first visit you will be asked to create (with the therapist's help) a family diagram. As Victoria Harrison, a faculty member at the Bowen Center, explains, the "family diagram is a graphic depiction of facts of family functioning over several generations." Using symbols for various family members and relationships, the diagram is much more than a simple family tree. Instead, it portrays the emotional connections within and across the generations, based on the assumption that the history of the family lives on in the present.

I spent an afternoon with Dr. Anne McKnight, the director of the Bowen Center, as we created my own family diagram. In preparation, I had tried to reconstruct my family history as best I could, going back several generations. I thought I had done a good job, but two hours with Anne showed me the limits of my awareness of family history and hidden patterns of interaction. Anne trained with Murray Bowen himself and has used the theory to help clients for forty years, so I knew I was in good hands. She explained the process to me:

> We take a three-generation family history, usually in the first session. We look at all of the different ways the family has managed anxiety. People may have the realization, "Oh, yeah, my grandfather did this or that!" That doesn't change the nature of the cosmos, but it does add the idea that a particular issue is not unique and it's a broader pattern

in a family. Somebody else did it before in the past. Then we can ask, "What went on with that?"

I was ready. Working with Anne, I learned that the family members in a generation are represented chronologically from left to right (e.g., the oldest child is farthest to the left), with females as circles, males as squares. After five generations were mapped out, from my grandparents down to my two young grandchildren (the diagram gets crowded!), I filled in more details. Conflict is indicated by a wavy line, divorce by two slashes, and cutoff by a broken line between two people. Time flew by as Anne led me through the complicated emotional landscape of my family.

I absorbed many things in this single session, but one lesson in particular stood out: what I had lost by a cutoff in my family generations ago. After I had thanked Anne for working with me, I stared at my diagram and marveled at this missing piece that I had never before considered. It led me to understand how one can lose connection to a world of family members because of actions taken before one's birth. The circumstances were rarely discussed in my family, but over the years I gleaned the basics.

My grandmother, whom we called Nan, had moved in with my family after the death of my father when I was three years old. Nan came to support my traumatized mother, a widow at age thirty-eight with four children, the oldest of whom was nine. When Nan moved in, she was already over seventy. In vibrantly good health, she took over the management of the household while my mother worked. It was Nan who was home for us after school, who patched us up after neighborhood altercations, and who maintained an even keel when our mother sank into periodic bouts of depression. She was a pillar of strength and an endless source of grandmotherly wisdom.

I spent much time talking with her as a child and an adolescent, but there was one topic on which Nan was largely silent: her family of origin. I knew she came from a family of five children, one of whom died as a young man. Of her remaining three siblings, her youngest sister, Bess, communicated once or twice a year by letter. There was no communication of any kind with her sister Mildred or her brother Wilfred. Nan never mentioned either of them. My mother and father were only children, so we had few relatives; it was surprising that those we did have were ignored. But answers were not readily forthcoming.

In college, my interest was piqued, and I badgered my grandmother and mother for information. Slowly I learned that the rift came about because of the family home, a stately, thirteen-room residence on a shady, tree-lined street in Selinsgrove, Pennsylvania. Built by my great-great-grandfather, a prominent Lutheran minister who helped found Susquehanna University in that town, it was inherited by my great-grandparents, who raised their children there. When both parents died, Mildred, the oldest, inherited the property. That event was the beginning of the end.

The family broke apart when Mildred decided to sell the house for a nominal sum to the university along with all the family furnishings, which included treasured artifacts such as the original patriarch's writing desk on which he penned his many articles and sermons. The other siblings were viscerally attached to the home, and bitter words were spoken in increasingly hostile arguments. After it was sold, the siblings died decades later without ever speaking again. I found these memories reemerging with surprising force as I shared them, and Anne swiftly and expertly diagrammed them.

Doing my research in preparation for the diagram, I learned that my grandmother's brother had four children, ten grandchildren, and thirteen great-grandchildren. A little web searching showed that they lived a half-day's drive from our home. I stared at the diagram and its broken line showing the cutoff between my grandmother and her brother, and I was struck with remorse at the missed opportunities it symbolized. Those connections could have been invaluable to me and my struggling family.

After my father's death, my mother became very isolated. With no siblings, she shouldered the burden of care for us with Nan, working long hours and coming home to the usual array of children's conflicts and problems. What might those first cousins have meant to her? How could they have grounded her in a sense of extended family and available support? As a child, I watched my friends spend time with their lively, noisy extended families. What would it have meant to my sense of security in the world if I had grown up embracing this extensive side of the family? My mother and I missed all these opportunities because a set of siblings fought over a house. Did anyone consider the collateral damage that might ensue? We will never know if the thought entered their minds as they quarreled, then cut one another off.

I have used this story from my own family because I know it well, and because of the questions it raises. But I uncovered many examples of people who suffered from the effects of a family rift years after it occurred. Some of the most poignant were from college students. I was fortunate in this project to have the assistance of Gregory Chen, an undergraduate at Cornell University who joined my research team. He recruited and interviewed dozens of his peers who experienced collateral damage from the estrangement of others in their families. As parents fight with their siblings, or with their own parents, I wish they could hear the voices of these young people who bear the burden of their elders' actions.

They should listen to James Doyle, who has been cut off from his mother's side of the family since he was in elementary school. Issues of inheritance divided his mother from his extended family, and contact was cut off. James told me: "It's kind of been weird, because we don't refer to my aunts and uncles and cousins as people we even know. But I still have memories of them, and I still consider them family."

James wishes that the family could reunite and cannot help feeling resentful that those involved are damaging his generation just for material gain. He explained: "I feel like I don't know when all of them will come to their senses and realize there is more to life than this money. It's kind of BS, because everyone is pretty well-off. They are definitely losing family over money. All of them are getting older, and it's definitely not worth it to cross out life connections for money."

James is not able to openly express his feelings to his uncles and aunts. I asked him what he would like to tell them if they were gathered in a room. He didn't hesitate to exhort them to consider the next generation:

> I would tell them that "you guys are brother and sister; you guys are supposed to take care of each other." It's not supposed to be everybody looking out for themselves. I would tell them to look at their grandchildren and ask them: "Is it worth it to stop family members from ever meeting each other because of money? Is it worth it to break family connections because of money?" I would tell them to hold your siblings close.

THE CONTAGION OF STRESS

Stress rarely affects just one person. Science supports that fact, but you can certainly go to your own experience for verification. If your sister is going through a divorce, for example, she is enduring one of life's most stressful experiences. She has her ups and downs, perhaps reconciling for a time, only to have the attempt fail. She suffers economically as she transitions to one income and must deal with the disruption to her children's lives. Her mental and physical health deteriorate.

Because you are close to her, you cannot avoid what social scientists call "stress contagion"—when devastating events to a loved one roll over into your own life. In this case, your sister is likely to rely on you for emotional support. You may have to sit with her through long evenings and take tearful calls in the middle of the night. She may need your help with child care, burdening your already busy schedule. You experience anger at her spouse, and you lose sleep ruminating about it. Most important, you have a front-row seat to watch someone you love suffer, which research shows is extraordinarily stressful. Our natural ability to empathize makes us feel as if we are sharing the difficult emotions. The same is true of an estrangement: By bearing witness to suffering you did not cause and cannot control, the stress becomes contagious.

One of the most challenging effects of living with a loved one's estrangement is the unpleasant experience of being caught in the middle. The innocent bystander turns into a mediator, referee, and ambivalent advocate for the opposing parties. Lois Miles provides an excellent example of how stress proliferated from her family members affected her daily life, health, and psychological well-being.

Lois was forced for years to act as a go-between for her mother, Sonya, and brother, Johnny. Lois's parents had a difficult and conflictual marriage, and divorced when she and her brother were children. Despite a chaotic early life, Lois has many positive memories about her brother: "We were thrown together and played together a lot and were very close. I looked up to him." She sighed and went on: "But he and my mother always had a very difficult relationship. He was a difficult child. He was exceedingly bright but also had emotional regulation issues."

As a result of these problems, Johnny was sent to live with his father's family. He dropped out of school and left home, traveling around the country and taking odd jobs. He appeared intermittently at Lois and Sonya's home, which was a source of both relief and stress. Lois told me:

> My brother would periodically turn up in the middle of the night and knock on the door. I would let him in, and he would have been hitchhiking and not have had a bath for days. All he would have was a bag with a couple of clothing items in it. Then my mother would come home, she'd be happy to see him, and they'd be okay for a little while. But inevitably she would find him difficult. She would begin to criticize him, saying things like: "Why are you such a bum? Why don't you go to school?" He would run off again.

As time went on, Johnny and Lois saw little of each other, and when they did meet, tensions inevitably emerged. Johnny continually complained to Lois about their mother, which Lois found highly stressful. Lois reported: "I had to listen to him talk badly about our mother. He would say, 'It's all because of our mother that my life is such a hell and

I'm a loser.' I started saying to him: 'You know, we're adults and we're talking about our mother all day long, every day. This is not healthy. You can't blame your mother for ruining your life.'"

As the negative interactions between Johnny and Sonya mounted, so did Lois's distress about negotiating between them. She was torn between the two, which led to angry confrontations with her brother:

> At one point, I told him: "You're trying to make me choose between you and our mother. If you make me choose, I'm going to choose her, because she has done the best she could. I cannot hold her eternally responsible for not being a perfect mother. She had a horrible experience of her own childhood and most of her life. She did the best she could, and I'm willing to forgive her for that." He became more and more angry with me.

Lois found it no easier to cope with her mother's distress. Sonya's emotionally tumultuous relationship with her son began to affect her health. Eventually, Lois's mother decided that the only solution was to remain totally estranged, even to the point of treating Johnny as if he did not exist:

> My mother had become ill. She had terrible back problems, and every emotion she had would make the pain worse. Just having interactions with Johnny practically killed her; she couldn't handle it. Finally, she said: "I just have to pretend that he's dead. I can't deal with it anymore; it's going to kill me." It made her very sad that she lost her son, but she convinced herself that he was dead to her.

Lois also was forced to break off contact with Johnny to reduce the intolerable tension. She became emotional as she told me:

> As long as our mother was still alive, I had an awful choice. If I'd gotten in contact with him, I could either tell her and cause her

immense emotional distress, or try to keep it from her so that she wouldn't know. But we were so close that she would inevitably find out that I was talking to him and keeping it from her. That was more than I could bear, and it would only end in heartbreak.

Lois admitted that she was barely able to cope with the contagion of stress from a situation she had not created. She was an innocent bystander caught up in a painful drama between mother and son. Like many other individuals who become collateral damage in an estrangement, she felt remorse at her inability to repair the situation: "This was a testament to the sad estrangement that our family was experiencing, and that's the real tragedy here."

Stress also proliferates through the emotional connection we have with others, which makes observing their suffering immensely stressful. Research shows that the closer we are to someone, the more we converge with him or her emotionally. Although this ability to empathize motivates us to help others, it also has a negative side. Studies demonstrate that we experience emotional contagion, that is, when others we care about are distressed, we experience similar emotions (for example, feeling sad when someone else is sad). When people undergo an estrangement, the tumultuous emotions do not stop with them. Those who care about them absorb and reflect the pain and suffering.

Nowhere was the effect of such emotional contagion so evident as in interviews with college students whose families experienced estrangement. The developmental task for a college student is to move from dependence toward autonomy, becoming more differentiated from the family and entering into adult relationships with parents and siblings. Living through a family estrangement interrupts a smooth pathway to adult development, drawing young adults into the turmoil of their parents and other relatives as they seek to be supportive at a distance. Emotional contagion from their loved ones can permeate their own experience.

Brenda Cisneros was the collateral victim of her mother's estrangement from her two brothers. Brenda's grandmother died, and her mother, Inez, was made the executor of the will. This decision caused resentment among Inez's siblings, who viewed it as a sign of undeserved parental favoritism. Increasingly acrimonious arguments arose about the distribution of the inheritance. Despite Inez's attempts at fairness, her brothers accused her of stealing from the estate.

The effect on Brenda's family was profound. She reported:

> They were really mean to my mom, and it caused a lot of problems on my mom's side. Because of the fighting, we lost contact with all my uncles. One of them was my godfather, and we were super close. Now he doesn't even send me birthday gifts anymore. It also affected my relationships with my cousins. There's an awkward tension, and I don't see them much anymore. There were times when we couldn't even see each other at all because the tension among our parents got so bad. It has created a distance between everybody.

Brenda has been deeply affected emotionally by her mother's distress over the estrangement, to the point of losing focus on her studies. She and her mother talk frequently, so she is exposed routinely to emotional contagion:

> Every time I was home, it would always be talking about the estate. It was always the topic of conversation, like, "What did your brothers say to you today, Mom?" There was always something new, so it was continually stressful. I tried to be supportive of my mom. Not only did she lose her mother, but she also had her siblings turn against her. Sometimes it would be too much to handle. There would just be too much drama going on in the family.

Brenda struggles with managing her own grief while trying to help her mother cope: "I was dealing with the fact that I have no family that I am close to anymore, while trying to be a support system for my mom. I've had to devote a lot of time throughout this situation, supporting my mom and listening to her, so I can try to make her feel better about it." For Brenda and other emerging adults, the ripple effects of a family estrangement are emotionally draining and tax their coping skills as they attempt to become independent. At any age, people drawn into a rift become immersed in the painful emotions of others, through no fault of their own.

TO THE SEVENTH GENERATION

I live in central New York, once the home of the Iroquois nation. Iroquois philosophy held to the "seventh generation principle." In this worldview, the Creator requires that we consider how our actions today will affect the seventh generation after us. It's a good approach to considering our effects on the natural environment, but it is also a powerful way to think about estrangement. Family rifts ripple into future generations, causing later cohorts to lose resources, knowledge, and loving relationships. A serious look forward can inspire caution when deciding that the best answer to family problems is a rift.

My respondents spoke with a single voice in offering this advice: If you are on the verge of entering into a rift, step back and consider the effects on others. Based on their experiences and mine, before cutting someone off, I suggest that you make a family diagram that is not of the past history, but *of the future*. For example, if you and your brother or sister declare that your relationship is over, what will it mean for your children, their children, and their children's children? What is needed, my respondents told me, is *legacy thinking*.

What do I mean by "legacy thinking"? Molly York provides a perfect example, in which she intervened in a budding estrangement in her own family. She told me:

> There was a time in my husband's family when two people were
> heading toward a rift. One of them was saying, "He needs to apologize

for what happened. He said this, this, and this. He needs to apologize." And everyone was asking, "What's going on with Uncle Oscar and Uncle Alan?" One day at a gathering, I found both of them and made them sit down. I said: "I have to tell you that this tension between you is now getting to the nieces and nephews. They are noticing, they are seeing it, and they are asking me about it. I think you two can do better, for the good of the whole family. I wouldn't worry about whose fault it was and who's apologizing. Open up and look at all these other people that are being impacted." Well, I've got to tell you, they got back on track the next week.

It is human nature to make decisions that feel satisfying in the short term, rather than looking toward the long-term implications. We do this on a small scale when that piece of pie looks so good that the long-range goal of losing weight recedes into the background. It's also clear on a large scale with societies that have trouble planning for long-term negative impacts, like the effects of climate change. It therefore may not seem natural to consider what example is being set for future generations when the primal urge hits to tell a relative, "I never want to see you again." However, it is important to stop and consider that decision in light of the collateral damage it may cause for generations to come.

No one put it better than one of my wise respondents. Diana Dyer became estranged from her mother after a tumultuous relationship in which boundaries were not respected. After having children, however, Diana became worried about the legacy of estrangement and its possible effects on them. With hard work and counseling, she was able to reconcile with her mother, who is now involved in the lives of her grandchildren.

Despite some ongoing stress in relating to her mother, nipping a flowering estrangement in the bud was worth it. Diana told me: "Because we overcame the estrangement, my kids have never known that behavior. They've never received it. They've never seen it. And they are themselves pretty good people, and when they go to raise their kids, I think they'll do a fine job of it. And that's what I wanted."

Diana is a spiritual and reflective person who has no difficulty taking the long view. As she considered my questions about why she overcame the estrangement, she shared this powerful example of legacy thinking:

Here's a little philosophy titbit for you, if you want it. I think everybody has around one hundred and fifty years of memory. Why? Because you talk to your grandmother, and your grandmother has talked to her grandmother. So your grandmother can tell you stories of her grandmother, and you get about one hundred and fifty years of history just sitting there in your kitchen. I can't go around treating my parents like they're jerks and model that behavior to my kids, and then have my one hundred and fifty years of future history turn out to be crap because I blew it.

PART TWO

THE ROAD TO RECONCILIATION

CHAPTER 5:

WHY RECONCILE?

Don't do what I did and wait ten years to heal your relationship. I say that because you just don't know when someone's time is up on this earth. You could wait too long and it would be too late. You don't want to have that weight and guilt on you for the rest of your life. But you do need to be able to have yourself at a place where you're ready to hold this conversation. So my advice is to get some help, go through whatever steps you need. Then go ahead and hold that conversation to start your life again, because the rift needs to be stopped before life can start again.

Whether you're the person that the estrangement happened to or you're the person who created it, you're both victims, and it's going to take one of you to make it happen. When you are successful at reconciling, it's almost like a rebirth. It's an awakening, and you become this new person, this energized, strong person, and you can take on the world. If you could take this on, and you reconcile, you can take on the world.

—MARTINA MOORE

We have explored the landscape of estrangement, immersing ourselves in the origins and painful effects of family rifts. We have seen how frequently they occur and the damage they cause to those directly involved as well as to other family members. Telling this part of the story was critically important, but much of it is familiar to readers who have experienced estrangement. Media coverage and online discussions of estrangement also focus on what causes families to fall apart, who is to blame, and the devastating effects that follow.

My goal in this book, however, is to move beyond the trauma of family rifts and the struggles of individuals to cope with them. As I discussed in the Introduction, I learned that there is an extraordinary reservoir of wise and practical information about why, when, and how to reconcile. I tracked down and talked to the true experts on reconciliation: people who overcame an estrangement in their own families. Instead of standing forever at the edge of the rift, against sometimes heavy odds, these individuals built a bridge across it.

I pulled out all the stops in my efforts to find people who bridged the rift. I gave them a special name, which I will use in the remainder of this book: "the reconcilers." Unwilling to dwell in the limbo of estrangement, they pushed ahead with restoring the relationship. The reconcilers were not in situations that were easy to resolve. Instead, their estrangements were as intractable and hopeless as those of others who never reconcile. They struggled with the same issues: harsh parenting, histories of conflict, poor communication, legacies of mental illness or addiction, and bitter fights over inheritance, the care of parents, or the choice of a partner. To help other people overcome estrangements, I believed that the most important thing I could do was to learn from them. I was not disappointed.

I was able to collect data on a large number of individuals who experienced an estrangement and later reconciled. (The details are in the book's Appendix.) The most important source is one hundred in-depth, personal interviews with reconcilers from across the country. In these interviews, I plumbed the depths of their estrangement and reconciliation experiences, asking not just for their general ideas but for specifics on what led them to reconcile, how they did it, and what challenges they encountered. In some cases, the reconcilers were interviewed more than once to examine how the restored relationship progressed over time.

The suggestions, strategies, and tips I offer thus come from the most extensive research study of family reconciliation ever conducted. The reconcilers are diverse in many ways. They were estranged from parents, children, siblings, cousins, uncles, and aunts. Many were in rifts for a decade or more. In some cases, both people desired a reconciliation; whereas in others, extraordinary persistence was required by one individual.

All the reconcilers, however, have two things in common. First, they are now back in contact with the relative from whom they were estranged. Second, whether they created the estrangement or were on the receiving end, no one regretted having reconciled. Indeed, some of them saw the reconciliation as one of their most important life experiences. As we will see throughout Part Two, the remarkable journey from a seemingly irreparable rift to a restored connection can be an engine for personal growth, a struggle that teaches invaluable lessons about what it means to be part of a family and, indeed, to be human.

The question comes down to this: *Are you ready to reconcile?* For many people, this question is both ambiguous and ambivalent. It requires taking risks and imagining an alternative future that is very different from the present. Whether you created the rift or not, it is important to consider precisely why it makes sense to try to create a bridge. If you ask the reconcilers, as I did, they offer a particularly compelling reason for why they are glad they made the attempt. They told me that the best answer to "Why reconcile?" is *Do it for yourself.*

DO IT FOR YOURSELF

Altruistic reasons are certainly one motivation for reconciling. We have seen the intense pain experienced by people who have been cut off. Few of us would willingly inflict suffering on another person when it is possible to alleviate it with limited burden to ourselves. However, there is an even stronger reason to give a relationship another chance: your own self-interest. Over and over, when asked why they overcame the cutoff, the reconcilers told me, "I did it for myself."

Cliff Miller was raised in a boisterous household in Kentucky; he was one of four siblings, all of whom had strong personalities. Cliff reported that it was superficially a "good childhood," but with an undercurrent of tension. He told me:

> There was a lot of sibling rivalry as we were growing up. My parents would favor one child over the other. So there was a lot of internal anger that manifested itself as we got older. My main problem was with my brother, Harry, who is three years younger than I am. He was always very self-absorbed and looking out for number one. It seemed like at times he'd just throw me under the bus. There was a lot of resentment there.

Harry moved to Connecticut while Cliff remained in Kentucky, raising a family and living near his widowed father. His occasional conversations with Harry were tense and strained. Past resentments were exacerbated by political differences. Harry became an "Eastern liberal," and although Cliff considers himself to be in the political middle, arguments over politics became increasingly irritating. The final break took place when Harry returned to their hometown in Kentucky for a visit. He suggested that the two brothers get together for a drink. It did not go well:

> He set me up to push my buttons. He made some crack about political crap. We're not hardliners, but his view is anybody that lives in the South is a right-wing wacko. That's not the case, but he just set me up, and he made a remark about political issues just to start something. I said, "That's it. I'm done with this guy." And I didn't speak to him for eight years.

To understand how remarkable this reconciliation was, it is important to hear the degree to which Cliff had abandoned the relationship. This was not a "let's wait and see" situation, with pathways to contact left open. Cliff was *done*:

I never wanted to be around him again. I have never felt that way about anybody, but the fact that he was a sibling probably compounded the intensity of my feelings. I never thought, "Someday I'm going to call him." I just thought, "I don't give a damn if I ever see him or speak to him again—he's toxic." I wanted nothing to do with him. He's just a guy I knew, and I was adamant that I cared nothing about him. He could have dropped dead, and I would have said, "What's for supper?"

As we have seen in Part One, the story could easily have ended here. Two brothers with a difficult history experience a hostile event and the relationship never resolves before it is ended by death. However, as he grew older, Cliff became aware of people his age who were becoming ill and dying. He told me: "At some point, I realized that time was running out and that if I wanted him back in my life to some degree, it was time. So I called him." To Cliff's surprise, his brother eagerly agreed to resume contact.

What is it like for the brothers now? Imperfect, as reconciled relationships sometimes are. They talk by phone regularly, usually about their wives and children and their eighty-five-year-old father and his care needs. Harry visits their father once or twice a year, and he and Cliff are pleasant to one another. Still, prolonged interactions with Harry are stressful for Cliff:

It's all cordial, but when he leaves, I'm exhausted. I don't know how to explain it. I kind of tolerate it and we get along fine, but I just could never hang out with him if we lived in the same vicinity. This is more than enough having him come back a couple of times a year. We just see the world differently.

And thus, we come again to this chapter's core question: *Why reconcile?* Cliff did not feel any need to do it for Harry's sake, given that Harry had treated him selfishly and dismissively. There was no pressure from his siblings or his wife. Even his father had come to accept that this was one relationship in the family that simply would never work out. So, why do it? Cliff's answer was simple: *He did it for himself.*

Over the years, Cliff's ambivalence about his brother would emerge to trouble him. It felt like an unscratched itch; it was unfinished business that had to be taken care of. When people are estranged, two very different ideas often exist at the same time, which psychologists term "cognitive dissonance." On the one hand, Cliff felt secure and justified in his decision to cut off contact. On the other hand, a soft voice kept insisting that the estrangement *just wasn't right*. He told me:

> You can't totally walk away from the relationship. I have all these connections to him through my other siblings, and one of my siblings would say, "Yeah, well what's going on with Harry?" Then I would realize he was gone out of my life. I was somehow cognizant of the need to forgive and move on, but I couldn't do it.

The reconciliation worked like a miracle cure, cutting through the murky unease and guilt about the estrangement. Cliff is not ashamed to admit that his motivation was selfish. When asked what prompted him to make the fateful call, he laughed and said: "I did it for me. Boy, it just felt good to put it behind me and move on. It was a feeling of relief." He went on: "It was very difficult for me to do it, because I was still angry at the way he had treated me. But you've got to put on your big-boy pants and do the right thing. It was difficult on the one hand. On the other hand, it was very liberating."

I asked Cliff what he would tell someone who was on the fence about reaching out as he did. His response:

> I would tell them to do it for yourself. You do take a chance— somebody might hang up on you if you called them. But I didn't care. This was all about me. I was doing this for me. Certain things just

came together, and I suddenly realized, "I'm going to have to take that heavy load off my back and quit marching." So do it now. Do it for yourself. It did immeasurable things for me.

Cliff's analogy of the heavy load was a common one. Many people described the years of estrangement as a weight, with reconciliation coming as a relief from having to carry that burden day in and day out. When Luann Carillo resolved a long estrangement, dropping the weight was one of the most liberating experiences of her life.

Luann's parents rejected her when she married a man from a different culture and class background. She described the situation: "My mother said to me, 'You won't have any family left if you marry him.' We got married anyway. My parents were not at the wedding. My dad did not walk me down the aisle. They told my brother, Shane, that he would be cut off as well if he had contact with me." Three years into the estrangement, Luann's twin sons were born.

At that time, Luann, Shane, and her parents lived in the same city. Luann was going to be transferred out of the country for several years by her company, and Shane arranged a dinner to see if the rift could be resolved before she left. It did not go well. Luann told me: "When Shane suggested we reconcile, they got up and left. They were not interested in any sort of reconciliation." Luann moved and another year went by with no contact. Then tragedy struck: Shane, with no prior symptoms, suffered a heart attack and died. Out of the grief came reconciliation. Luann told me:

> My mom was just broken then. She told me she realized how much time she had wasted that we could have spent in a relationship. She apologized. I was broken too, because Shane was my best friend. It brought us back together. I came and visited, and we had a long talk and set some boundaries. She was happy to spend time with her grandkids. We prayed together about it.

Luann is extremely grateful that the reconciliation occurred in time for them to enjoy the renewed ties:

> Our relationship was completely restored. Unfortunately, it took losing my brother to restore it. Then my mother got cancer and there was no treatment. I spent a week with her before she died. I'm so grateful. You know, Jesus says to forgive; he doesn't say to wait for them to apologize or wait for them to realize they were wrong. You just do it.

Like Cliff, Luann experienced reconciliation as the release from an enormous burden. She explained:

> The estrangement was really hindering me. It was hurting me more than my parents, my holding on to things and not forgiving. It was like a dead weight on me. I'm just glad that we did get to experience peace and healing and forgiveness, because when they passed away, they had peace and I had peace with them. That is what forgiveness is about. It's for you to be able to love them and get rid of that extra weight. Because that's what it is. It's an extra weight of negativity, of hurt feelings, of anger, of these bad feelings that you're carrying around with you all the time. I realized that it was only hurting me, and the only way was to give it all up.

Perhaps the best personal reward for reconciliation is summed up in the beautiful expression "peace of mind." Most narratives of estrangement include its opposite: anxiety, uncertainty, rumination about past harms, and guilt. Reconciliation brought about for many people a release from those emotions and a movement to a more peaceful state of mind and outlook on relationships.

If you are debating reconciling with a relative, it can be helpful to consider the reconcilers' message: The best reason is to do it for yourself. Even if the restored relationship is superficial or less than fulfilling, you may share the experience of Martin Kovac, who, after ending a twenty-five-year estrangement with his brother, had the sudden realization: "Hey, it's not in the back of my head anymore, the thought that I haven't talked to my brother in twenty-five years!"

No one summed up the "do it for yourself" mentality better than Marisa Gallagher. Her father was abusive to her, her siblings, and her mother. Marisa escaped the family when she went to college and refused any contact with her father for twenty years. Over time, her father became a better person and reached out to her occasionally to express his remorse over his behavior. Marisa wanted nothing to do with him. Then she went on a spiritual retreat. She told me: "One exercise was 'find a way to forgive somebody.' I did that and I wrote him a letter. I told him I forgave him for the crap he's pulled, and I talked about what I did, too, that helped keep us estranged." They began with first limited and now regular contact.

After such negative childhood experiences and twenty years of estrangement, I could not help wondering why Marisa made the effort. Was it for her father's sake, now that he has grown old? She laughed, shook her head, and said:

> I'm not doing it for him. I'm doing it for me! I'm doing it for me, for
> my sense of well-being, for my health. I realized that this is what's
> going to heal a person like me the best. And never mind Dad. In this
> situation, as far as I'm concerned, Dad can go jump in the lake.
> Healing me was what I was going for.

THE FOUR BENEFITS OF RECONCILIATION

The reconcilers have a unified message: When it comes to ending a rift, being selfish is a good thing. They believe that reconciling was transformative, resulting in a burden lifted from their shoulders. But given the anxiety, risk, and effort that a reconciliation attempt can take, you have every right to ask, What, specifically, will I get out of it? The reconcilers identified four key benefits of reconciliation. Of course, not everyone will experience all of them, but consider these potential gains as you debate whether you are ready to take steps to end the rift.

THE FIRST BENEFIT: AVOIDING REGRET

Many people told me that they were prodded to reconcile by a nagging sense of *anticipated regret*. Usually, we think of regret as believing that our current situation would have been better if only we had made a different decision. Research shows, however, that anticipating regret can be a powerful motivation for action. Psychologists who have studied this issue have asked, How can thinking about future regrets affect the actions we take? They have found that when people are faced with difficult decisions, a critical factor for many is the regret they think they may feel in the future for an action taken or not taken. Thus, anticipating possible regrets can serve a very useful function: It helps us make better decisions.

Avoiding future regret was the motivation for many people who reconciled with family members after an estrangement. Perhaps a bout of insomnia led to a late-night rumination, or hearing a passage from scripture in church about how little time we have (along the lines of "teach us to number our days, that we may gain a heart of wisdom"). As they get older, some people realize that soon it will forever be too late to apologize, to forgive, or even to click the Add Friend button on Facebook. A powerful motivation for taking the first, tentative step is a small, recurring voice murmuring, *"Will I be consumed with regret it if I wait until it's too late to reconcile?"*

Lois Miles, whom we first met in Chapter 4, decided she needed to attempt a reconciliation with her brother, Johnny. As Lois continued to think about her brother, feelings of anticipatory regret grew:

> About five years ago, I realized that we were getting older. I had lost so many friends to cancer. I had this feeling in the back of my mind: "I don't know what I'll do if I hear that Johnny's dead and I've never spoken to him again. I don't know how that will affect me or whether I'll be able to bear it." That inspired me to write him one more letter

saying, "I just can't not make one more attempt." I had to do it for myself. At least I would have known I tried that last time. He agreed to try again.

Lois and her brother had a successful reconciliation—but she almost missed her chance. Not long after their reunion, Johnny died. Lois told me: "One day we had an amazing phone conversation and processed the past a little more and talked about the future. We hung up, and within days they called that he had died during the night of a massive stroke. They found him dead out in his workshop, which was a place he loved. So I felt good about having reached out to him before it was too late."

Lois is overwhelmingly grateful that she allowed anticipatory regret to guide her decision to mend the relationship:

> It was an incredibly healing thing. I am so, so glad that I did it and that we had that time to reconnect and share again the closeness that we'd had when we were children. I can't even imagine how much I'd be suffering now if that had not happened and he had died before we reconciled.

Stories of reconciling "in the nick of time" make powerful arguments for reconnecting. Paula Bright became estranged from her sister, Sally, after a difficult childhood and continued conflict into adulthood. Following a decade of no contact, Paula received a life-threatening diagnosis that precipitated a reconciliation. As the illness brought them together, Paula noted a dramatic change in her sister: "She softened a lot. She stopped treating me like a pawn in the family. She started asking how I was doing and if there was anything she could do." The relationship became a warm and loving one.

Paula recovered from her illness, but after less than a year of reconciliation, Sally died suddenly and unexpectedly. Paula is grateful every day for the time she had with Sally. It even cast her own illness in a different light: "I don't regret having cancer, because it bought some time with my sister that I would not have had otherwise. If I had to do it over again, I would choose cancer so that I could have that time with Sally."

After the reconciliation, Paula was freed from any feelings of regret, because she had bridged the rift with her sister. Paula offered a moving description of what that year together meant:

> Before Sally died, we had some time where we were connected as sisters. It wasn't about somebody else. It was just about us being sisters. Some of my fondest memories of her will be just spending time together. I breed dogs, and I would bring out the puppies and show Sally how they played together, because she loved stuff like that. We enjoyed the simplest kind of things together. It made me so happy to have that time that was just about something silly and light, like playing with the puppies. We were both so happy.

THE SECOND BENEFIT: GETTING BACK INTO THE FAMILY

We have seen in earlier chapters how an estrangement between two individuals can have powerful ripple effects on the entire family. In some cases, family members take sides and recruit others into their camps. Even if family members remain neutral, the hostility between the two warring parties makes it impossible for them to be at the same events. For the reconcilers, a desire to reintegrate into the family was an important motivation to reconnect.

Sidney Kelly had a difficult relationship with his father and after a number of angry incidents decided to cut off all contact with him. However, this estrangement could not be separated from his relationship with his mother. In addition, his younger brother remained close to his father. Sidney considered his options carefully and made a decision to reconcile:

> When you're estranged from your whole family, it's one of those things where you're going to see each other and you're going to be in the same family gatherings. Your lives are still going to be connected in some

way. If my father had been the only one, then it might be different—we might still not have a relationship. But with my mom and brother choosing to stick by his side, it was to either continue to be estranged or to ignore some of the issues and problems and put them aside to maintain relationships with the other family members.

Families constitute a system in which any two members' interactions are likely to affect the relationships between other relatives. An estrangement can make almost any family gathering tense: Do we invite Ted if we are also inviting Alice? Can we really leave Bob out of the wedding just because Carol won't be in the same room with him? What if there is a huge scene? By the same token, reconciliation can be a path to greater family solidarity and integration. It also leads to more tangible benefits, as we will see in the next section.

THE THIRD BENEFIT: ACCESS TO RESOURCES

In contemporary society, we tend to think of the family purely in emotional terms. After we reach adulthood, few of us are fully dependent on our families to support us financially, provide us with work, or care for our children, as was the case in earlier times. Therefore, we focus on the quality of the interpersonal relationships, such as whether we feel loved, supported, and cared for. The reconcilers agree, but they also insist that bridging the rift can bring much more tangible rewards. You will recall my earlier discussion of the idea of "social capital," those sources of practical and financial support that are available to us even if we infrequently use them. Reconciling with one's family makes it possible to tap family social capital—something that cannot happen while estranged.

Mindy Russell experienced a devastating rift with her sister, Florence. Their father changed his will and told only Mindy, who was the executor. Although Mindy worked tirelessly to be as fair as possible in the management of the estate, her sister was furious at the arrangement, and they became estranged for twenty years. Their children, who had previously been close, witnessed bitter fights between the siblings and gave up contact with one another. The tragic death of one of Florence's children brought the sisters back together, and they restored a relationship that, although not as close as it was before the rift, involved enjoyable activities and pleasant visits.

For both sisters, the reconnection created a source of practical assistance that neither would have had while living with the rift. Mindy told me:

> The fact that we got back together was really a good thing, because a few years later she had a heart problem that was life-threatening. Her children work and would have had trouble caring for her, but I was able to go and stay with her when she got home from the hospital. Her children didn't have to worry about it. Then there was another benefit. Later on, I had my eyes operated on at different times. Florence came down to where I live and stayed with me each time after my eye surgeries.

Amy Sanders found similar tangible rewards from reconciling. Her estrangement began over three years ago. Amy's father entered into a dispute with his brother over money he felt was owed to him. Amy's father and uncle each firmly believed the other had cheated him. According to Amy:

> When my uncle did that to my dad, it hurt him immensely. We lost all contact with my uncle and his sons. My father passed away a year and a half later, and they did come to the funeral. But they did not sit with the family, and we didn't welcome them in our homes because of what happened. After my dad passed away, my mother and I had no connection with his side of the family at all—none.

Fully three decades later, one of the reconciliation miracles I had come to expect occurred. For reasons she cannot explain, Amy began to think about, and miss, the other side of the family. A few years ago, an idea popped into her head that was both unexpected and eventful. She told me:

> I started thinking about the photographs I'd seen of my dad as a boy. I remembered one where he's about eight years old in this photo. He was in a 4-H club where they raise animals. I kept thinking about that picture of my dad with a sweet little calf that he had raised for his project. He often talked about how much he loved that calf and how proud he was of having raised it. So I wanted that picture very much. But the problem was that we believed my uncle's widow, my aunt Adele, had it. My mother said to me, "You know, Adele and I don't have that many years left, we're both in our late seventies. So I'm just going to reach out and ask her about that photo."

Amy was surprised, but she supported her mother. She went on:

> My mother sent her a letter and she included some other family photos. She asked about the old photo with the calf and suggested they meet. Time passed with no answer, and my mother got the nerve to call. Mom said: "I don't know if she's going to hang up on me or what. But I'm just going to reach out and try it." She called, and to her surprise my aunt said, "Well, I've looked for that photo and I can't find it." She hesitated and then went on, "But you're welcome to drive over and help me look for it." She lived about an hour away.

Amy's mother was anxious about a meeting, but she said to Amy, "Well, if she acts too hostile, I'll just leave." However, her aunt was welcoming. They found a box of family memorabilia in the attic. Amy shook her head in amazement as she continued: "And so, she gets this big box of pictures and they root through the pictures for hours. They spent hours visiting and getting reacquainted by looking at old photos."

Unable to find the photo with the calf, the sisters decided to go out for a walk together. They came back to the house, and Amy's mother sighed, saying, "Well, I guess I'll give up on this and go on." To which Adele responded, "Well, come on in for a cup of tea, and we'll look one more place." Amy thoroughly enjoyed telling what happened next:

> Of course, in the last place they looked, there was an old family photo album. At the very back of that photo album was the picture of my dad with his prize calf that we'd been looking for all along. And so, that photo was what brought the two families back together. Of course, my dad is gone, my grandmother's long gone, my uncle is gone, but it's been a blessing to reconnect with them. Sadly, my aunt is gone now too, but my cousins and I have become close. We are five cousins, and it's been nice reconnecting with them and getting acquainted with their families.

For Amy, the social and practical benefits of reconnecting have been enormous. She said, "Tears came to my eyes last Christmas because my cousin, Kiki, sent a wreath and a bottle of wine for us, just to let us know she's thinking of us. And when my mother and I were on vacation, Kiki met us and took us out for dinner and to her house." The benefits of the new resources went both ways. Amy's aunt had been lonely since her children had moved away, and at her age, she had little social contact. Amy was able to keep an eye on her for them.

More intensive help was needed, as well:

> At one point she broke her ankle and had to go into a rehab center near here. We went to see her and I talked to them on the phone about her. When she got out, they were worried about her. I said, "Well, I can take your mother to where she needs to go." They responded: "Oh, would you, Amy? Oh, that'd be great." And so, you know, we're blessing each other on each side."

THE FOURTH BENEFIT: SHARED LIFETIME

With the longevity revolution, we are living (and staying healthier) longer than ever. One effect of this demographic change is the increase we have in shared lifetime with our family members. Parents may have a half century or more of relationships with their children after they become adults. With siblings or cousins, we could be looking at a century with one another. For my first book, *30 Lessons for Living: Tried and True Advice from the Wisest Americans*, I interviewed a 108-year-old woman who was in daily contact with her two brothers, ages 100 and 103! Of course, this will not happen to all of us, but even in our middle years we can expect decades of relationship time with a brother or sister.

In an estrangement, shared lifetime stops dead. That expression is particularly apt here, because in many rifts, someone declares that the other person "is dead to me." In my interviews with estranged people, the family story came to an end, and the years of absence began to roll out, one after the other. If you are in such an estrangement, you might take a moment to imagine the alternative future. A benefit of reconciliation is shared (rather than separate) lifetime. Is it worth the risk? The reconcilers think so.

For these individuals, the benefit was pleasure and enjoyment in a future they had not anticipated. In some cases the relationship never reached previous closeness. In other families, however, the reconciliation brought a renewed and vibrant relationship. Some reconcilers were appalled that they had so long deprived themselves of friendly interactions with their relative. Good reasons to reconcile are to do it for yourself, to avoid regret, and to gain resources. But one possible payoff is simply this: It can be life-enhancing, providing a source of enjoyable experiences that you otherwise would have missed.

Naomi Unger loved her sister, Vera, and was dismayed when Vera married Marvin, who did not like her family. The family attempted to tiptoe around him, but his negativity ruined every interaction. Naomi and other relatives were pushed away from the couple. For over two decades, Naomi saw her sister only a few times, at obligatory family gatherings.

Then, Vera contacted Naomi and told her that she had left Marvin. Naomi did not hesitate; she jumped back into the relationship without a second thought.

Now, Naomi can barely believe her good fortune. The years of shared lifetime after separation have far exceeded anything she hoped for. She told me:

> We picked up right away. Vera came up and stayed with us for a period of time. I went to visit her and we just hung around, basically reconnected. And it was like no time had gone by at all, and it was fun. We talked about things in our childhood, and there were things she'd forgotten, there were things I'd forgotten. We laughed our brains out. We discussed differences we had about things and how we felt similarly about things.

Discovering shared interests and guilty pleasures was part of the fun:

> One of the favorite things that we do now is watch *The Bachelorette* together whenever the season is on. She watches at her house, and I watch at my house; we text back and forth and have opinions about everything, of course. She has joined my husband and me on a few vacations, and if it's on, we sneak away to watch the show together. We probably drive him crazy with our loud opinions.

I asked Naomi what it meant for her to have the relationship back. She told me:

> Unbelievably, we're like best friends. We're very different people, as it turns out. I'm more easygoing and freewheeling, for example. But we accept that about each other—that's not a problem. The relationship just continues to blossom, and we just enjoy the heck out of each other, and our families are enjoying each other.

Naomi paused and then added, a little wistfully:

> My sister and I have said: "Wouldn't Mom be thrilled if she could see
> us sitting here having a cocktail together or watching TV?" Because she
> knew that we were estranged. That kind of broke her heart, because
> my mother and her own sister were really close. And so my sister
> sometimes says, "Wouldn't Mom love it if she could see us now?" And
> we think, "Yeah, well, she can. You know, she's looking down, being
> happy from someplace."

Of course, not all experiences of reconciliation turn out to be as life-
enhancing as these examples. But the stories I have shared in this chapter
are by no means exceptions. There is a celebratory feeling when what
seemed like the end of shared lives turned out not to be the end after all.
Especially when the earlier phases of the relationship had a positive side,
many people were able to recapture the pleasure of the past connection.
Indeed, a common feeling was, "Why did I wait so long?"

Olivia Polanco grew up in a blended family. Her brother, Leon, did not
get along with their father, and in high school, he left to live with his
mother. For nearly a decade, there was no contact; Leon had disappeared
from their lives. The death of their grandfather, to whom Leon had been
close, brought him back into contact with the family, and he and Olivia
have a very warm relationship. She told me:

> If I could do anything differently, I would have reached out to him
> sooner. I ask myself, "Why didn't I?" I don't know. Maybe it's just so
> easy to not do anything. I feel sad for my dad and my brother and
> their relationship. They are so close now, and I think it's sad that they
> missed out on a lot of life together. If anybody is really thinking about
> reconciling, I would tell them to reach out, to do it, to take that step if
> you feel in your gut that it's what you should do. I should have done it
> earlier.

ARE YOU READY TO RECONCILE?

When people are in an estrangement, they typically think about it a lot. Except for the most traumatic and damaging circumstances, people in rifts shift in and out of reflection on alternative futures. They wonder what it would be like to reconnect and how life might be changed. Among individuals I interviewed who were currently estranged, the question of whether or not to attempt a reconciliation loomed large.

To borrow from the world of advertising: "There's a social science for that!" Psychologists and sociologists have studied extensively the topic of behavior change: What are the steps that lead someone to move from Point A to Point B, whether it be a decision to buy a car, change jobs, improve their health, or get married or divorced? And social scientists love to give their concepts ponderous names, so here's one you can feel free to drop at cocktail parties: the "transtheoretical model" of behavior change. I'm not going to go into what "transtheoretical" means here. Instead, there's one very helpful insight it teaches us.

Decades of research using this model have shown that when we move toward a major life decision, most of us begin in the same way. We enter a stage called "contemplation." In that stage, we recognize the existence of a problem, and we start to think about it and consider the pros and cons of acting. We contemplate the change, often going back and forth on whether to proceed. When contemplation leads to a decision to move ahead, we prepare and take action.

The reconcilers told me about three "nudges" they experienced when they were in the contemplation stage. Be sure to pay attention to these three signs that you may be ready to reconcile:

1. THE CIRCUMSTANCES HAVE CHANGED

As we will see in later chapters, estranged relationships become frozen in time, given the end of contact. Because people are cut off, they may not be aware of how circumstances have changed. In some cases, however, the change is obvious, as when a problematic in-law moves out of the picture. Glenna Redmond successfully reconciled with her sister, who had married an angry and controlling man. As long as her sister was tied to him and "under his thumb," there was no chance for bridging the rift. She told me: "I wanted to do it for a really long time, but when her husband was alive, I didn't even consider trying. Well, then her husband died. I emailed her, and I told her I was coming up to see her. And without the husband, our relationship just started again, as good as it had been before." New circumstances can make you ready to reconcile, and it is important to be aware of them.

2. YOU START DEVELOPING A PLAN

One sign of being ready to reconcile is finding yourself working out concrete plans. You may imagine alternative ways to reconnect, sometimes in detail. Katrin De Jong went through this process before she decided to take action on reconciling with her son. Perhaps you recognize thoughts like these:

> Leading up to offering to reconcile, I tried to picture myself in the situation. I asked myself, "Okay, how am I going to feel twenty-four hours after I make the attempt?" Am I going to be ashamed of myself for, say, blubbering into the phone? Am I going to be able to keep myself in check enough that I'm going to be able to make a request to meet me for a coffee? If he's not receptive, how am I going to feel? What if he says yes—what will my next move be? I had started asking, "What are the pros and cons?" I didn't want to go in unprepared.

When your vague inclination to reconcile makes way to pondering concrete strategies, you may be ready to move forward.

3. YOU GET A SIGN

The reconcilers offer one more piece of advice for knowing when and if you are ready to reconcile: Look for a sign. No, I'm not being spiritual or mystical here. But when we are feeling ambivalent about making a change, we can become aware of the topic all around us. It's like when you learn a new word and then you see it all the time. You may hear a sermon, read a book, find an old letter, attend a retreat where forgiveness is discussed. A surprising number of reconcilers pointed to a particular moment when they knew it was time to reconcile, and they paid attention to it.

What might a sign look like? One of my favorite reconciliation stories comes from Fletcher Inman. He and his brother, Arlen, had an angry incident when their children were young. Fletcher told me: "His son continually bullied my kids. I asked Arlen to make him stop. That led to some very harsh words, and we stopped speaking to one another." This situation went on for thirty years. By the time of Fletcher's interview, I had become accustomed to unexpected turning points and surprising revelations. However, even I was not prepared for a real Christmas miracle. Fletcher recounted the experience:

> We're not very religious, but we do go to church on Christmas. So we went to the morning service, and the preacher gave a sermon. It was all about forgiveness and letting go of things that drive you crazy. It sunk in. Suddenly, I thought, "That's it. I'm going to call Arlen and say, 'I apologize for being so angry.'"

Fletcher reacted immediately to the sermon's message without analysis or second thoughts. He told me:

> We got home from the service and I told my wife, "I'm going to call Arlen and apologize." She was surprised, but all she said was, "Go do it." So, that was it. I called him up and I apologized for being so angry with him and we had a nice chat. And he admitted to some things and that's been it. It's history. We now we get together a few times a year and talk on the phone. The argument that caused all this seems trivial now. It's kind of a Christmas miracle, isn't it?

In the remaining chapters of this book, the reconcilers will offer more concrete and specific advice on how to plan and carry out the reconciliation process. In "The Tool Kit" section of each chapter, I will share their experiences of what worked and what didn't. This practical information can be very important in making the decision to bridge the rift or to live in it for a while longer. Of course, the choice is up to you, and the reconcilers tell you to trust yourself.

I leave the last word to Max Whitney, who advises that ultimately you need to examine, and then follow, your feelings:

> You're not a bad person for being estranged. Just be gentle with yourself and understand that you're not wrong for your feelings. You're not a bad person for not wanting to talk to someone for a while. Maybe you just needed that time apart. When you're ready to try, you'll know. You'll know when the time is right to talk again.

CHAPTER 6:

VOLCANIC EVENTS

We had argued before, but there was something different that day. She kept telling me that she wanted a tiny wedding with just the parents, brothers, and sisters. I knew it would deeply hurt her grandparents not to be invited. I guess I told her that one too many times and in too strong words. She exploded, shouted at me, "Well, if that's the case, I don't want you to come!" She stormed out, and since that day three years ago, I haven't seen her again.

My husband and I were not invited to her wedding, and we have not seen our first grandchild, who is one year old. I think about that moment—I even dream about it—over and over. How could everything turn on just that one time, just that moment? Well, I guess it did, because I'm sure paying for it now.

—ELLA LANDRY

My grandmother came of age at the beginning of the last century. In those days before television or the internet, creating scrapbooks was a popular leisure-time activity. My grandmother left us several such volumes of the highlights of her young life at the turn of the twentieth century. Her scrapbooks are filled with mementos of important events: a dance card where eligible men signed up for a waltz or fox-trot, a menu from a formal dinner, a theater program, a poem, a lock of a child's hair. Photographs had pride of place, as picture taking was a costly luxury.

Paging through an old, treasured scrapbook, one thing strikes the viewer: Each object is frozen in time. Photographs, clippings, souvenirs are all there to be remembered and mused about, but they will never change. Taped to the pages or under cellophane, their function is to represent the historical moment in which each emerged. The items in my grandmother's scrapbooks highlight past events and invite nostalgic reflection, but they do not have a future.

As I sought to understand family estrangement from the stories of people living through it, I found that I was assembling my own version of a "scrapbook." In computer files, rather than on the pages of a weathered binder, I had a collection of powerful events that instigated family rifts, many of which could be summed up in a single image. Like mementos in a scrapbook, they are frozen in time but open to endless interpretation. They symbolize a longer history and a larger world of relationships that go beyond the specific issue on which the event turned.

What kinds of things are in my scrapbook of estrangement events? Here's a plane ticket, never used. Gail Ziegler bought it for her brother to come see their dying mother. She told me: "My mom lived in Florida and was desperate to have him come visit. We bought him a plane ticket and arranged to have him picked up at the airport. He never used it. He just didn't come. At that point, I decided I didn't want to have anything to do with him anymore."

There's a photo of a beautiful, antique porcelain vase. Anya Kozlov had looked forward to one day inheriting this family heirloom, which had been promised to her by her grandmother. But her father forgot about the arrangement; when he died, the vase was left to her sister. Anya asked her sister to reconsider and allow her to have the vase, but her sister refused. "What I had been told was mine ever since I can remember was instead to become my sister's. That felt like a slap in the face. When she told me that I wasn't getting what had been promised to me, that was the end of the relationship."

And here's a wedding invitation. Gwen Houston dreamed about the wedding of her daughter, Veronica, for years. However, after Veronica and her fiancé moved to the city where his family lived, Gwen's fantasies were shattered. "She was planning the wedding, and they were excluding me; everything was about her husband's family. At the wedding, I felt like an acquaintance. It was supposed to be one of the happiest days of my life, but it turned out to be one of the darkest days of my life. We haven't spoken for two years."

When people share such stories of how a rift began, they typically do so with extraordinary clarity. As I listened to their descriptions, I was reminded of those old-fashioned press conferences you see in films from the 1940s. The politician, movie star, or police chief steps forward and suddenly flashbulbs go off, riveting the brilliantly illuminated speaker in place. Estranged individuals often describe such a "flashbulb" episode—a snapshot memory of how the relationship ended. It was, as several of them put it, "as if the world had turned on a dime." The event constitutes a clear before-and-after moment in which everything changed irrevocably.

Over the course of many interviews, I became obsessed by the question: *Why is a single event so important in generating a family rift?* Do such signature incidents truly take everyone by surprise, or are they the crystallization of ongoing but obscure processes? As so often happened, I was led to an answer by one of my respondents, who are, after all, the true experts on estrangement. Eliot Dahl's rift began on what otherwise had been a normal visit to his mother's home. The memory is as vivid today as it was thirty-five years ago:

> My mother and I became estranged when I was married to my first wife, Betty. I was visiting my mother at her home in another state. My mother had paid for other grandchildren's college, and the subject of Betty's son, Derek, came up. I said, "I hope you consider my stepson as family and you will also help with his college expenses, the same as the son I had with Betty." My mother said, "No, I will not do that."
>
> I told her, "Well, Mom, he's my son. He's as dear to me as my own son is." She was adamant: "No, I will not do that." Things got more heated. Finally, I walked out. I called up someone I knew out there

and said, "Come get me. I'm leaving. I'm out of here." I stayed with this friend the rest of the time and then flew back home. I was furious that she wouldn't consider someone I loved as part of the family. For five years, she made no effort to get in touch with me, and I made no effort to get in touch with her. She wouldn't accept my stepson, so the hell with her.

I was so absorbed in Eliot's story that without much thought I asked him: "But how can one event be so important?" I told him that we had surveyed hundreds of people, and many of them pointed to a disastrous incident or event as the trigger for the estrangement. So why, I persisted, is a single event like this so important?

Eliot thought about the question for so long that I was certain his response would be a simple "How should I know?" Instead, he provided a key to understanding why single events are so important:

> Let's go to a metaphor. Think of a volcano. The fire's inside and steam is coming out of the top. But all of a sudden, it's not from the top but from a fissure that opens up on the side where lava comes pouring out. It's not what you might expect, not the dramatic blowing of the top, but something relatively minor. All that gas and lava comes spewing out. A relatively trivial opening can be just as devastating as the top going off of Mount St. Helens.

It's hard to resist geological metaphors in a book about rifts, but I realized that considering these incidents to be "volcanic events" is strikingly accurate. If you remember your earth science, you know that the rocks underneath the earth's surface can melt, becoming magma. The magma rises upward, and when it reaches the surface, an eruption occurs. The more difficult it is for the pressure to escape as the magma rises, the more violent the eruption. Just as the circumstances leading to a volcanic eruption build over the course of years, the powerful estrangement event is the culmination of a long history of tension and disappointment.

Eliot thus provided me with the key to understanding the outsize role of specific events. A small fissure opens up floodgates of pain and resentment. In his case, Eliot had long felt that his mother disapproved of his marriage and of his wife. His family was one in which people rarely discussed their feelings, so his resentment simmered beneath the surface. The signature incident embodied long-standing, unresolved conflicts, which then exploded in an unexpected way. For many people, the volcanic event crystallizes everything that was wrong about the relationship. Out of many similar moments, they are pushed toward dramatic action by this particular event, even if they do not understand precisely why.

WHY IS A SINGLE EVENT SO POWERFUL?

When estranged people tell others about the event that led to the rift, they often encounter the response, "Wait—that's all that happened?" However, research shows the power of a single event to cause a dramatic change in a relationship. My own studies make it clear that volcanic events can take on such outsize power that they stand in the way of reconciliation. After the initial shock, they harden over time and are reinforced by rumination. Social science helps us unravel the mystery by showing that it is in fact normal to be profoundly affected by negative relationship events.

One reason we are puzzled by the powerful impact of an event is that we think of our relationships as unfolding in a predictable, linear progression. However, studies show us that dramatic events are in fact major engines of change. Relationships researcher Colleen Harmeling and her colleagues have studied "transformational relationship events." They find that such events force a reinterpretation of what the relationship means to the person, how important it is, and whether it should be continued. As they sum up the research, transformational events "test the very fabric of the relationship, including the partners' identity. Turning points can create the worst enemies or best friends, with fundamentally altered affective and psychological connections." One incident, the research shows, can cause "dramatic, discontinuous change to the relationship's trajectory."

Studies find that negative relationship events have a particularly powerful impact on lowering the level of commitment to the relationship. Further, because estrangement events are strongly emotional, they are remembered vividly. A highly charged incident can become a reference point for how we remember everything about the relationship leading up to the event. The past history shifts as it is interpreted in light of the volcanic event.

There is an additional factor that increases the power of estrangement events. If you are in a rift, you have probably spent many hours thinking back over a moment that transformed the relationship. Psychologists have a term for this mental process: "angry rumination." They define "angry rumination" as "perseverative thinking about a personally meaningful anger-inducing event." The event may have happened to you or to someone else; indeed, some estrangement events happen to other people (as in the case of Gail Ziegler, whose brother failed to visit his dying mother).

Of course, it is natural to reflect back on a troubling incident, but angry rumination is different from that kind of self-analysis because it is repetitive and intrusive. It involves keeping up the thoughts about the event and playing the episode over and over in one's mind. Such rumination is often invasive; you may relive the event mentally as you are driving to work, taking a shower, or making dinner.

Estrangement events thus take on part of their power from our inability to stop thinking about them. Wesley Austin has spent years ruminating about the event that ended his relationship with his sister, Marcie. The two had never been close, although they interacted occasionally at family gatherings. Then Marcie did something so deeply offensive that Wesley ended the relationship. He told me, "It may have seemed small to others, but I was never able to get over it."

For Wesley, the incident felt like a flashbulb, an unforgettable moment emblazoned in his memory. It hinged on something seemingly innocent:

a video created for a family event. If you ask Wesley why he never speaks to his sister, he provides an immediate answer:

> My parents have birthdays near one another, and they were turning seventy. So we decided to have a big party, and the entire family was going to be together. My sister made a video for the occasion that compiled old home movies, family pictures, that kind of thing. It had everybody in it, everybody's kids. It was playing on a loop, and I enjoyed it at first. Then I watched again, and I was stunned.
>
> I watched it about five times, and my son's not in there. My adopted son was totally left out in the video of all the family. That was the final straw. That was the end of it. I unfriended my sister on Facebook. She sent me a message saying, "I thought we were friends." I just ignored it. That was the end of it then.

Throughout our conversation, Wesley returned many times to the story of that video. He vividly recalled his initial appreciation that his sister had done something unexpectedly nice. His pleasure turned to confusion, and then to fury as he saw every family member featured in the video—except his son. The video engendered a long-simmering resentment that the relationship could not withstand. Viewing the family video, and ruminating about it afterward, Wesley felt that this failure to acknowledge his son seemed to illuminate every flaw. To him, his sister showed her true colors:

> When we adopted our son, it's just like having a baby, so your family should send congratulations. I never heard once from my sister. That continued, as she never even acknowledged that he existed. Why did she do this? Well, my adopted son is a different race, and she doesn't accept him. I was hurt by that video, that she was so prejudiced and unconcerned about him. She can't accept him because he's different.

After many years of reflection, Wesley is now aware that the video symbolized a history of dissatisfaction with the relationship. He admits that this one incident stands in the way of reconciliation. He told me:

> The final straw was that video. Everything led up to how much I was hurt by that. My sister and her husband haven't accepted my family. I didn't tell her about it; I didn't confront her about it. I know that if I had, she would have just said, "Tough luck," or "Too bad." She wouldn't have been sensitive to my feelings. So I just shut it off. I know what family should be, but you know, wishes don't make it what it should be.

Thus, volcanic events are anything but trivial; instead, they help shape the nature of estrangements. It may, therefore, seem surprising that I have placed this discussion of these critical incidents in the part of this book that is devoted to reconciliation. After all, isn't the event a cause of the rift, rather than part of the pathway to overcoming it? I learned, however, that understanding such events and our response to them can be a key to decoding the causes of a rift, as well as to finding a path forward. People who moved beyond *"I can't believe he or she did that to me!"* discovered avenues toward reconciliation. In "The Tool Kit" below, we will explore different ways in which the reconcilers dealt with volcanic events.

THE TOOL KIT

Based on their experiences, the reconcilers offer a strong piece of advice: Whether or not you initiated the estrangement, take the time to reflect on the meaning of the volcanic event and on the way it embodies problems in the relationship. They argue that the "cause" of the estrangement is not the event itself. Rather, the momentous incident serves as a critical turning point that emerges from a long history of interactions. The first strategy they propose is working to understand the event. By doing so, you can go a long way toward uncovering the cause of the rift. The second strategy is to take action immediately after the rift, before the emotions harden and are difficult to change. In the final strategy, they turn the idea around, proposing that we look for events that can lead to reconciliation.

THE FIRST STRATEGY: UNCOVER THE MEANING OF THE EVENT

The reconcilers recommend taking a careful, objective look at the estrangement event. Armed with the knowledge that one incident can exert undue power over a relationship, the goal is *to understand the deeper meaning of the event.* Yes, they told me, the event was traumatic and unpleasant, and there is a strong temptation to either prod the memory like a painful tooth or to avoid thinking about it at all. Stepping back and analyzing the incident, however, is a unique key to unlocking the dynamics of the rift.

Susie Herrera found herself locked in an estrangement and feeling helpless. Susie's relationship with her son, Rafael, became difficult during his adolescence and conflicts persisted into young adulthood. After living on his own after high school for two years, Rafael was unemployed and came home to live with his mother. Susie believed that his life had changed and that he wished to make amends. A volcanic event occurred, however, and Rafael moved out and cut off his mother for over a year.

The event that started the estrangement stands out in Susie's mind: her refusal to drive Rafael to see friends who she felt were not a good influence on him. She explained:

> I remember it like it was yesterday. We lived in the suburbs, so you
> have to drive everywhere. He didn't have a car. The whole thing started
> because I wouldn't drive him into town to hang out with his friends,
> who I thought might be using drugs. I was asking him, "Why do you
> want to go into town so late and hang out with your friends? Why do

you want to do that?" Well, he called me awful, horrible names, so I said, "You have to leave. You can't stay here."

Her son packed up and left. Susie was in a state of shock, because she felt she was helping Rafael to get back on his feet. She told me: "When this happened, it really came out of the blue for me. Because up until that point, things were going pretty well."

Eager to pursue a reconciliation, Susie realized that she had to come to terms with the event that had precipitated it. She went back over the incident and wrote down her memories, thoughts, and feelings about it. Slowly, she came to see that the "out of the blue" incident was in fact indicative of long-standing problems in their relationship. More important, she became aware that her own actions had contributed to past problems the event symbolized. She saw how her overprotectiveness had affected the relationship:

> I didn't feel comfortable driving him into town late at night so he
> could hang out with his friends. I wasn't going to do that. To me, it
> made me a responsible parent. In reality, he would have gone with his
> friends, they would have hung out in town, and probably everything
> would have been fine the next day. But I wasn't good with that.

Susie realized that her own inflexibility was part of the problem: "I would not bend what I believed were my standards. And that meant: in my house, my rules." Ruminating over the incident, she realized that she had focused on blaming her son for his irresponsible and unreasonable behavior. Now she began to see the relationship in a different way that opened her up to reconciliation:

> I realized that every single one of us is one hundred percent responsible
> for fifty percent of the relationship. I asked myself a hard question:
> "Was I overprotective?" Yes, probably. I looked back at the history of
> the relationship. He was my firstborn; I was terrified that things were

going to happen to him. I now see I went overboard. I realized that I was that crazy mother. I look back now and—wow! I was that mom. I was so stressed out and I was so anxious with him. I was so protective of him. Did that make me a "smotherer"? To me, it made me a responsible parent, but maybe not to him. I saw that's where my responsibility lies in it. So I needed to take some responsibility.

They recently have reconciled, and Susie now sees her son regularly. The situation is in progress; as Susie put it: "It's a guarded reconciliation at this point. I'm being very careful and cautious with the relationship. It's still not where I would like it to be, but it's better than it ever was. I'm able to do things for him, and I value that. He thanks me for it, and I'm sure he appreciates it very much. That's the kind of relationship we have right now."

According to Susie and other reconcilers, tracking back from the incident and understanding it from the other person's perspective is extremely useful. (See Chapter 8 for more on understanding your role in the rift.) Ask yourself: What in our shared history created the background for this event? What did it symbolize to the other person, and to you? Expanding the event to focus on its context can reshape your thinking about it. In Susie's case, she was able to explain to her son, without blaming him, why the incident was powerful for her and how it threatened her, which helped facilitate their eventual reconciliation.

THE SECOND STRATEGY: ACT QUICKLY

I learned from my interviews that the viewpoints of both parties harden quickly after a volcanic event. In a relatively short time, it becomes easier to stay in the rift. The new reality sets in fast; therefore, the time to "make things better" is as soon as possible after the blowup. In a large interview study I conducted with older people, I encountered Janice Carpenter and James Gallegos, who made this point as their strongest recommendations.

Janice had always had a somewhat tense relationship with her older daughter, Gloria; in contrast, she enjoyed warm companionship with her younger daughter, Beth. Things came to a head when Gloria decided to go on vacation instead of attending the wedding of Beth's only daughter. The anger she felt ruined the event for Janice, and the money she had contributed for the wedding felt wasted. When Gloria returned from her vacation, Janice refused to speak to her, becoming angrier with each passing day. According to Janice, this event was the "last straw," a turning point at which she "saw Gloria's true colors." She felt humiliated in front of her closest friends and relatives and began to speak of Gloria's behavior as "unforgivable." For her part, Gloria felt fully justified and had difficulty understanding "what the fuss is all about."

Looking back at the rift, Janice reported: "I should have had a heart-to-heart with Gloria right away. After a week or two, we were both so angry, and I guess hardened. It was terribly difficult even to start a conversation." Days turned into weeks, and over time Gloria simply got used to the lack of contact. Recently, Beth has worked to reinstate contact between her mother and sister, but all agree that the situation would have been greatly eased had a frank and honest discussion taken place immediately after the rift occurred.

That's what happened in the Gallegos family. Although he lived nearby, James Gallegos failed to help his mother, Maria, when his father suffered a stroke. When her husband died several weeks later, Maria found her anger toward her son to be so intense that she was alarmed. She decided she would act as soon as possible, sensing that the situation would only get worse. Within a week, she sat down with James and told him exactly how she felt. James confessed that he was so upset by his father's illness that he was incapable of helping out. Maria, although still harboring some resentment at what she felt was James's selfishness, allowed the reconciliation to take place. She told me: "It's worth it not to feel like I might lose what I have that's good with my son."

Both the reconcilers and those who remained estranged argued that relationship "first aid" is needed after a major blowup. As each week goes by, it becomes more and more difficult to pick up the phone or write an email asking to discuss the incident. One reason why speedy communication is so important is that the incident may have been based on mistaking the intentions of the other person or reading things into his or her actions. If for no other reason, engaging soon after the event can help identify whether the cause is a misunderstanding, attributing malicious intent that was not really there.

Leda Dawkins had a difficult relationship with her mother during her childhood. In her thirties, Leda became determined to, as she put it, "figure out why things are how they are and try to fix them." Little progress was being made, and in a moment of frustration, Leda sent her mother an email. In it, she told her mother that they both needed to work on the relationship. Leda delivered an ultimatum: "I suggested that until she was ready to talk to me about the relationship, and not just about trivial things, we shouldn't talk anymore. I felt certain that she would say, 'Okay, let's fix this.'"

To Leda's disappointment, and then dismay, her mother never contacted her again. She told me:

> Instead of my email leading to an agreement to fix things, she just said, "Okay, let's not talk anymore then." I wanted us to be honest about our relationship. I didn't want to pretend that we're this ideal mother-daughter relationship, because we're not. I wanted us to call it what it is, and move on from there and see what happens. But she thought that meant that I didn't want to talk to her. So I haven't talked to her since.

Two years have passed since that email. Leda wishes she had acted soon after the email communication. "I should have continued communication and told her, 'That's not what I meant.' But at the time, I was so beaten up by the fact that she thought it was fine not to talk to me again, and I didn't fight for it." Her advice to others is this:

> I would tell them to go back soon and clear things up. Just try to talk to the person as honestly as possible. Because the more you beat

around issues and avoid them, the more compacted they become, the worse it is, and the harder it is to try to get to the core. The longer you wait, the harder it will be.

Some reconcilers suggested that outside mediation can help resolve events. Such assistance can be especially appropriate if the estrangement revolves around a concrete decision, such as distribution of family heirlooms after a death or decisions around finances or property. Becky Yost experienced a volcanic event with her father, one that was so emotionally charged that she preferred not to offer details. She told me:

> He overstepped normal boundaries and we had a blowup. Then he lied to others about what happened. I cut all contact with him for a year. We were helped to get over it by a mediator, and I would recommend this to anyone in my situation. I think people should seek out somebody who can identify the problem and help each of them avoid it in the future. Each person is so entrenched in their victimization that they can't see their participation in the blowup. Find a mediator who is an objective third party and does not have a dog in this race. Because there's no way that you can have clarity when you are so emotionally invested.

Mediation to deal with an estrangement event is different from counseling or family therapy (which are discussed in Chapter 10). Mediation should occur during or immediately after the incident to untangle the practical aspects of the situation. For example, if a family rift has occurred because of sibling disagreements about parent care, a geriatric social worker (sometimes called a "care manager") could help resolve the conflict. Some reconcilers sought out clergy or trusted friends to assist as mediators following a dispute.

A useful resource that may be available locally are community dispute resolution centers, which offer short-term mediation to families experiencing conflicts. Staff in these centers are trained to help people with opposing positions work together to come to mutually acceptable solutions. A relative who is resistant to family therapy may be willing to participate in targeted, short-term dispute resolution. If communication about a volcanic incident seems too difficult to do on your own, take a look at available mediation resources available in your community. Many individuals who remained in estrangements wished they had sought mediation while the issue was fresh.

THE THIRD STRATEGY: LOOK FOR YOUR "LIGHTBULB MOMENT"

Just as the volcanic event serves as a turning point to end the relationship, a decision to let go of it sometimes occurs via a single episode. Some reconcilers who had ruminated endlessly over an interpersonal transgression found that they were eventually able to release their anger and start over. It took a special moment of insight for Leah Aguilar to decide to let go of the volcanic event. Leah's estrangement from her sister began on a family vacation. She told me:

> We'd had problems on and off, but we still got along when we needed to be together. In the early 1990s, there was a blowup while we were on a family vacation with our parents. My sister and I got into a big fight. I just kind of ignored it, like, "Boy, this is the way it's always going to be, between her and me." But when we all got back to our respective homes, she called me and said, "I don't want to have anything to do with you. We will never get along, and I don't want to deal with it." And I was like, "Okay, maybe she's right. We really haven't ever been that supportive of each other." I reached out once and got no response from her. I wasn't upset by that, because we hadn't been in each other's lives much at all.

Then, fifteen years into the estrangement, Leah got a sign that it was time to reconcile. She told me:

I have two adult children, and they don't get along very well, unfortunately. So I was having lunch with my son, and I was lecturing him that he should try to get along better with his sister. And he turned to me and he said, "Like you do with *your* sister?" That was my lightbulb moment. I called her that day, and we both decided to try again. We are so close now. I have felt nothing but joy that we have reconnected.

I am very grateful to Leah for giving a name to the instant when reconcilers decide it's time to let go. They suggest that you stay attuned to your own "lightbulb moments." Perhaps you find yourself listening carefully to messages that have to do with estrangement and reconciliation. Such awareness may mean you are ready to let go of the event that led to the estrangement. Pay special attention when a nudge hits you strongly. Just as one incident can begin an estrangement, another event may occur that hits at a gut level with the message: *It's time to let go.*

The act of letting go of the event was experienced as an enormous relief. Erin Travers, who ceased having contact with her father after an angry encounter, attended a spiritual retreat on the theme of forgiveness. At one point, the image of the last time she had spoken to her father came vividly to mind, and as if someone were speaking to her, she heard the words "It is time to move on." She immediately contacted her father, and the relationship resumed. She told me: "It was the greatest thing in the world, I feel like he and I both released each other from this stricture. I knew in my heart that I had done the right thing, and it was wonderful."

CHANGING THE NARRATIVE

In this chapter, we have seen that despite a long developmental history that precedes an estrangement, many people see it as encapsulated in a single event. We also learned that traumatic relationship events have precisely this kind of effect; they can change the path of a relationship, and they gain power through retelling and rumination. I will offer one final piece of advice from the reconcilers: Just as you have created a narrative about the event (one you may have shared many times), you can also *change that narrative*. Indeed, taking a hard look at the story one has been telling can lead to a shift in perspective.

Many reconcilers who changed their narratives were able to move beyond the event. Reflection is an important part of this process, in which one goes back over the facts of the event and what they meant. It is possible to rethink the narrative of the volcanic event and incorporate it into a more positive life story. Psychologists have found that going beyond just remembering an event to analyzing, interpreting, and explaining it can lead to wisdom. Thus, although you do not have the power to go back in time and change the event, it is possible to construct a different narrative, which may help you to let it go.

I will close with an example of precisely this process. A volcanic event devastated a mother and nearly led to a permanent estrangement from her daughter. But by reflecting deeply on the event and rewriting the story, they were able to reconcile.

Julia and Juan Hernandez had had a rocky relationship with their daughter, Alma, for as long as they could remember. According to Julia, Alma has always been volatile, from childhood into college and beyond. Julia reported: "She is prone to frustration and perfectionism and to outrages and things like that." The situation deteriorated when Alma was visiting Julia and Juan with her children. A volcanic event occurred that led to estrangement. The experience was so traumatic that Julia seemed to be witnessing the incident again while she described it to me:

> Alma and my husband get into an argument. They are fighting about something, and she gets up to run into the garage. He follows her while they're yelling at each other, and she tries to slam the door on him. He curses her out, which is very unusual for him. Then she told him she was leaving because of his behavior. She said: "I am going and I will never come back! I don't want to see you again!" She called her kids:

"We're leaving. We're leaving, we can't stay here." She yells at me: "You're siding with Papa, and I never want to see you again either!" So they left.

Even though there had been many blowups in the past, Julia knew in her heart that this time was different:

> She lives in another state and she went home. We didn't hear from her again. And she didn't respond to any phone calls or emails or apologies or anything. Nothing—she just didn't respond. I knew that this event had changed everything. That last episode when she told us she was leaving, I knew she meant it. I can't explain it to you, but I knew she meant it. It seemed very final to me, whereas other times it would just end on a bad note, I always knew we would see her again. This time it really felt final, and that's why I was devastated.

For over a year, they did not see one another and had only a few contacts via email. After suffering through this period in which she deeply missed both her daughter and her grandchildren, Julia came to a powerful conclusion: "I decided I was not going to live with a family estrangement—I would rather have a relationship on her terms. Part of it may be that we are Latino; family is just so important in our culture."

She went back and reflected on the traumatic incident, and she came to a revelation that amazes her to this day. She told me:

> This lightbulb went on in my head that all these years I was trying to establish a relationship like I thought it should be. I had this ideal image of an equal, healthy, adult relationship, and I came to the realization that I had to understand her personality and her ideas. It hit me that I wouldn't try to make her see things my way. I would just stop all of that. I changed my thinking from the idea that I have to fix her to something like this: "It's okay, you're not in that role anymore of trying to help her. Just take what you can get." And I would have never accepted that before.

Reflecting on the volcanic event, Julia mentally rewrote the story of what occurred, adding in her daughter's perspective to the narrative:

> I would think about that terrible time at our house, and I'd ask myself, "What have I done? You know, all I've done is try." And then one day another lightbulb went off: "All I've done is try?" That's exactly what I've done! I've tried too hard. That's my fault in this. I've tried too hard and too much. When Alma blew up, she was pushing against those efforts from my husband and me. Why all those years did we keep trying to take her on and make her see reason, or see things the way we did? So I came to see what happened that night in an entirely different light, and it changed the way I saw the entire estrangement.

Just as events shape us, the stories we tell about them give them meaning—and give us the power to change what they mean to us. A saying is attributed to one of my favorite spiritual writers, Anthony de Mello: "A lost coin is found by means of a candle; the deepest truth is found by means of a simple story." The reconcilers suggest that if you remain haunted by a volcanic event even after many years, rewriting your event narrative may help you see the incident in a different light and point toward a new direction for the relationship.

CHAPTER 7:

LET GO OF THE PAST

When I was still living at home, my father and I had terrible arguments, and he then refused to speak to me or interact in any way. We were estranged for several decades and it's been a theme that shaped my life. As he became older, I realized that I did not want to be that person who left the world with a grudge, or with someone having a grudge toward me. So I reconnected with my dad. So many things had gone on between us that it was tempting to bring up past hurts. But I could tell that he was more interested in seeing who I was and me seeing who he was than hashing up the past.

We both found that we were focused on more important things in life, and on connecting with one another. So in a way it was like a new relationship. I don't have a lot of time to dredge up anything from the past. There's too many exciting things going on now. I would tell someone, "You can't change it. You can't change the past." Unless it makes you happy, stop looking at it. You don't owe this person anything, you don't have to take anything from them, but you can clear your own path. In terms of your own soul, you'll never regret it.

—KENDRA WHITE

"The past is never dead. It's not even past." William Faulkner's profound observation came to mind as I talked with people dealing with estrangement. In many families I interviewed, past and present were so interwoven that they became inseparable. For some, the history of the relationship almost entirely overwhelmed the present moment. It is as if family members are aware of two realities, seeing the contemporary relationship through layers of old anger, insults, betrayals, and tragedies. Any action in the present is interpreted as a sign or symptom of an underlying, decades-old pathology. What might seem to an outsider as a routine remark or social media post is perceived as part of a pattern of hostility or disapproval. It all feels the same way it did ten, twenty, or thirty years ago.

Of all the dilemmas that confront estranged relatives, among the most challenging is this: *To what extent must the other person come to agree with my version of the past?* Over and over, I encountered individuals who remained cut off from a relative who simply could not "see the light" about the past, and denied significant events or patterns of behavior that the other insists occurred.

One way in which estranged relationships differ from conflictual or poor-quality ones lies in their static quality. The relationship becomes frozen at a particular moment in time. The past takes on critical, and unchanged, importance because new information is unavailable. Particularly after a long estrangement, individuals who try to reconcile have missed the changes life brings about, both in the circumstances of the other person and in how he or she has developed over the years or decades. Overcoming the rift requires learning how old ways of communicating and relating have changed.

Reconciliation attempts thus suffer from the overwhelming presence of past events, discord, and dysfunction. For people with a troubled childhood, the vestiges of the eighteen years during which the family shared a home can overshadow the current realities of those involved. In Charles Dickens's *A Christmas Carol*, the Ghost of Christmas Past takes Scrooge to earlier scenes in his life. Scrooge becomes a shade, a kind of ghost of his present self, who lingers unseen as events transpire. The past is something like this in estranged relationships, a figure in the background who haunts the present, creating a lens through which the participants view their current interactions. The past isn't past at all.

In an estrangement, the issue is not simply coming to terms with one's own past. Instead, people wish to impose their vision of the relationship's past on others. They insist that the other person must understand what *really* went on and admit his or her critical failings. A child demands that her mother confess her failure to protect her from an emotionally abusive father, whereas the mother believes that she did the best she could. A man wants his brother to acknowledge that his childhood teasing scarred him for life, but to the brother, nothing occurred beyond the usual sibling rivalry. A son wants his parents to see that they were unwelcoming toward his wife, whereas the parents feel they were merely cautioning him against a potentially bad match.

With one family, I had a unique opportunity to witness the weight of the past on the present. The Morris family allowed me into their lives for a remarkable occasion that cast into stark relief the dilemma between resolving old hurts and letting them go to focus on the present. This experience made a powerful impression on me and led me to one of the major revelations in this book.

CONFRONTING THE PAST IN THE PRESENT

I was filled with anticipation as I drove to a retirement community in the Sunbelt. I turned off the highway and into a senior-living development where identical beige stucco dwellings were arrayed on small, meticulously landscaped lots. I pulled up at one of these dwellings and walked through the heat to the air-conditioned cool of Sadie Morris's home.

I have been in many older people's homes for my research, so the décor was familiar to me— comfortable furniture, knickknacks on display shelves, family pictures on the walls. And I was ready to talk to Sadie, because I have interviewed hundreds of older people about their families. However, unlike in my other interviews, this time I was not alone.

I was accompanied by Sadie's son, Eric, who had been estranged from his mother for twenty-five years. With us as well was Eric's older sister, Paula, who remained in reluctant, limited contact with her mother. Now in their fifties, the siblings were facing the first opportunity to be together with their mother in nearly a quarter century. Knowing my interest in estrangement, Eric had invited me to join them, and even to interview his mother as part of the visit.

Immediately upon our entering, Sadie fussed over us, offering us food and drinks. I could sense the tension mounting in Eric and Paula, who viewed these behaviors as a familiar smokescreen to cover the tension. Eric paced nervously, barely able to sit still, while his mother expressed her amazement at the fulfillment of her decades-long wish that she would see him again. I knew from our prior conversations that he was not at this moment fully in the present. A half century of family history was pressing down on him.

My presence helped reduce the tension, and given that an ostensible reason for my being there was to conduct an interview about the family relationships, I got out my tape recorder, and Sadie and I moved into a room by ourselves. We began at the beginning, and Sadie told me of the difficulties of her early family life. Her first husband, Eric's father, suffered from mental illness and abandoned the family when the children were very young. After a period when the family lived with her parents, Sadie married Stanley, who eventually adopted the children. That was where the story began to diverge.

Sadie believed that she had found a safe haven for her children with a husband who was a "good provider." She acknowledged that Stanley had limitations; he could be gruff and insensitive, and was prone to dark moods at times. Stanley also had custody of his teenage son, who, Sadie admits, was "a handful." But for Sadie, the important thing—as a single mother in the early 1960s—was to find a partner who would again make them a family and keep them from poverty. She told me: "I did everything in my power to help my first husband get help and nothing worked. I felt then the best thing I could do was provide a father for my children. I believe we all had a good life together."

Eric, however, believed that he had experienced the dark side of family life. The arrival of Stanley had brought the imposition of discipline that in Eric's view bordered on child abuse. His stepfather was a small-business owner, and Eric was made to work with him while his friends engaged in typical childhood activities. He watched his mother withdraw into passivity, allowing Stanley to increasingly dominate the family. The older stepbrother engaged in antisocial behavior and was at times threatening to the two younger children. Perhaps most important, Eric felt that his mother was habitually dishonest with herself and with her children, portraying family life as idyllic to others. For Eric, this was the beginning of a pattern of deceit.

Eric and Paula continued to struggle in their relationship to their mother, and the core issues lay in the interpretation of what occurred forty or more years ago. Their very descriptions showed the gap in what is considered to be "reality" itself. Talking about both of her children, Sadie told me:

> I feel like I have done everything I can to show that I'm a loving, caring parent. But they don't see it that way, somehow. Nothing really makes sense to me. I mean, I always ask myself, "What part was abusive?" They went to good schools, they did extracurricular activities, there was always good food on the table. Where is the disconnect here? You know, we didn't have alcoholism, we didn't have physical abuse. We didn't have any of that in our family. They don't have any reality check on this. And if the parents try to bring that side, it's just, "No, you're negative and a toxic parent," instead of the reality.

After the visit, I sat with Eric and Paula at a nearby restaurant. Their mother had given me permission to share her interview with them, and I described her view of the relationship history. They nodded wearily, showing that this story was familiar to them. Eric told me:

> When we were growing up, she lied all time. She's manipulative. After about age twenty-five, I just didn't want to have anything to do with her. Neither did my sister, but she was more tolerant of her than I was. I just had had enough. If you met her, you'd think she was nice, but

everything was in service to her needs. She wasn't like a normal
mother. Yes, she was involved with us, but she was so narcissistic. You
get so tired of it. The reality of our lives was that she put us in the
hands of an emotionally abusive stepfather and detached herself from
that reality.

Over and over in my interviews with people who remained in estrangements, I heard the term "reality." At the risk of redundancy, each person's
reality is the real reality, and the other's view is biased, reconstructed, or
delusional. I discovered in my studies that one of the major barriers to
reconnection is the urge to *align two views of the past*. Many people remain estranged for that reason alone: The other person will not give up
his or her view of past events and subscribe to the "correct" one. Such
individuals were prone to ambivalence: The drive to reconcile is at war
with the need to have others change their narrative of past events.

Alan Benson's estrangement followed one pattern we observed in
Chapter 2: the family's perception that he had "married the wrong person." His mother and father believed that his then girlfriend, Inez, was
spoiled, picked fights with him, and made him unhappy. Alan became
angry when he learned that his parents and his brother referred to her as
"the princess" behind his back. In Alan's view, they entirely misjudged
Inez and were instead motivated by their own needs. Family solidarity
was a high priority for them, and they could not accept the fact that Alan
now had a competing relationship that drew him away. For her part, Inez
came to a point where she was barely civil to her parents-in-law and eventually refused to attend all but the most obligatory family events.

Eight years ago, the stress level became unbearable, and Alan and Inez
decided to cut off all ties with his parents. As his parents have grown older,
Alan recently has become concerned about letting the rift continue indefi-
nitely. Every attempt at a family discussion, however, ends up with angry
disagreements about what "really happened" in the past. For Alan, it is es-
sential that his parents adopt his view of past events and give up their own.
For even first steps toward a reconciliation, they must accept blame:

What we are looking for is my parents to apologize and acknowledge that their concerns about Inez were false, and that these were their own issues that they needed to work through. In the past, I approached my parents about this, and they took the stance of, "No, the problem was just her, and we're not going to apologize for anything." My family was very much in denial, and they still are. I have told them: "Instead of blaming Inez, why don't you look in the mirror? This was a problem that originated from our family." I was trying to use logic to get them to understand.

Alan's parents do not agree that they must adopt his view of the past: "They would like to just start over and not process what went on." Alan, however, cannot move on without aligning their views of the past. Otherwise, he feels that a reconciliation is impossible. There was resignation in his voice as he told me: "I can't just sweep this under the rug. That's what my family wanted, for us to sweep it under the rug and just let it go away. I have taken the stance that we just can't do that; we can't let bygones be bygones." The past stands in the way of a relationship with his parents and their relationship with their three grandchildren.

Because the past overshadowed the present so often, I was eager to learn how this issue was overcome in families that bridged the rift. As I heard the reconcilers' stories, a pattern emerged that grew stronger with each interview I conducted: It may take many years, but a point was reached when the past mattered less than the present and future did. We will explore their advice for moving on together without a shared narrative of past events.

THE TOOL KIT

Our Tool Kit begins with a recommendation that may pose a challenge for some people in long-term rifts, but I encourage you to reflect on it carefully. The reconcilers are nearly unanimous on one strategy: Bridging the rift requires abandoning the urge to align the past. Indeed, it was only when imposing their view of past events no longer mattered that they were able to reconcile. The second strategy is based on this principle: Time spent waiting for an apology is time wasted. Third, they offer a strategy that many found effective: Focus on building a new future that can eclipse the past.

THE FIRST STRATEGY: ACCEPT THAT YOUR PASTS WILL NOT ALIGN

In many estrangements, past hurts play a leading role in the minds of those involved. As we saw in Chapter 5, traumatic relationship events become prominent, reinforced through sharing them with sympathetic others and angry rumination. Not only do events feature prominently in narratives of rifts, but so do patterns of behavior. For example, perceived parental favoritism, emotional neglect, or disapproval loom large in adult children's estrangement stories. In all cases, the individuals involved develop narratives based on what is necessarily selective memory.

Thus, we can look at how the different parties explain an estrangement as diverging narratives. Decades of psychological research show the power of narratives; indeed, they form the way in which we think about relationships. Rather than representing an objective "truth," narratives tend to support our own identity. The psychologist Robyn Fivush puts it succinctly: "Narratives move beyond simple chronological accounts to include thoughts, emotions, motivations, intentions, and evaluations, essentially describing a human drama of self and others." In estrangements, both parties have composed narratives that place them at the center of the family drama and support their sense of self.

The creation of such ego-centered narratives is not in itself a problem. In fact, it is the way we make sense of our lives. But understanding how narratives work leads to a critically important conclusion: It is unlikely, especially after years of estrangement, that someone is going to simply accept your narrative of what caused it. Even agreement on the existence of specific events is not enough, as people disagree on the details and the meaning of those events.

It was common for both estranged individuals to cite the same critical incidents but to disagree dramatically on their meaning. The Sharpe family provides an example of how narratives of the same events differ. Brandon Sharpe and his son Nick have been estranged for over ten years. Both Brandon and Nick agree that there were difficulties in his childhood. But after that, their accounts break off—so much so that they could be describing two different families.

Brandon admits that his divorce from Nick's mother was painful for his three sons. In Brandon's narrative, however, he and his wife agreed to the divorce and he was not to blame. As he put it: "Divorce is mutual. There's no absolute winner or loser or person at fault. The answer is always in the middle." He also acknowledges that his work issues contributed to the family's difficulties. His business failed, and he felt he was a failure as well. However, he asserts that he was able to provide for the family and that they remained comfortable. He feels he is a true "family man." He told me: "At the end of the day, we are a family and you love your family. Sure, there are days you'd love to kill them. But at the end of the day, we are in this together. We are going to look out for one another."

Other than the fact of the divorce, it is hard to find overlap with Nick's narrative. In Nick's story of the relationship, he is the victim of extreme parental favoritism. He told me: "I have two brothers, and growing up they were my father's favorites, and I was left out. The favoritism was really difficult." Nick feels his father portrayed the family to others as ideal, whereas Nick was miserable. Nick's view of the basic facts differs as well. According to Nick, Brandon's business went bankrupt because he had made bad financial decisions. He asserts that his mother held the family together financially and provided stability, while his father just gave up.

Brandon touts his attempt to stay connected with Nick, pointing to visits that occurred. To Nick, however, such attempts were unwelcome: "I do remember visits with him, but they were unpleasant. He was trying to get me and my brothers to be against my mom and come to his side. My mental health suffered pretty severely." Over time, his father has attempted to contact him again. The possibility of seeing Brandon upsets

Nick greatly. After much deliberation, he finally concluded, "It's much better not having somebody like him in my life." Brandon, on the other hand, believes both their lives would be enhanced by reconciling. The two very different views of the past, however, get in the way.

I offer this detailed example to show in clear relief how difficult (and in most cases, impossible) it is to align such diverse views of the past. For one person, an incident that started the rift was truly a volcanic event that changed the relationship forever; for the other, it was a minor occurrence that is barely remembered. One sibling reports that he had a good childhood growing up in the family, but for his brother it was a Dickensian nightmare. And over and over among the estranged, I heard the claim that the other person simply refused to "see the reality" of what went on.

What do the reconcilers have in common? It is stunningly simple: *They let go of the need to align two versions of the past.* After years or decades, individuals who made an overture to reconcile, or accepted one, came to the conclusion that consensus would never be reached on what went on in the family. They did not abandon their individual view of events in which they were deeply invested. They decided, however, that it was no longer important that the other person subscribe to their version of events. They did not give up the past, but rather they gave up imposing their narrative on their relative. As they often put it, rather than remain frozen in the past, they decided it was "time to move on."

We met Leah Aguilar in Chapter 6, in which she shared the "lightbulb moment" that brought her together again with her sister, Tamara, after a long estrangement. After the sisters agreed to reconcile, the issue of aligning their narratives of the past emerged. Both sisters quickly rejected a need to process past events. They did spend a brief time discussing why they had not gotten along well, but they moved on almost immediately. Leah told me:

> It wasn't like we were looking for reasons, you know? It was just an "it is what it is" kind of thing, and we just went along our merry way, not trying hard to figure out where the chasm came from. I don't recall

either one of us apologizing. We just pretty much started from present. We did dip into our mom and dad's history and their relationship, but not about each other.

When asked what advice she would give others seeking to reconcile, Leah emphasized letting go of the past:

I would tell them not to go over old wounds, to just start from [the] present. Later, maybe you can go back and take inventory about how you got there. But to get back together, keep it in the present day and don't dwell on past insults. I felt that way, and my sister didn't want to go there either. We were both winging it, but neither one of us felt like we had to go back and dig something up. It was already buried, and we left it there.

For Leah, the benefits of abandoning the past have been extraordinary:

I am so glad. We now find ways to meet whenever we can. It hit me, "Wow, you don't have anybody else that you can call 'sister' but her." And we say, "I love you" on the phone when we get off. We don't have to do that, but it feels like you want to, you know? So my life is so much better for her being in it. I feel really loved, you know, in a way that nobody but your sister can love you.

The ability to forego aligning the past may seem easy in cases where the discrepancy revolves around a single incident or is relatively superficial. I learned that deep-rooted differences in narratives about core family issues also can be released, if both parties are willing. Letting go of one's own narrative is not easy, however. Some reconcilers admit that they gave up imposing their view of the past at a cost to themselves. They did it because they believed the restored relationship was more important.

Toni Carpenter became estranged from her sister Marsha in early adulthood, in large part because they disagreed dramatically about the past. Toni believes that their family was "seriously dysfunctional" and feels that her own lifelong problems with relationships stemmed from her damaging upbringing. Her sister does not agree:

> If you ask Marsha and me about our parents and our growing up, you're going to have two different stories. But I'm the oldest, and I'm right and I know it! She didn't want to hear any kind of criticism of our parents, but the atmosphere in our home was abusive and it rubbed off on us. One time, I was telling Marsha this, and she got very upset and very agitated. It turned into a terrible argument, and she never did get what I was talking about. She got mad at me about it and refused to speak to me again. We did see each other at a few family events; we would have a few words then, but they weren't good ones.

Toni also was estranged from her mother, whom she blamed for not protecting her from her father's abusive behavior. Toward the end of her mother's life, their relationship improved, and Toni visited and assisted her. A turning point occurred at her mother's funeral, where the two sisters found themselves drawn toward each other. Toni recounted what happened: "Marsha and I had a tentative kind of relationship at the end. We hugged each other goodbye and said we loved each other." They now get together a few times a year and talk frequently on the phone.

Toni still firmly believes in her version of family events. Giving up trying to align the past has been difficult for her:

> We're letting sleeping dogs lie and we're not letting loose the snakes. At the beginning, I wanted some acknowledgement of what I went through as a child and teenager. But she just thinks that I'm carrying a grudge, so I just need to completely let go of it. If I'm having trouble with it, I don't need to talk about it with my sister; I can work with a counselor for my side of it. If she wants to think our father was a wonderful man, fine. I don't, and she knows how I feel, but she just thinks that I'm wrong. So what's the point? She doesn't agree with me

and she's not going to believe me. Yes, that bothers me, but it's still better than being estranged from my sister.

Despite these concerns, Toni is adamant about the need to let go of the past. She offers this advice to others wanting to reconcile:

> Don't discuss whatever happened between you. Let it go away, just forget about it, start anew. Some things are not going to be the same. Some things are going to be a sore subject, so we avoid those subjects. I'm just happy about where we're at now, and I'm not going to do anything on purpose to mess it up. I think we're probably as good as we can get, and it's not at a bad place. We didn't ever really talk anything out. We just came together because of my mother's death and realized this was a stupid thing. We were all each other had.

THE SECOND STRATEGY: ABANDON THE APOLOGY

In addition to the urge to align the past, the pathway to reconciliation may be blocked by a requirement that the other person apologize. We saw in the chapter on volcanic events that a swift and sincere apology can be important "first aid" to repair the relationship. Among people in long-term estrangements, however, there is often a desire for something broader: an apology for how the entire relationship was conducted. Indeed, what some people want is for the relative to apologize for being the person he or she is. The issue is not one of "Apologize for this thing you did to me." Rather, the demand is "Apologize for how you have treated me for my entire life." It is asking others to abandon *their* lifelong narratives, to which they are equally attached. Narratives form our sense of identity; we do not give them up easily.

The reconcilers managed to overcome this barrier. They acknowledged that after years or decades of estrangement, the positions were hardened and the relative was no more likely to apologize now than he or she was when the estrangement began. Therefore, the reconcilers focused on *changes in behavior* in the present relationship, rather than repentance for past infractions. Many came to understand that a verbal acknowledgement of long-ago bad behavior would not be as satisfying as the actual end of the behavior.

Randall Abbott had a falling-out with his parents over behavior he found unacceptable. Randall felt that the relationship had been generally a good one, but it became strained when his parents began to express disapproval of his career choices and of his girlfriend (whom he later married). The tension boiled over at a family event. He told me:

> We were all gathering in my parent's vacation condo on the beach in North Carolina. It was set up to be a celebration of my wife's and my engagement. Well, everybody gathered, but the entire aspect of the engagement celebration just was overlooked, ignored, gone right out the window. In addition, my family communicates with a lot of teasing and sarcasm. My fiancée hadn't seen that side of them before, and it was very difficult. So things came to a head with a major argument.
>
> We ended up leaving early and heading back to Chicago, where we live. It was a revelation to me. I realized that they started treating my fiancée as a member of the family—in other words, poorly. I stood up against it, which was a shock for the family. Usually my reaction to their behavior was to check out. But this time I didn't check out; I pushed back for very first time, and that was a huge shock.
>
> After this happened, my parents kept trying to blame it all on me and my wife-to-be. They tried to convince me that I should dump her and then we'd all be reconciled, and I just said no. One time, my mother was in Chicago on business, and she called me to meet for lunch. We hadn't spoken for quite a while, and I thought this might be her attempt to reconcile. We had a nice conversation, but after lunch, as we were walking down the street, she tried to convince me to leave my fiancée. I said, "We can't have this conversation." And I just turned my back on her and walked away, because an argument would just go nowhere.

After three years of estrangement, Randall's mother's health problems led both sides to make overtures toward one another. Randall told me that he knew there could be no meaningful discussion of what had gone on in the past, let alone an apology: "My parents' attitude was, 'Yes, fine, why do we have to talk about it? Let's just act like nothing happened.' Another of their attitudes was, 'We'll be happy for you to admit that you were wrong.' And I realized that I had the same attitude toward them: 'When are you going to admit you're wrong?' So I was just as bad."

Randall decided that he did not need an apology—but he did need his parents' behavior to change. He and his wife made it clear what they would and would not accept. Randall related:

> We took the attitude of "operant conditioning." You know, rewarding positive behavior, and backing off when they went to the negative behavior. As a result, they began to modify their behavior. Our approach was, "No, we're not going to get into button pushing or anything." It was simply that good behavior will be rewarded. Instead of demanding an apology, we developed that strategy. I put my foot down and said, "No, I will not stand for this at all anymore."

Randall knows that he would have waited forever for an apology from his parents. Instead, he focused on behavior change in the present moment, without a need for agreement on the past. The payoff was a restored relationship: "We had a lot of things that we liked to do in common. So having them back was just like getting a friend back." In this case, as in those of many other reconcilers, the perspective was that actions speak louder than words. If one cannot reconcile the views of the past, one can make sure that the past behavior does not continue into the present.

Interestingly, a number of reconcilers found that the apology came later, rather than preceding the reconciliation. Once the relationship was reestablished, the relative began to feel, and eventually express, remorse. Bethany Richardson had a troubled relationship with her mother. Her parents divorced soon after she graduated from college. Her mother behaved erratically, alternately making overtures and giving gifts to Bethany, then angrily rejecting her.

The relationship reached a breaking point when Bethany lost her job and her mother suggested Bethany live with her. Her mother's demands and hostile behavior precipitated the end of the relationship. Bethany moved out, and they did not see each other or speak for over a decade. During the estrangement, Bethany did her best to substitute friends for the family she was missing. Peace of mind, however, escaped her. She told me:

> My experience over the estrangement was one of asking myself the same questions: "Am I being unreasonable? Should I just let this go? Am I crazy for making this decision to put my own family on hold?" There are a lot of questions you ask yourself, and some of these things were pretty serious. You wonder if you are just crazy and a person who's wildly overreacting.

After a decade had gone by, Bethany realized that her mother had changed for the better, in part because she was now in a stable second marriage. Bethany's brother was planning his wedding, and he wanted Bethany and their mother to attend. Both agreed, and they saw each other for the first time in a decade during activities leading up to the wedding ceremony. Bethany felt drawn to a relationship with her mother, but the need for an apology stood in the way. She told me:

> I wanted her to acknowledge the problems she had caused before I was willing to reconnect. During the estrangement, she would write me letters saying things like, "Can't you let this go?" Or "Can't you just give it up?" But what I wanted was, "I'm sorry—all that shouldn't have happened." I needed her to apologize and say what's going to be different. I needed a conversation about it. It bothered me for a really long time. When she sent a card and it said, "Miss you. Merry Christmas!" I was like, "Where's my apology note?"

By the time of her brother's wedding, Bethany had decided to let go of her need for an apology. She had worked on herself extensively and had lost the need to change how her mother viewed the past:

> When I finally got back into the relationship, I knew I wasn't needing anything from her—I had no expectations. I had been through counseling and realized that I didn't want to step into this journey unless I was willing to go to a place of full forgiveness on my part. I need to give her a break, consider her past and her circumstances, and then be willing to just take the relationship as far as it would go.

A few months later, something remarkable happened. Bethany had continued to see her mother occasionally and found it very fulfilling. Bethany has a daughter with health problems, with whom her mother established a strong bond. On one visit, they went out for dinner and the moment Bethany had long desired occurred:

> During the dinner, my mother sincerely apologized. She started to cry and said: "I wish all that wouldn't have happened. I behaved badly. I really feel bad about it." And that was the moment where I healed a lot. I just needed to hear her acknowledge, "Yeah, that was not what should have happened." It wasn't like she said a lot, but it was enough to know that she thought about it. I'm glad I didn't wait any longer for an apology, because she could only make it after we reconnected.

THE THIRD STRATEGY: BUILD A FUTURE

The reconcilers discovered one more key to overcoming a legacy of past conflict, hurt, and misunderstanding. The answer for many was to focus on the future—on building a new relationship that left the past behind. When they resumed contact after a long estrangement, they envisioned it as an opportunity to start over, in which they discovered things they had in common with each other. These reconcilers told me that the key to bridging a rift was to focus on what could happen *next* in the relationship, rather than what had *already* happened.

Nadine Perry had a series of upsetting interactions with her daughter, Edie, with whom she previously had been close. In her early thirties, her daughter experienced a series of job and relationship setbacks, which, according to Nadine, Edie wanted to "dump on" her mother. Edie became angry at her mother's attempts to give advice and a vicious argument took place. Nadine criticized her daughter about her choice in men in terms she later regretted:

> I said something that really upset her, she blew up at me, and I didn't see it coming. I pushed back and pointed out a bunch of stuff that she's already beating herself up about. I said things a mother should never say to her kid. And Edie, in turn, said a bunch of really horrible stuff. She didn't want to see me for a while, and I didn't know what to do about that. So I just kind of let it be. But part of me was just like, "Well, screw you. You haven't been able to achieve your goals. That's not my fault. Don't blame me if you can't find the right guy. How's that my fault?"

Nadine's husband got the relationship back on track:

> He reached out to Edie and told us both: "This is not going to be a permanent state of affairs. You have to reconcile with one another." And it was a very important relationship to me. I made a decision that even if she was going to be a jerk, I was going to take a different path. We got together and made a decision in that meeting to rebuild our relationship.

The question then became: How to move ahead? Instead of going over the angry events of the past, Nadine had a powerful insight that changed the course of the relationship: "I decided that if it feels like there's no way forward because of the past, find something new to own together in the future. I remember at the time thinking: 'I see what's happening here. I am going to invest in this strategy.'"

Nadine knew that her daughter was interested in weaving, and Nadine herself was an aspiring weaver. She proposed that the two of them attend a three-day weaving workshop together. Nadine paid for it, so cost was not a barrier. Nadine laughed as she told me, "So the only barrier for Edie was, 'Do I want to hang out with my mother for three days?'" The experience served as a new beginning: "It was a really good time because we got together in the evening and talked about all the stuff we were learning. It gave us something to own together moving forward, this shared interest."

Focusing on the future paid off for Nadine and Edie:

> Now we couldn't be closer, and the story had the happiest of endings. We talk all the time, we email all the time. But it could have gone in a really different direction, and a bad one. I think that you should find something, almost anything—it could be the silliest thing, it could be a craft thing, some kind of movies you both like. It should just be something that's not in your history that you can enjoy together, that's a completely clean slate. That worked for us.

Building a shared future does not need to be a major project, organized around creating a brand-new life together. Some reconcilers found that settling on simple activities they could share helped build a common future. One seemingly intractable estrangement was solved, surprisingly, by penny slot machines. Johanna Payne and her sister, Rita, became estranged after angry arguments over the distribution of their parent's estate. Johanna told me: "It was really, really nasty. She just completely stopped speaking to me. That went on for several years. This is how mad she was at me and how much of a grudge she had. She felt like she had been cheated."

When she heard from another family member that Rita had lost her job and was depressed, Johanna felt sympathy for her. She told me: "I wasn't so much mad at her as a person. I was mad that she could believe all that bad stuff about me. I didn't know how in the world I could ever get through that wall." However, Johanna emailed Rita and said, "I'm coming to see you." The initial meeting did not go well: "I sat down in her kitchen, and she managed to squeeze out a few words. It wasn't the most cordial meeting in the world."

Johanna and Rita found a way through the tension. Johanna explained:

> We never really talked about the past much. I think she holds a lot of guilt about it, and she thinks that if you open up a can of worms, everybody's going to get eaten. I was really hoping we could process it, because I quite frankly had been so very hurt over the years by the accusations that were made against me. But we decided just to find things we could do together.

Rather than rehashing the past, they found a simple activity they could do together. Johanna laughed as she told me: "I went to her local casino with her. That's one of the things she likes to do, so I went with her." By focusing on future plans that could be easily accomplished, the sisters avoided the past. Johanna reported:

> We got together at first maybe once a month. I would always take the train and we would go to the casino. We never spent much money; we'd play the penny slots and have lunch. That was how we related for a long time: going to the casino and then coming home and watching a movie on TV. Then eventually we started talking a little more and visiting a little more. And slowly but surely, we rebuilt the relationship. Going over the past was just not going to work for us; we learned how to move ahead together.

LIVING LIFE FORWARD

When I was in college and trying to understand the world and my own beliefs, I came across the work of the Danish philosopher Søren Kierkegaard. Like others, I struggled to understand his complex, existentialist philosophy. One of his statements, however, stayed with me throughout my life. It is as profound today as it was almost two hundred years ago: "Life can only be understood backwards; but it must be lived forwards." If you are struggling with the role of the past in an estrangement, let that saying wash over you for a bit.

To me, this sentence sums up precisely what the reconcilers are telling us. You have every right and reason to look back and try to understand how your relationship evolved in the unique way it did. You can and should, perhaps with the help of a counselor, piece together the incidents that led to a rift, understanding your role and that of others involved.

However, when it is time to reconcile, the relationship *must be lived forward*. For many people, the attempt to create a shared "backward understanding" will fail, because our narratives are our own and form part of our identity. If you are considering an attempt at reconciliation, you must ultimately move forward together, whether or not the two pasts can be aligned.

I will close with a story shared with me by Erin Travers. It encapsulates what happens when we give up the need to align the past. Erin and her father both felt betrayed by each other and did not speak for many years. As her father grew older, Erin felt a strong drive to get to know him again. Father and daughter both agreed to let the past lie and focus on the present. They developed a warm relationship, full of discussions of ideas and politics. Nevertheless, there were mysteries in the relationship for Erin, aspects of her father's behavior that she never understood. She let those issues go, believing that he would not be able to give her an honest answer. She summed up her attitude: "I saw no benefit to hashing things out."

Several years after the reconciliation, Erin's father became terminally ill. When it was clear that he had only days to live, Erin flew back to be with him one last time. In their last conversation, an unforgettable moment occurred. Erin told me:

> At one point, right before he died, my dad said to me, "Ask me anything you want—anything—and I'll answer you." And so my brain raced. All these scenarios went through my mind. I realized I could ask

him: "Why did you reject me when I was young? Why did you leave us?" Then, in that moment, I asked myself: "Is that the question I wanted to be the last I asked my dad? And was the answer anything I really needed to hear?" I mean, it just doesn't make a difference. So, what I asked him was, "Dad, what were you looking for all these years?" And he looked at me and said: "Treasure. And I found it too." There's my legacy from him.

CHAPTER 8:

TAKING RESPONSIBILITY

My brother and I were very close as children, but he had a terrible relationship with my father. When he was an adult, his life was pretty much a disaster. Eventually there was a blowup with my father, and I took my dad's side. We did not have contact for around twenty years. But I never stopped thinking about him, because he had been such an incredibly important part of my childhood. Finally, around the time of his birthday, I wrote a letter to him. He wrote immediately to me and said, "I'm so sorry I didn't write to you sooner. I would love to talk to you." I called him and we talked for hours. We had a great relationship until he died, sadly, a few years later.

Why did it work out after such a long estrangement? The most important thing I did was realize what part I played in it. As long as you think everything is the other person's fault, you're never going to have any kind of communication. If you want to reconcile, you have to have some understanding of that and stop throwing blame totally on the other person. In fact, drop the blame altogether and say, "This is the situation, and this is what happened" and accept that.

—BEVERLY GLOVER

Early in the last century, a sociologist named George Herbert Mead taught at the University of Chicago. Interestingly, Mead was not a good writer but was a talented speaker. Much of what we know today about his ideas comes from his students' diligently taken notes. One of the most important concepts they recorded was what Mead called "taking on the role of the other." As humans grow up, we develop the ability to "see through another person's eyes." We learn to imagine how someone else might think and feel about a situation, and we orient our behavior by mentally stepping into his or her role. This capacity to shift your perspective to that of another person allows you to make a satisfactory business deal, avoid saying the wrong thing to your fiancé's parents, or choose a birthday present for a loved one that delights rather than disappoints.

I confess that I had not thought much about George Herbert Mead since I was made to read him in an introductory sociology course many years ago. But his core concept leapt to mind as I heard the stories of people mired in long-term estrangements. There are few situations in life where the ability to see the world from the other person's point of view is simultaneously so important *and* so compromised. A cascade of events often precipitates estrangement, leading both sides to become locked in a standoff. The buildup of negative interactions, hurts, and slights leads to stonewalling and silence, as attitudes toward each other crystallize. The capacity to "put oneself in the other person's shoes" is lost.

This hardened position shows up in a phrase I heard over and over from estranged family members: "It's not my fault." And my research revealed that few greater barriers to reconciliation exist than an absolute belief in that statement.

June Lucas provides an example of this perspective. Estranged from her children, she urges parents in similar situations to stop looking for their own possible contribution to the rift:

> One thing I would say to estranged parents is, "Don't look for fault in
> yourself. It is not your fault." That's the one thing we know: It is not
> your fault. You did not do some horrible thing that deserves this. This
> is something that is coming out of the ground right now—I don't
> know why. But it wasn't your fault, and so that's one thing you can be
> comforted by. And you stop beating yourself up. Stop looking for that
> answer, for what you could have done better. It isn't there, it just isn't

there. There's nothing you can do. There's no love that you can give them. Just know that it wasn't you.

Estranged parents sometimes extend the blame to the younger generation as a whole, labeling the entire cohort as selfish and uncaring. Kevin Ellis spoke for many others when he told me:

There's an awful lot of narcissism. You know, it's all about them. They call it the "entitlement generation" that we're running into. They seem to completely lack empathy, compassion, and regret, and they feel no accountability for anything they do. They are on a different planet, and I feel sorry for them. It's a devastating thing going on in this country.

Adult children adopt the "it's not my fault" perspective as well. Carmen Clayton has been estranged from her mother for over twenty years. Her mother has attempted to contact her, but Carmen has no interest whatsoever: "I just never responded. I didn't acknowledge the phone calls, I didn't respond to any of the letters." Carmen places the responsibility entirely on her mother, attributing the situation to her mother's personality characteristics:

She's a mean person, yelled all the time. She lied all the time. She's manipulative. She's a bully. And so I was just like, "You know what, this makes my life much easier," and so I cut the ties. She acts nice and must have said "I love you" a thousand times every time I saw her. And it just makes me want to throw up every time I hear it, because it doesn't feel real to me. It's just something that you say. It is really better that she isn't in my life.

In contrast, my own research and insights from the family therapy literature point to a different principle: *Estrangement is rarely one person's responsibility*. This insight may sound simplistic, but it is in fact one of the most important points in this book. Estrangement is a process that involves hundreds or thousands of small interactions over time, in which both relationship partners make choices that can distance them or provide opportunities to connect. The claim "it's entirely his or her fault" is almost never accurate and forms a major barrier to reconciliation.

According to the reconcilers, taking a step back and examining one's own role is transformative. After years or decades of blaming the other person, they found that acknowledging shared responsibility was liberating and empowering, whether or not the relationship was restored. Reflecting deeply on their own actions helped remove the mystery about the rift and opened doorways for action. Even if you eventually conclude that you were not at fault, the analysis of what you might have done differently is still enlightening.

But there's a big problem with this recommendation: It's extremely hard to do. Both from personal experience and from my interviews, I know that exploring one's own role in a family rift is really, really tough. Having difficulty seeing the rift from another's point of view is one thing that is definitely *not* your fault! Social psychological research on interpersonal relationships reveals that humans have a natural response to a traumatic event like estrangement, which paradoxically protects us in the short term but can harm us in the long term: our propensity to *defensiveness*.

Many individuals in long-term estrangements adopt an impenetrable defensive posture. As time goes on, the actions and inactions of the other relative become magnified and serve as additional justification for why he or she shoulders all the responsibility. Social psychologists who study close relationships would expect precisely this reaction. It occurs because we humans have well-documented ways of responding to threats.

We are highly motivated to see ourselves as good people. An event like an estrangement threatens our self-image. Research suggests that we possess a mental system that is designed to preserve a high level of self-esteem. When our self-esteem gets damaged, we try to repair it. One of the most common mechanisms we use is dismissing negative feedback as irrelevant, biased, or just plain wrong. That is, we get defensive.

Psychologists David Nussbaum and Carol Dweck point out that although such a defensive attitude is natural, it has one big drawback. Defensiveness can give us back our self-esteem, but at the expense of ignoring the underlying reason we got the negative feedback in the first place. Instead of actually confronting the problem, we simply adjust to it psychologically. When people approach an estrangement non-defensively, they can look at the facts of the situation, ask what's wrong with the strategies they are using, explore opportunities to improve, and make adjustments. By becoming aware of our natural defensive tendencies, we can understand how estrangement threatens our self-esteem and adopt more flexible and less defensive strategies.

Later in this chapter, I will provide strategies from the reconcilers (who are the real experts on this topic) for ways to examine one's own role in the rift. But first let's look at the question: *What keeps people from an objective evaluation of their own role in a rift?* Through my interviews, I discovered that many estranged persons adopt a stance of what I term "defensive ignorance." This standpoint cuts them off from information that might help them understand their relative's perspective and stands in the way of reconciliation.

DEFENSIVE IGNORANCE

Over the course of hundreds of interviews, a process of discovery sometimes unfolds. You hear something once, then twice, then more and more often. It sinks in slowly, followed by an "aha" moment when a pattern suddenly shows itself. (Indeed, this kind of revelation makes interview studies so fascinating and has kept me at them for more than thirty years.) That's what happened when I discovered defensive ignorance.

At the outset of many interviews, respondents declared ignorance of why the rift occurred. When asked what caused the estrangement, they would reply, "I have no idea," or "I only wish she would tell me!" Ignorance of the causes made it impossible for them to take action, such as making amends or devising an effective apology. They commonly asserted that they would take steps to address the rift "if only I knew how."

As these interviews progressed, however, I would catch myself thinking, "But wait a minute . . ." Because in almost every case, the respondent actually provided clear reasons for the estrangement, ranging from long-established patterns of separation or conflict to specific arguments or disagreements. Some people described actions of their own that objectively appeared to be causes of estrangement, but they did not interpret them as "deal breakers."

Typically, the person who cut them off provided them with a detailed description of the reasons, often in the form of a letter. Respondents dismissed such messages as "crazy" or "just plain wrong." Estranged relatives described themselves as walking in a fog of ignorance, struggling to understand how the rift could have occurred in their families. But they also offered reasons, and sometimes plenty of them. I came to describe this paradox as "defensive ignorance"—and overcoming it is no easy task.

Let's take a look at a family in which defensive ignorance vied with clear reasons for the estrangement. John Cobb was deeply troubled by being cut off by his son. He told me: "I feel terrible about the estrangement. This is not something I ever thought would happen between a child of mine and myself. I feel down about it. I go through periods of disbelief and feeling depressed. It's a terrible situation. I wouldn't wish it on anyone." When it comes to his role in the rift, however, John showed the paradox of defensive ignorance.

John had two sons in his first marriage, who were two years apart. His wife died, John remarried when his sons were young adults, and he is in a happy relationship with his second wife. John was estranged from his older son, Randy, but maintained a good relationship with his younger son, Harry. Like many other people in a rift, John claimed ignorance of what caused it. Randy began to distance himself soon after he got married. The relationship, from John's perspective, changed. He told me:

It was shortly after Randy's marriage when things started to crumble between my son and me. He'd been distancing before that, but it became more overt. He announced at one point, shortly after he got married, that he didn't know how much he really wanted to interact with my wife and me. He started to act strangely toward me, and it kept getting worse. He also didn't want me having anything to do with my grandchildren. He didn't want much to do with me at all.

Around two years ago, Randy cut off the relationship entirely. John told me he is baffled by his son's reasons for cutting him off:

He was accusing me of not being there for him, of never visiting, of not helping him out with his children. He would rant to me, accusing me of crazy things. When I tried to reason with him, it was impossible. He'll lie. He'll exaggerate. He'll misconstrue. Then when you go to defend yourself, he'll go on to something else. He accused me of having chronic anger and rage, but I don't have any of those things.

By the time I interviewed John, I had begun asking directly whether the person could identify his or her role in the estrangement. I put it like this to John: "You describe yourself as not knowing why the estrangement happened. But from what you have said, it sounds to me like a pretty conflictual relationship, where you didn't get along and were critical of each other for quite a long time. Am I wrong about that?"

Frequently, my interviewees responded by defending their own position and reiterating the complaints about the other person. So it was with John:

I know I was supportive and always there for him emotionally. I'm just as human as the next person. But I do know that I've always been conscientious, always, and tried my best in parenting. I cannot for the life of me think of anything I would have done different. I was very conscientious, not perfect, but conscientious, and they know it. My kids know that.

What struck me powerfully was this: *During the same interview, John pointed to major events in the relationship that could explain the estrangement.* In so doing, he was not alone. Many people who had been cut off by a loved one both declared ignorance of the causes and yet provided ample grounds for estrangement. As we will see later in this chapter, a key task is to acknowledge and investigate these reasons.

As our interview progressed, John laid out a long list of his son's shortcomings and the conflicts they have had over the decades. Problems began early on; John compared Randy with his favored son, Harry:

> Randy had, from day one, been a very strong-willed child, not the most affectionate child, and that's fine. I accepted it. That's who he was—he was very strong-willed. He's the one that you certainly don't want to say, "Oh, no, you can't do this. You can't do that," because he will double up his effort, always been strong-willed. Harry is way more of a laid-back personality, way more reasonable, a very fair person, and more affectionate than Randy.

Despite his conviction that the reasons for the estrangement were unfathomable, John described a number of specific conflicts:

> There have been many throughout the years: for example, accusing me of not having interest in his kids; not coming to where he lives in Texas enough to visit; not being empathetic during his hard times; I didn't care enough to be there for the kids' birthdays. Right around the time he pulled the plug, one of the things he said to me was, "You pretend to have an interest in me now, but you were never there when I really needed your help."

John acknowledged the possible truth in some of Randy's complaints but explained them away. For example, he reported that his son accused him of speaking badly about him to others. John did not disagree, and even provided examples of that behavior:

> He would say that I was two-faced, that I would talk about him behind his back. Maybe he thought I talked with Harry about him, and maybe I did. I mean, he used to waste his money buying junk that he didn't need. We all thought it was just horrible, wasteful, and mostly to buy status symbols. We didn't get it. We still don't get it, and his wife used to have a fit too. Maybe I did talk about him, but not to his face. I was never judgmental.

Perhaps most tellingly, John was able to point to a specific volcanic event that precipitated the final rift. As we saw in Chapter 6, it is a near-perfect example of how a single event can symbolize years of conflict. As John reported it:

> There was one thing that really ended this relationship. And I don't know, I doubt if it'll ever be fixed, and this was a crazy thing. My son started posting pictures of things he would buy on Instagram. I guess he thought he was some kind of "influencer." He was going on about his good taste and offering advice on what people should buy. My other son, Harry, saw pictures of him surrounded by all this crap and showed it to me. I wrote Harry an email that said, "If that's good taste, I wonder what bad taste is?"
>
> Well, I copied Randy on it by mistake, so he saw this email. I couldn't believe it. He gets back to me immediately, says, "Wow, that's a nice thing to say about your son." I tried to say, "Look, it was meant as a joke, Randy. I saw all that stuff on Instagram that looks kind of bargain-basement, and I thought it was funny, you know, 'good taste.'" I said, "I was joking. I meant just to send it to your brother, and I'm sorry I sent it to you."

Well, he didn't think it was funny, so that did it. We haven't talked since then, and that was over a year ago. This Father's Day, there was no phone call, no text, no nothing. I don't know what I've done to him, honestly, aside from that email, which everyone who knows about it says that's crazy that he would cut things off because of that. That makes no sense.

Reading this narrative, it's easy to ask: How is it possible to both describe relationship-long conflict and a volcanic incident while simultaneously feeling that one is entirely in the dark as to the causes of the estrangement? The psychological research on defensiveness provides an answer. Defensiveness encourages us to selectively edit information we receive, treating as "facts" events that help protect our self-esteem, and discounting those that may threaten a positive perception of ourselves. As a rift deepens, both sides come to believe that they possess the truth. Bridging the gap in hardened viewpoints becomes a daunting task.

Even people estranged from multiple family members resisted exploring their own responsibility. Katrina Orr described herself as frustrated, confused, and angry. She had been cut off by all three of her children and was baffled by it:

It primarily started with my older son when he started to become a young adult. Then it spread to my daughter and my younger son. This is extremely bizarre to me, because I have been nothing but kind and loving to my children. It's probably the most bizarre thing I've ever experienced in my life. And when you think about it, you can't help but start obsessing over it. Because in your rational mind, you're trying to understand why it's happening: "Did I ever do anything?" I am willing to admit anything I've done wrong and apologize for it. I just don't know what the heck it is.

However, Katrina went on to describe long-term patterns of conflict and provided numerous examples of her own confrontational behavior.

In a lengthy interview, she recounted a troubled relationship history, which included the effects of an unpleasant divorce from their father. She described ongoing conflicts with her children over their desire to have a relationship with her ex-husband, whom she detests. With each child, she recounted a set of grievances and difficulties. These included arguments about weddings, their partners, and her need to "walk on eggshells" around them.

Rather than exploring how her own patterns of criticism and verbal aggression might have contributed to the rift, Katrina believed that her children's character flaws caused the estrangement. She told me:

> They just became self-centered as adults, and it's all about them. And when it's not about them, they are not interested. They seem to completely lack empathy, compassion, regret, and they feel no accountability for anything they do. It's almost like they've been possessed. Like they got introduced into a cult, taking those values.

Katrina's view was not influenced by the fact that all three children cut her out of their lives. According to the reconcilers, this kind of self-defense can protect against the emotional effects of estrangement, but it makes it nearly impossible to overcome it. Defensive ignorance puts up a formidable barrier to exploring one's own role in the estrangement: dismissing and disregarding concrete reasons that are actually provided by the relative.

Yusuf Aydin provides a classic example of a phenomenon I encountered many times over the course of my studies. There is both a desire to know why the estrangement occurred and simultaneously a dismissal of the reasons provided. Estranged from his children, he told me:

> I'd just like to know why they're doing this. I mean, if I can ever find out why, I would at least have an answer to what's going on. When you're just out here in limbo, and all of a sudden your kids say, "I never want to talk to you again!" They never tell you why, never sit there and

say, "You did this," or "You did that," or "I feel this way about you." They never answer that question.

I had my follow-up question ready. I asked: "Some people tell us that they did get a letter or another explanation, but they go on to say, 'Yes, they gave me reasons, but those reasons were crazy.' They didn't want to accept the reasons. What do you think about that?" Yusuf didn't hesitate in his response:

> Well, you're going to find out a lot, too, that they lie. There's been a lot of lying going on in my situation to justify their position. That does anger me. I don't mind them telling the truth. Give me something, but don't tell lies that aren't true to justify your position. I can certainly accept fault if it lies on my shoulders, but when they're lying to make up stories to justify what they're doing, that isn't tolerable. When they're saying that I didn't spend time with them or help them or that I criticize them, that is about as far from the truth as it could possibly get.

Doug Ingram, a son who struggled to reconcile with his parents despite a difficult and conflictual relationship, shed light on this issue. When I asked him about defensive ignorance, he smiled knowingly and said:

> You know, the estranged parents, they're saying, "Well, I don't know why my kids aren't talking to me." I don't say "guarantee" a lot, but I guarantee somewhere in their dresser they have a heartfelt letter from their kid that's ten pages double-sided that says in detail why they're not talking to the parent. I can almost guarantee it. I've written those letters, I've known many people who've written those letters, I've sent those letters. I've tacked my hope and my heart onto those letters, and they're summarily ignored.

A family rift is a powerful and disruptive experience. We have seen how natural it is to become defensive after being cut off. Over the course of time, the relative comes to be seen as "the other," a person whose actions are inexplicable and deliberately harmful. People reinforce this viewpoint by seeking out like-minded others who reinforce their view (social networking sites provide ample opportunity for such reinforcement). As an outsider listening to the accounts of hundreds of estranged individuals, I found it easy to track back over the course of a relationship and identify flash points, volcanic events, major conflicts, value differences, and personality conflicts that might lead to a rift. But to those in the thick of a cutoff, it may not be obvious at all.

The reconcilers believe that there is a way to move beyond defensive ignorance: stepping back and taking a more detached view of the facts of the estrangement. They are not demanding that you accept fault for the rift. What they do insist is that you examine as objectively as possible *whether or not* you may have contributed to the rift. Fortunately, they offer several valuable strategies to help you get to that point.

THE TOOL KIT

The reconcilers believe that everyone can benefit by exploring their role in a rift. It is difficult, and it may be stressful, but it is well worth the effort. They offer three specific strategies that worked for them. First, they recommend that you experiment with seeing the rift from the other person's point of view, even if you do not agree with it. Second, they encourage you to get some distance from your own view by writing from the point of view of the other person. Third, they propose that you go beyond the network of people who are already on your side to more objective outsiders.

THE FIRST STRATEGY: TRY PERSPECTIVE-TAKING

It's easy to identify defensive ignorance and recommend moving beyond it. Actually carrying out this task is much more difficult. Fortunately, the reconcilers have an answer, and one backed up by psychological research. You can explore any role you might have played by thinking about the rift *from the other person's perspective*. Before you object, let me be clear that they are not telling you to sympathize with or to have compassion for your relative. You are not accepting blame, and you are not looking only for how you may be at fault. What you will do, however, is take the perspective of the other person. You do your best to see their side of the story, but no one is asking you to feel their pain.

We tend to think of empathy as feeling the way another person does; that is, when we see someone crying, it makes us sad. But that's only part of empathy, and not the one that concerns us here. Empathy is also a cognitive skill that allows us to put ourselves in another person's situation and imagine his or her viewpoint and emotional state. In any intimate relationship, conflicts occur because each person has his or her own perspective, values, and expectations for the relationship. The challenge is to get into their minds to understand how they see the world. Psychologists call this ability "perspective-taking." It allows us to consider a situation from the other person's viewpoint, and it is a skill that can be improved over time.

As the researchers Nicholas Epley and Eugene Caruso found, perspective-taking requires that we move beyond "our own psychological point of view to consider the perspective of another person who is likely to have a very different psychological point of view." This hurdle fits well with what we have learned about estrangement: *If we want to adopt another person's perspective, we must see beyond our own egocentric experiences.* We understand our own perspective easily and automatically, but that won't happen when we try to reason about someone else's perspective. Taking on the other's perspective requires hard thinking and mental endeavor. But according to the reconcilers, it's well worth the effort.

Let's look at how Connie Dunn's efforts at understanding her sibling's perception helped end a rift. Connie and her younger sister Patty had a rocky relationship growing up. Their personalities clashed and they competed with each other. As they grew older, the sisters became closer when they both married and had children. They cooperated in the care of their mother until the end of her life.

However, the seeds of a long estrangement were sown by decisions regarding their mother's estate. Their mother owned a vacation house on Cape Cod to which Patty was very attached. Connie, however, was experiencing financial pressure and wanted to sell the vacation home and split the proceeds. Connie believed selling the property and dividing the proceeds was a sensible approach. Patty had a very emotional reaction and was unwilling to work on a compromise arrangement. Arguments ensued and the two exchanged angry letters. Connie told me: "And that was the end of our relationship for twelve years. We each felt very justified in our feelings. And angry, hurtful words were spoken and written."

The estate was finally settled, but that did nothing to heal the relationship between the siblings. Connie, however, thought frequently about her sister. She told me: "I would be watching Lifetime, and a movie about sisters would come on, and I would think to myself, 'I have a sister too.'" But Connie could not see a way to bridge the broad rift between them. Then the unexpected happened. She practically glowed as she told me:

> And then three years ago, I got a Christmas card from her out of the blue. Patty wrote that it had been long enough, and we needed to put the past behind us and be sisters again. I was so happy! She gave me her phone number, and I called and told her I wanted to make up too. We went for a walk on the beach together, and we exchanged quick catch-ups and history. We tacitly agreed to let our disagreement stay where it belonged—in the past. I feel as though having almost lost my sister for a time, I appreciate how special her friendship is to me.

Asked why the reconciliation worked so smoothly, she replied:

> I think my sister did it beautifully. She did it by mail, so it's not so personal; it's not like picking up the telephone or whatever. She did it on Christmas, which said to me, "I remember how much the holidays

mean to you." It said to me, "I still care about you." I've told her that I was really thankful that she took the initiative.

How was she able to say yes to her sister's offer of contact after a long history of anger, perceived betrayal, and then silence? Connie was un-equivocal: *The key was examining her own role from her sister's perspective.* Connie described the process she went through in locating her own responsibility—and it is one that can work for many other people.

Connie decided to drop her defensiveness and take a good, hard look at whether she had contributed to the estrangement. She posed some dif-ficult questions to herself: "So, okay, how would I like this to turn out? How did we get to this point? What happened, and what was my in-volvement in it? What part did I play in how we got to where we are? And what can I do about fixing my part?" She went on: "You have to honestly be willing to admit whatever the situation is and how you were a part of it. You know, it is not all one person's fault."

By moving off her hardened defensive posture, Connie was able to take on the role of the other person more effectively and locate her responsi-bility:

> I processed the fact that I didn't handle the situation with the vacation
> home well. I acknowledged her pain and the emotional component. I
> know now what was a mistake: my refusing to keep the property at
> least for a few years, until we could get over my mother's death. Also,
> when she rebuffed my ideas, I should have said: "Well, you know
> what? Let's get a professional mediator and see if we can't work this
> out. Because I want to save our relationship." I would have tried
> harder. Instead, in the way I often handled things then, I retreated.
> That turned out to be a bad thing for both of us.

Connie and her sister have reaped the rewards of her self-examination, bridging the rift with a more balanced view of the relationship history and an appreciation of their differences: "You sometimes feel there has to be a winner, but as we both took responsibility, we didn't feel like there had to be a winner in this. Greater maturity has brought me to really appreciate the person that she is."

This example shows that a deep and meaningful understanding of the other's perspective in an estrangement is possible. Our fundamental tendency to protect our self-image when we are attacked may be a formidable barrier, but we can overcome it. Indeed, the reconcilers taught me that if persistently asked to describe the relative's interpretation of events, most people can do it. Whether you initiated the estrangement, your relative did, or you both had a hand in it, it's worth taking a step into the other's perspective.

THE SECOND STRATEGY: HARNESS THE POWER OF WRITING

A lot of writing goes on during the process of estrangement. People write letters, long emails, and Facebook posts. Much of the writing is to the other person involved, and often it is done from a place of anger. Nowadays, of course, people text one another, using our newest communication medium to spit out their point of view in terse messages. From my research, I've found that it's a rare rift that doesn't have at least one pivotal incident that hinges on something someone wrote. (John's unfortunately misdirected email is just one of many examples.)

The reconcilers recommend a very different kind of writing. Rather than penning a list of grievances and a catalog of evidence of the other person's bad behavior, the reconcilers suggest writing about *the other person's side of the story*. That is, take on the perspective of the person from whom you are estranged and write his or her view of grievances, incidents, and problem behaviors. In my interviews, I often told the respondents: "Imagine that your relative is having lunch with a friend, and the friend asks, 'What's up with the two of you?' What would your relative say?"

Writing an answer to that question can be enlightening. Connie Dunn found that journaling was key to her resolution with her sister. She told me:

I journal a lot. That's my cheap therapy. And I think that if I were giving advice, I'd first of all tell people to write about this question: "Okay, perfect world, how would you like this to turn out?" Write about that, because sometimes just the act of writing about something makes your brain work differently, and things come up. So, "How would you like this to turn out?" And then, "How did we get to this point? What happened, and what was my involvement in it?" You know, honestly being willing to admit that whatever the situation is, you have a part of it. It is not all one person's fault. So, you can write about "What part did I play in how we got to where we are? And what can I do about fixing my part?"

Creating a narrative from the other person's viewpoint is the key to perspective-taking. Writing lets you, in the very apt expression of researcher Jiyoung Park and colleagues, "step back to move forward." Instead of being immersed in the negative events yet again through your own eyes, you can step back and reason about the relationship history, which in turn helps with emotional processing.

Do you find it too difficult to see the causes of the rift from your relative's perspective? If so, psychologists have another suggestion: Try writing about the conflicts you have with him or her from a third-party perspective. If it's hard to get into your relative's head, then envision the causes of the rift from the viewpoint of a totally neutral individual—a third party.

Although this method hasn't been tested with estranged family members, Eli Finkel and his colleagues asked married couples to perform a task. They wrote about a marital disagreement from the imagined perspective of a neutral person. This simple exercise improved the quality of the marriage—even over years. Based on their model, here's a writing task you can try:

Think about the problems you have had with your estranged relative. Think about these problems with him/her from the perspective of a neutral third party who wants the best for all involved; that is, a person who sees things from a neutral point of view. How might this person think about the causes of the estrangement?

The point is to find a way to step back from your own highly emotional reactive viewpoint and write the history from another perspective. Whether you take on the role of your relative or of a neutral third party, writing down what happened from a different point of view is an important part of the tool kit for understanding—and possibly reconciling—a rift.

THE THIRD STRATEGY: EXPAND YOUR FEEDBACK LOOP

When we experience stressful events, and in particular when our self-esteem is threatened, humans have a natural tendency to seek out people who are very much like them. In the case of individuals in long-term estrangements, my research found that many of them eventually find themselves in an "echo chamber," in which they hear only views similar to their own. This tendency to find and listen to sympathetic others forms a major barrier to reconciliation.

The exclusive interest in similar viewpoints is brought into stark relief by examining online posts and forums regarding estrangement. It is very telling that no site exists for estranged persons of all types to come together to discuss their situations with one another. Instead, there are groups on Facebook, Reddit, and other platforms for estranged parents *or* estranged children. Reading these forums provides an example of the stark contrast between different viewpoints and the inability to explore a different perspective.

There are forums where adult children encourage one another to "go no contact" and share stories of parental behaviors that range from the irritating to the abusive. Parents are referred to as narcissists (nicknames are used, such as "Nmom" for "narcissist mother"). Forums and Facebook groups also exist for parents of estranged children who share parallel complaints, reinforced through posts and comments.

Striking examples of the hardened viewpoints emerge when a member of one of these forums "sneaks over" to the other side and reports back to their own forum. One can find children criticizing and mocking the posts on estranged parents' forums. For example, one adult child posted:

It's always something like: "I, an innocent little old lady, was harmlessly sitting in my living room when my crazy bitch of a daughter stormed in and started screaming and spitting on my face. She called me the worst mother who's ever lived simply because I didn't attend her eighth-grade graduation ceremony. Then she said that I would never see any of my grandchildren! Oh, and she said it all with a smug, evil, emotionless smile on her cold lips." It's all very exaggerated, so you'd look like a complete jerk to question it.

Similarly, here is a mother who visited a "go no contact" thread for adult children who believe they were raised by narcissistic parents and need to cut them off completely. She told members of an estranged parents group:

I have news for you. They are all reading a script. They did join the same cult. What they are doing is called "Going No Contact." It's literally a scripted plan that they follow. It starts when they judge us as not just humans with whom they disagree, but "evil" because we don't see things their way. They complain online, and meet other complaining children who honestly believe, thanks to the self-esteem movement, that any time they were uncomfortable for a moment equals abuse. If their parents disagreed with them or made them do something that they didn't like or whacked their fresh asses when they talked back or refused to follow rules, they add this to their pile of justification. Lacking coping skills, they believe that anytime they are not happy, they have been wronged, and the person who dared to "make" them feel bad is a Narcissist.

It's not just the participants in online discussions who rely on like-minded other people to justify their higher moral ground in the rift; we are all prone to the same tendency. We discuss our family issues with individuals who are likely to agree with us, and we stop sharing them with people who disagree. Because rifts often create different "camps" within a family, we turn instinctively to those relatives who are already on our side. A strong push to consider our own role and responsibility is unlikely to come from these friendly sources.

The reconcilers offer this simple but highly effective advice: *Talk to people who may not agree with your position.* The reconcilers suggest that you seek out friends and relatives who are concerned about you but who are not already on your side. Such conversations serve as an effective means of "stepping back to move forward" in the relationship. When we are in conflict, we naturally seek out others who bolster our own viewpoints. For those in an estrangement, seeking out neutral or even unsupportive others can be enlightening.

There are many ways to find an objective listener. Grace Brock decided to take a long, hard look at her role in a family rift. Estranged for years from her brother after a series of angry arguments, she engaged in perspective-taking and came to understand her brother's side of the story. Grace told me:

> It's so easy to blame the other person. It's just so much easier to say, "Well, he did this or he did that." But of course everybody has a part in it, and if you don't look at your own part in it, you can't reconcile. If you're only looking at their part, it's just not possible, because it won't work. I realized that I blew up and said some things I shouldn't have said. I did insult him in unkind ways. People need to think about what they did, what's their part in it. And if you're going to make an apology or reach out, stick to your part in it and not their part.

When I asked Grace how she had been able to "step back and move forward," she gave credit to her 12-step group. She told me: "It just depends on the situation, but for me the best was a group. Some kind of group, wherever you can find it." She went on:

I'm in a 12-step program. I go to Al-Anon for adult children of alcoholics, and everybody in there gets it. It's not a therapy, counseling thing. But when I share about my brother, everybody understands, because there's so many that had fractured families where people didn't know how to listen. So I've gotten great advice from my Al-Anon friends, and that was one of the reasons I reached out to my brother when I did.

Grace found that members of her 12-step group were uniquely helpful because of their greater emotional distance from her estrangement. She explained:

You should have feedback that's not just from family members, because they're already emotionally involved. Good friends can help, but good friends will just take your side. In my 12-step program, however, I shared my story, and then people gave advice. And it's different from a counselor. When you go to an Al-Anon meeting, there's twenty people there, and I can get their feedback. So I would tell people to find some kind of group, maybe a group at church or some kind of a group that will help you step back and understand your situation.

The reconcilers offered another excellent piece of advice about how to gain perspective on a rift. They suggest that you reach out beyond your immediate family to more-distant relatives for their viewpoints. It is likely that you have discussed the estrangement with family members who are already on your side. The next step is to seek out relatives who have more distance from the rift, and thus can assist you in stepping back and getting perspective. What you learn may surprise you, as it did Klaus Jencks.

Klaus became estranged from his parents and his brother over their negative treatment of him and his wife. Klaus believed that he had been unfairly treated much of his life by his parents, who clearly favored his brother. Klaus moved in and out of contact with his family, withdrawing when conflicts occurred with his brother, who was invariably supported by his parents. Saddened by the rift in his own family, Klaus sought out more distant family members. He developed a relationship with an uncle and aunt with whom he had little prior contact.

Klaus told me that the extended family members were invaluable in helping him understand the rift. Interestingly, they provided evidence that Klaus may not, in fact, bear responsibility for the estrangement:

> I gained insights based on candid conversations with my uncle and aunt this year. We talked for the first time about my relationship with my parents. My uncle said that when they see my parents, my parents only talk about my brother and avoid talking about me. They talk about my brother, and what his kids are up to, and that they love being grandparents to my brother's kids. The insight that my uncle came up with was that my brother can do no wrong in their eyes. That's how it's always been.

Klaus's uncle provided a specific example that was enlightening:

> He told me about an incident that occurred when my brother and I were young. They were visiting my family. At one point, my brother hit me really hard. My dad yelled at me instead of my brother. My uncle said, "I told your dad that it was your brother who had done the hitting. I told him you hadn't done anything wrong. But you were the one who got in trouble." I told them that that's how it was growing up all the time. It was constant, where my brother would do something and I would get in trouble. My brother completely took advantage of that.

This information helped Klaus to understand one of the barriers to reconciliation: his parents' insistence that he apologize to his brother for his behavior, rather than mutual acknowledgment of mistakes on both their parts. The revelation about the past shed light on the present: "It's still that same dynamic, even now, where my parents still insist that I owe my brother an apology for this whole family conflict. Yeah, it was eye-opening to me." By seeking the perspective of family members not involved in the estrangement, Klaus found himself less to blame than he had imagined.

STEPPING BACK TO MOVE FORWARD

In this chapter, I have shared a fundamental lesson from the reconcilers: A key to moving forward is stepping back, taking on the perspective of others who are involved, and exploring what role all parties played in the rift—including your own. To move beyond defensive ignorance, it helps to write from another's perspective and to seek input from people who are not already one's allies. Perspective-taking can point the way to a resolution or to a better understanding of why an estrangement cannot be resolved.

I will leave you with the advice of one of my youngest interviewees, eighteen-year-old Eleni Andreou. Eleni was one of the college students who shared their stories of estrangement. She experienced the "collateral damage" of a rift that separated her parents entirely from her father's side of the family. Eleni is an innocent bystander who watched as her family was torn apart. To other families in similar situations, she offered this wisdom of youth:

> I would tell them that even though they're very upset and they don't
> feel like communicating with that person, it's okay for a short time,
> but long-term, it's not a solution. The best way to solve the problem is
> to think of the other person and to try to consider their perspective,
> even if it seems unfathomable. Then you can come to a resolution
> without the selfish perspective of "I'm right and they're wrong." A big
> factor that leads to people not to talk to each other is the idea "Oh, I'm
> very right, and they're very wrong." I would give the advice to be a
> little bit selfless, consider the other person's perspective, and try to
> work through it.

CHAPTER 9:

CHANGING EXPECTATIONS

When my parents were ill, my brother refused to help me care for them. I became very angry with him because he was easily within distance to help. I decided that I was no longer going to speak with him because it just took too much from my energy. It was an unpleasant part of my life that I just wanted to forget about for the time being. We later reconciled, in large part because I learned to accept his limitations. It doesn't do me any good to expect anything more from him, because it's just not there. I would tell people that you may just have to let go of your expectations for the person. It is liberating. You stop wasting emotion expecting something that's not going to be there.

—DINA SANDOVAL

Most of us carry around unrealistic expectations regarding family life. I know, because in that department, I am guilty as charged. I want each family event to be the "best ever," and I can set up high expectations that are hard to fulfill. I have been compared to Chevy Chase's character Clark Griswold in the iconic Christmas movie *National Lampoon's Christmas Vacation*. In the film, there is this bit of dialogue with his long-suffering wife, Ellen:

ELLEN: You set standards that no family activity can live up to.
CLARK: When have I ever done that?

ELLEN: Birthdays, weddings, anniversaries, funerals, holidays, vacations, graduations . . .

Clark and I are not alone; family life is built on expectations for one another's behavior. At its best, this shared understanding of how we expect our relatives to act keeps family life running smoothly. When we interact with our families, we play a role in relation to the roles of others. That is, in fact, how a social role is defined: a set of expectations for how we are supposed to behave.

Just as we have individual expectations for our family members, we also have broader expectations about what family life should be like. These beliefs are sometimes framed as "family values"—that is, our judgments about what is important in family life and the moral system that guides us in interactions with relatives. Family values are expressed in phrases like "Siblings should have your back," "Children should always respect their parents," and the famous "Blood is thicker than water."

Expectations aren't necessarily bad. Without them we would have difficulty knowing how to interact with others. But when it comes to family estrangements, the problem is a profound mismatch between the expectations of the parties involved. Over and over, I encountered rifts that resulted from one person's failure to live up to the high expectations of another family member. In most cases, a relative believed that his or her expectations were the only correct ones. Many estrangements are born, I learned, from the belief that *my* expectations are universally valid and that *your* failure to live up to them is grounds for ending the relationship.

In this chapter, we will look at the role of expectations both as causes of estrangement and as pathways toward reconciliation. I will focus in particular on the differing expectations of parents and children and how they contribute to long-lasting rifts. In "The Tool Kit" below, we will explore the recommendations of the reconcilers about how changing expectations can lead to reconnection.

EXPECTATIONS ARE RELATIVE

No pun intended—okay, pun sort of intended. Most of us have clear expectations for our relatives, and we believe those expectations are correct. That is, we give our expectations for the relationship *absolute value*, rather than understanding them as products of our individual upbringing, the historical period in which we grew up, our cultural background, and our personal experiences. To understand an estrangement, the reconcilers told me, one must acknowledge the possibility that our values are not absolute and that family members may not share them.

In cases of prolonged estrangement, I heard stories of what happens when such absolute expectations are violated. Family members render judgment on one another based on hardened views of what is right and wrong. I encountered a saying (attributed to various sources) that could have been created for family estrangements: "Expectations are resentments waiting to happen." The author Brené Brown states the idea even more clearly: "Disappointment is unmet expectations, and the more significant the expectations, the more significant the disappointment." Over and over, I saw the power of family-related "shoulds": the relative *should* have done this or *should not* have done that.

Here's a story about the power of *should*. Jonas Krevsky and his wife, Olga, experienced a volcanic event that initiated estrangement with their son Peter. Jonas and Olga planned to spend time with their son and his wife after their first grandchild was born: "Peter called me and said his wife is in the hospital and that the baby was born sooner than they expected. We were all excited." What happened next, however, violated the parents' expectations. Jonas told me:

> We said, "Okay, we're going to get tickets to fly out." Then Peter calls me and goes, "Oh, you're going to need to rent a car." I asked, "What are you talking about?" He says, "Well, you're going to have to stay in a hotel." We were stunned and could barely ask him why. He said,

"Oh, you can't stay with us. We're just too exhausted. We can't have company."

Jonas's reaction was immediate:

I told him, "But we're not company!" He says, "Well, you can stay with us for a couple of days, but then you really have to go to a hotel." I ask why. He replies, "Oh, it's just too much having you all here and dealing with the baby and everything." Long story short, Olga and I ended up canceling the trip because we didn't want to be treated like that.

Jonas and Olga were deeply offended because the young couple failed to live up to their expectations for how a son and daughter-in-law should behave. They blamed the failure on Peter's difficult personality and believed they were standing up for what is right:

It's always been that you have to do what Peter says. Well, we started having a backbone. We started speaking up. Not in a mean way, but when he wrote to me and said, "Okay, you guys can come just for these days and then stay in a hotel," I wrote him back and I said no. I said, "We have discussed it together. We believe you have to do it the correct way."

As an outsider, you might be inclined to ask, Why is staying with the parent of a newborn an absolute value? Might it not be worthwhile to compromise one's expectations to be able to see a first grandchild? One could imagine an alternative scenario in which someone considered whether staying with new parents in their own home was indeed a value that could not be compromised. In the view of Jonas and Olga, the refusal to allow them to stay in the same house was a fundamental violation of the parent-child relationship. But another couple might, with equal correctness, say, "So what?"

Of course, this incident was not the only reason why the estrangement occurred. A long history of similar events preceded it, in which Jonas and Olga's expectations for their son's behavior were not met in a satisfactory way. Nevertheless, like many people we met in Chapter 8, Jonas told me he does not know why the estrangement occurred: "My wife and I had many lengthy conversations trying to unravel the mystery, because the big deal to us is just the *why*." Because they are convinced of the absolute value of their expectations, they could not comprehend their son's request. Peter's expectations for their roles, however, are different. He expected that his parents should accept his wishes and allow him independence in making decisions regarding his family.

Who is right? In some cases, the answer may be clear, such as when a relative engages in violent, abusive, or illegal behavior. But most of the time, the different expectations involve gray areas in which our society provides little concrete guidance. For example, there are no firm and fixed rules for how an estate should be divided, or exactly how much each sibling should help a frail, older parent. In these cases, we need to ask the question "Is the failure to live up to my expectations worth ending the relationship?" To gain additional clarity, let's look at the special case of the differing expectations of parents and their adult children.

THE PARENT-CHILD DIVIDE

A major theme of this book is examining common elements of family estrangement across different types of relationships. However, on the topic of expectations, there is good reason to single out parents and their adult children. Social science research, as well as my own studies, shows that expectations differ systematically between parents and their offspring. These relationships do not have one single history; instead, parents and children have distinct views of both past events and current obligations. Most important, their different life histories and positions in the family lead to unequal investment in the relationship.

Research demonstrates that parents are more invested in their adult children than adult children are in their parents. Studies show that parents feel more positively about their children than offspring report feeling about them. In addition, parents view the relationship as more important and express greater commitment to it. This imbalance comes from the different relationship histories and developmental stages of each generation.

Because of their investment, parents see their children as a continuation of themselves—their legacy. The offspring, although attached to their parents, strive for independence and autonomy. This basic feature of intergenerational relationships helps explain the differing expectations of parents and adult children in rifts and how they create a barrier to reconciliation. Put simply, the accumulated research points to this fact: *In general, parents care more.* They, therefore, have more to lose in an estrangement.

Many of the estranged parents I interviewed, however, operated on two principles. First, they expressed the view that the provision of the basic elements of an American childhood should be sufficient to ensure lifelong contact with the child. Second, they believed that family loyalty should prevail over problems and conflicts in the relationship. In the view of a number of parents, children are obligated to remain in the relationship because of all they have done for them and an absolute value that "families stick together no matter what."

Maxine Wells's story provides an excellent example of both these expectations. Maxine became estranged from her daughter, Faith, after years of on-and-off contact punctuated by angry confrontations. Maxine disapproved of Faith's husband, her social life, her choice of jobs, and her approach to childrearing. She admitted that it was difficult to keep from expressing her disapproval. She was stunned, however, when her daughter declared that she was "done" with the relationship and refused any contact. Maxine told me:

> There's something that really nags at me. Let's just say she really
> believes that I didn't make enough effort to see her kids. Let's say she
> thinks I'm critical of her. Let's say that she thinks that I didn't approve

of her partner. Let's just say all that. Here's the thing: If I had a parent like this, I would say to myself, "Boy, she was always there for me. She was always good to me and did the right things. For all those years, she did so many good things."

You don't cut off communication with such a parent. You maybe talk to them about it. As a rational adult, you don't cut off a relationship like that. Because your conscience should tell you, "Maybe I didn't like certain things, but boy, she always did the right thing for me. She was always there for me." So, she might really feel these things, but you have to weigh it. You don't cut off contact.

To provide additional justification, Maxine described "hanging in there" with her own difficult mother:

I had a mother who did some awful things—it would blow your mind. Not just to me, but to other people too. She was a very self-centered woman. I had every reason, as an adult, to totally break it off with her. But I said to myself, "I don't have to be super close with this woman, but I'm not going to break it off with her." So, we had a relationship until she died. I think that's the norm, rather than a person like this totally breaking off connections with their mother. I cannot believe that her conscience doesn't creep in, and she doesn't get glimpses of the good childhood that she had.

Parents' belief that family ties were unbreakable led to shock that a child could sever them. Jingfei Chen reflects that view. After many years of a difficult relationship, her son refused any further contact with Jingfei and her husband. For Jingfei, this decision violates a fundamental contract between parents and children:

Family is supposed to be there to help you through everything in life. Your family is your roots and they're there for you. He has burned the roots, He has burned the legacy. He just threw it all away. Family is always there for everything, and he's just never going to have that. He's broken one of the commandments already: "to honor your parents." And honor does not necessarily mean love, but it does mean "be respectful."

She used a metaphor that highlights how deeply she perceives the violation of basic values to be, comparing a cutoff to a dereliction of duty: "Kids who cut off their parents have committed abandonment, they have committed desertion. If a soldier deserts, you don't say, 'What's wrong with the military?' You say it's shame on him. It's the same for the kids: It's shame on them."

Thus, many estranged parents held firmly to two sets of expectations: that their past provision of support to their child obligates the child to remain in the relationship, and that family ties are so binding that even chronic stress in the relationship should not undo them. However, the social science research on different levels of investment between parents and children shows that such assumptions are faulty. Although they are seen as *absolute* values, they are actually *relative* values. A parent may pride himself or herself on having been a good provider. A child, however, is likely to view providing a stable childhood as a basic expectation of the parent-child relationship, not one that requires lifetime loyalty in the face of a pattern of aversive interactions.

This difference came through clearly in many of my interviews with adult children. Zoe Hartmann had an ambivalent relationship with her mother, Alice. Although her mother could be supportive at times, she was prone to outbursts of rage. When Zoe was in college, these combative incidents escalated, and she decided that the negatives of the relationship outweighed the positives. She cut off all contact with Alice.

Although she may restore the relationship at some point, Zoe felt that the rift was consistent with her values regarding family life. She told me:

My view of family is that it can be a very strong support system. However, for me it's not a guarantee. I don't see family as "Blood is thicker than water." It's not like you can assume these relationships should always go on. So I have a different outlook on family relationships from my mother. I don't think that you are necessarily close to everybody you are related to. And people who aren't related to you by blood can be family. I don't feel like the estrangement is the worst thing in the world. It's not like, "Oh my gosh, her not speaking to me is taking away the air I breathe!"

Many adult children do not subscribe to the view that they are obligated to remain in the relationship in the face of persistent unpleasant interactions. They are much more likely to weigh the positives of remaining connected against the negatives of stress and discomfort. Bridget Zaretsky's experience is a typical one, showing how adult children eventually decide that the parent-child tie is not, in fact, absolute.

Bridget's father was distant in her childhood, traveling for extended periods of time and making only small investments in the family. Her parents divorced, but she maintained a tenuous relationship with her father. The relationship took a turn for the worse when her father remarried. Bridget began to see the relationship in a new light. She told me:

> I came to realize that whatever seeming closeness we had was really a falsity. It was close as long as I minded him, and as long as I didn't exert any self-will or opinions. Then we could be close. But if I challenged him in any way or disobeyed in any way, then the relationship was going to be fractured. If you served him, if you served a purpose, you had a relationship. If you didn't serve him any longer, or if you pushed back, he blew up.

Bridget's father continued to believe that the family relationship was unbreakable. They would meet in restaurants, and on several occasions he became angry, shouted vulgarities at Bridget, and stormed out. He believed that because this was "family," normal limits on his words and actions did not apply. He was, therefore, stunned when she cut off the relationship and did not allow a reconciliation for five years. Monitoring or modifying his behavior did not occur to him because he believed that "children stick with their parents no matter what."

Like many of the adult children in my studies, however, Bridget had a different set of values and expectations. The quality of the relationship matters—or it can be ended. She told me:

> I think family is very important, but I don't think that you have to work on toxic relationships forever if they're not going to work. Just because you're my blood relative does not mean that you are my family. I don't see biology necessarily as family. I see it as mutual care for each other and a reciprocal relationship that both parties can benefit from. If you're both not doing that, then I don't consider that as family. I see that people who are not my biological family have been more like a family to me.

Rather than it being an ironclad obligation, Bridget views exiting the relationship as a viable decision, however difficult it may be:

> Make a concrete decision about whether this is someone you want in your life or somebody you feel you could do without. You can decide between blocking that contact or working on that relationship. If your parent responds negatively after many tries, you can go back to the first option, cutting off that tie. It takes being aware of yourself and the relationship, and making a decision and standing firm.

As we turn to "The Tool Kit," you will see that the reconcilers suggest carefully weighing whether holding firm to one's values and expectations is worth an estrangement. This consideration is particularly important for parents because of the imbalance in commitment to the relationship. Generally, it is easier for children to exit. Therefore, parents must weigh whether they have more to lose than their children do by holding to inflexible expectations.

THE TOOL KIT

Most of the reconcilers had to grapple with the issue of unmet expectations, and they have clear advice about how to deal with them. One strategy they propose is abandoning the idea that we can change the other person. They also suggest exploring the possibility that your relative may have changed over time, and thus moved closer to your expectations and values. Finally, they propose a strategy that can guide decisions about reconciliation: asking yourself, *What is the least that I can accept?*

THE FIRST STRATEGY: CHANGE YOUR EXPECTATIONS

For individuals wishing to reconnect, one of the strongest pieces of advice the reconcilers offer is this: "Accept that your relative is not going to change to meet your expectations; it's your expectations that need to change." As they examined the history of their relationships, most of them came to agree with the statement "Expectations are relative, not absolute." The reconcilers assert that it is a fool's errand to expect the other person to become someone he or she is not. It will almost certainly leave you angry and unfulfilled. Not everyone is able to adjust their expectations, which is a primary reason why they remain in rifts.

Steffy Poole became estranged from her brother when he violated her expectations for parental care. Despite living nearby, he never volunteered to assist with their parents' health crises, grudgingly helping for brief periods only after intense persuasion. Thinking back on the experience, she said:

> We got along pretty well as siblings. But when he was needed in a different sense, he just couldn't do it. He just didn't feel like he needed to be part of it. One excuse was that he has a very stressful job. To me, that doesn't cut it as an excuse. I mean, these are your parents. They're not strangers. These are people that have cared for you and taken care of you for the vast majority of your life. Where are you?

Steffy broke off all contact with him for over a year, ignoring his calls and emails. As time went by, she discovered that she had a desire to reconcile. She told me:

> I couldn't sustain my anger anymore. I didn't think that I ever could get back to being close again, but I wanted to be able to at least get along at holidays when we had to be in the same room. For the sake of keeping the peace, I thought, "I'm not going to ignore you, but I'm not going to embrace you either." I was disappointed in him. I felt he had let us down and I couldn't go back to viewing him as the same person I thought he had been.

The only way the reconciliation could be achieved, Steffy found, was by accepting him exactly as he is. She was moved toward reconciliation by a revelation she had about her brother: *She could not change his limitations, and he would never live up to her values.* As she put it:

> I realized that his comfort level is narrow, and he doesn't give family duties a lot of thought. I don't think he has a lot of depth or ability to understand my situation as the main caregiver. So I decided that you have to accept the limitations within people. He is not a bad person. But there is definitely some limitation in his ability to deal with our parents. This is a situation where you have to have so much empathy and compassion and patience.

I asked Steffy what advice she would give to estranged family members in similar situations. Her recommendation is clear:

> Stop wasting emotion on something that's not going to be there. It takes a toll on you when you let yourself become sad or angry about it, because it's not going to change. It's better to just accept it and move on. It's hard to maintain that mentality, but you need to do

it. Because you still get angry, you still get sad. But you can stop making it so important and just realize that's what it is—it's not going to be any different. When your expectations go down, you let go of a lot of that anger and sadness. If you bring your expectations in line with the other person's reality, it's possible to reconcile with them.

It can be particularly difficult to give up expectations for one's parents. Shirley Malone's mother and father divorced when she was an adolescent, and she had strong feelings of resentment toward her father because of his treatment of her mother. After she graduated from high school and left home, the relationship became worse, to the point that she cut off all contact with her father for five years.

During that time, her parents got back together and her siblings had reconciled with their father. Shirley found it challenging to maintain a relationship with her other family members while excluding her father. They eventually returned to limited contact. Shirley told me: "We do not have a full father-daughter relationship, and certainly not the relationship that he would want, but we're cordial. I visit and sometimes I'll even give him a phone call to check in. It took a very long time for me to be comfortable with things like having conversations and eating dinner together."

The reconciliation was possible because Shirley changed her expectations for what a father should be:

I used to really wish that I had a normal father-daughter relationship, one where we connected, we could talk about things, and I could turn to him for support and encouragement. I used to try to do that, but it always just ended in tears. Now I accept that although we're not estranged, it's definitely not a father-daughter relationship, but more like acquaintances. He's just someone that I know, if that makes sense.

From individuals who had given up expectations, I heard various versions of the phrase "It is what it is." Although this may be a cliché in some contexts, it deeply expresses the sense of acceptance of the other person "as is," which for many people is key to the journey back. After weighing the benefits and the costs of reconciliation, they decided to drop unrealistic expectations and make the best of the restored relationship. No one regretted the decision, even if it was not easy. Shirley spoke for many when she told me:

> I think that if you want to reconcile with somebody who hasn't changed and hasn't grown, or who's not emotionally very healthy, you just have to accept them how they are. Accept that you're never going to have that perfect relationship that you might be hoping for. You have to be okay with whatever relationship you get, and then do the best you can to protect yourself. But at least open the door for that relationship. It's important to have a realistic sense of what might be possible and not to be hoping for something that never will be.

Giving up on absolute family values and unattainable expectations may be difficult, but for many people it also was liberating. By letting expectations for behavior go, they were able to end a cycle of anticipation and disappointment. The first step in this path to a more realistic assessment of family members was becoming open to the facts of the relationship, rather than one's own idealized worldview.

Some parents accepted that their child would remain loyal to a new partner and not remain tied to them. Adult children looked at the facts of their parents' own upbringing and became less judgmental about their parenting. Siblings discovered that their hopes for support and responsible behavior would not always be realized. The relationships, they learned, would never be ideal. However, as Steffy Poole told us, "If you bring your expectations in line with the other person's reality, it's possible to reconcile with them."

THE SECOND STRATEGY: SEE HOW YOUR
RELATIVE HAS CHANGED

As a child, I was fascinated by a scene from the Disney movie *Sleeping Beauty*. When the title character pricks her finger on the infamous spindle, she falls asleep along with every inhabitant of her castle. When she awakes a century later, everyone is in the precise position they were when the spell began: servants balancing trays, ladies and gentlemen dancing, musicians with their hands poised to strum their instruments.

Estrangement has this frozen quality because at one point in time, *contact and connection stop*. Except through secondhand accounts from other relatives, you miss experiencing in real time how individuals and circumstances have changed. Compounding this issue, when people are in middle age and beyond, we have the ageist stereotype that they are "set in their ways" and cannot change. In fact, that prejudice is simply not true; psychologists who study life-span development tell us that the second half of life is a time of growth and change. Many people actually become better with age.

Most important, research shows that over the course of ten years or more, your relative may have changed in ways that make restoring a relationship possible. Studies from Stanford University demonstrate that as people move into their later years, they learn to better regulate their emotions and they place a higher value on interpersonal relationships with family. They often become happier. It's true—just about any way you measure it, older adults are generally happier than younger people. People may not transform from miserable to wonderful overnight, as Scrooge did in Charles Dickens's *A Christmas Carol*. But they do change, and often for the better.

These facts are extremely important if violated expectations caused your estrangement. The failure of your relative's behavior to align with your values may have led to doubts about his or her character. Violating what you perceive as absolute values led to the "I'm done forever" decision. However, there is one potential flaw in holding to this view as years go by. Specifically: *It is possible that the relative is no longer the same person with whom you originally had the rift.*

You, too, are also likely to be different in many ways, and the conditions that negatively affected the relationship may have eased. Therefore, to continue to make assumptions about a relationship based on data that are five, ten, fifteen, or twenty years old does not make sense. The reconcilers suggest that you take the opportunity to test the relationship to determine if the circumstances that led to your expectations being violated have changed.

Courtney Lutz found herself in classic conflicts with her mother-in-law: "It was kind of like being in a bad mother-in-law joke." After getting married, she and her husband, Jack, settled in Dallas, while her parents-in-law lived in Atlanta. Courtney told me:

> She was very intrusive to our marriage. She was calling all the time and very demanding. She was disrespectful of our privacy, and especially disrespectful to me. It got to a point where early in the marriage, with my husband's approval, I wrote my in-laws a letter saying, "We're married now, and it would be nice if you didn't call me five times a day. We need our privacy, and please understand that." All hell broke loose right then and there, and things deteriorated.

Courtney entered the marriage with high expectations for in-law relationships. She expected that her mother-in-law would welcome her into the family, if not for her sake, then for her husband's. Her spouse, like many others, was caught in the middle:

> My mother-in-law believed I was not good enough for him and would denigrate me at every possible chance. I finally said, "That's it. You are never allowed to talk about me that way. And if you do it again, I'll throw you out of this house and you'll never come back again until you apologize." We had a lot of things like that.

Finally, a series of interactions was so extreme that Courtney reached the end of her ability to tolerate her mother-in-law's behavior:

> She did several things that I found to be unforgivable, and I just said, "This is it. It's come to the point where it's either her or me." I said, "That's it, I'm done." We told her: "You're not allowed in our house until you apologize." I didn't talk to her, Jack kept in touch with her, but I had to keep her out of our lives. It was the only way that we could stay married.

Failed attempts at contact served to make things worse:

> There were a few times I did actually reach out to her, and she was extremely nasty on the phone. After the last one, I got off the phone and was like, "I don't care. I tried." That's how horrible it was. It just confirmed that I had made the right decision, and we had made the right decision to just keep her away and that I wasn't going to talk to her. I felt bad. I mean, I would have loved her to be in our life, but she didn't make it possible. I was done.

As we have seen before in this book, however, estrangements sometimes take unexpected turns. After nearly two decades of a complete cutoff, Courtney's mother-in-law made a bid for contact. Courtney and Jack's daughter graduated from college, and to their great surprise, her mother-in-law sent a gift. Courtney saw this action as an opportunity. She explained:

> I took that as a chance to talk with her. And I'm glad that I did. I called her, and we had a very good talk. She knew that Jack and I are extremely proud of our daughter, and our daughter is extremely close to us. And so she did something that was very thoughtful. That's when I said that maybe we would come to visit her. And we did.

I must admit that I was a bit bewildered about how such a reconcil-iation could possibly have taken place, given that the degree of overt hostility and conflict was extreme even among estranged individuals. Courtney's attempt was successful because, over the long period of the rift, her mother-in-law had changed. She was no longer the relentless critic engaged in a struggle for her son against his wife. Her attitude and behavior had moved much closer to Courtney's expectations. I asked Courtney how that first visit went, and she replied:

It went well. By that time, she was an old lady, and I think she was really happy to get any kind of visitors. She was grateful. Of course, I was on edge. You know, she was a person who had been so powerful in terms of her ability to cut me to the quick, and here I had chosen to go to her, on her turf. Well, she was very respectful and very nice, and she was pleasant. I did all the right things. She actually complimented me.

I started calling her and we would chat. As her health was failing, Jack and I went as much as we could to see her, and so it was all good, you know? We did whatever we could to help out. I lived up to my own expectations that I should be a good daughter-in-law in spite of her bad behavior all those years. I'm glad that we did reconcile. It even went so far as when she was extremely ill, she would want me to sit next to her. So I'm glad for that.

For Courtney, the key to reconciliation was understanding the changes her mother-in-law had undergone:

My mother-in-law was past the point of making me miserable. When I saw how she had changed, I was happy to make her happy, and she was grateful to see us. I was in charge of the relationship. She made no demands on me. At the end of the day, you know what? I'm a big enough person to say, "I'll take the chance." I felt like, "Hey, she did one small kind thing, and I'm going to take that as the door cracking open. I'm going to run with the person who she is now, not who she was."

The reconcilers' message is clear: The passage of time and shifting circumstances may have profoundly changed the relative. The irresponsible person who let you down again and again may have become more reliable; the angry person may have mellowed; the harsh parent may be experiencing remorse over his or her behavior. After years, you may find a relationship partner who comes closer to your values. Expect the unexpected: Many reconcilers found that the estrangement had brought about important changes, allowing for reconciliation to take place.

THE THIRD STRATEGY: DETERMINE THE LEAST YOU CAN ACCEPT

In contemporary self-help literature, there is an ongoing campaign against "settling." Many bloggers on love and romance post about the dangers of settling for someone who is less than ideal, arguing that you are selling yourself short if you do so. Similarly, the legion of life coaches tells you not to settle for an unfulfilling job. They urge you to keep looking until you find a career that aligns with your hopes and dreams.

If you subscribe to such views, I am going to ask you to suspend them when you think about reconciliation. In most cases, both parties have to settle for less than they desired to restore the relationship. As I analyzed the interviews of individuals who reconnected, as well as those whose reconciliation attempts had failed, one clear piece of advice emerged: *Decide what is the least you can accept in a restored relationship.*

Some scientists who study relationships use a perspective called "exchange theory." The idea is that people weigh the costs of a relationship (for example, time spent maintaining it and the emotional stress involved) with the rewards they get from it (for example, pleasure, support, and material resources). Many of the reconcilers made just this kind of calculation when they decided to reenter the relationship. They concluded that if they could not get everything they wanted in a restored relationship, they could live with what the relative was willing to offer. They moved from seeking an ideal relationship to realistically attempting the best connection possible.

Polly Thorpe lived through a troubled, unfulfilling marriage, choosing to stick it out until both her daughters graduated from college. She assumed that by then the impact of divorce would be minimal and that they would be able to sympathize with how difficult the marriage had been. Her older daughter did indeed show such understanding, but her younger daughter, Brianna, had an extreme reaction and rejected her. Polly was estranged from Brianna for six years. Polly told me:

> Brianna did not want to hear my side of the story. The divorce was
> extremely messy, and she refused to even listen to my side of it. Over
> the years, she graduated from college and got engaged; I was not
> invited to the wedding. There was nothing. She had this blind spot
> when it came to the divorce and her loyalty to her father.

Polly's strategy was to exercise patience, waiting until her daughter was ready to reach out. Opportunities for reconciliation were limited, however, because her daughter's job involved periods spent out of the country. Then the unexpected occurred. As the sixth year of separation came to a close, she received a call from her older daughter, who alerted her that Brianna planned to call her. Brianna was making a critical financial decision, and she knew Polly had useful guidance and contacts. They decided to meet and had a warm interaction that restored the relationship. In both their views, they have returned to past closeness.

But to get to this positive ending, Polly had to carefully consider the question: *What is the least I can accept to reconcile?* For Polly, after six years of separation, the answer was an easy one: She would unconditionally accept whatever terms her daughter proposed. The pain of the estrangement was so prolonged and intense that she discusses it with difficulty:

> Being estranged from your child—I do not wish that on my worst
> enemy. It was horrible to live through. I would sit there and cry, and
> my husband would sit there and pat my hand and say, "It's okay,
> you're going to get through this. We're okay." I was obsessed with

reconnecting with my daughter. I feared that I would die before we reconnected. You know, she's my child, I love her no matter what. People tell you to hang in there. Well, oftentimes, the way I was hanging in there, I was hanging by a thread.

When Polly considered the benefits of reconciliation with her daughter against the pain of the estrangement, she decided she was willing to accept whatever terms were required. She abandoned the need for an apology for her daughter's lack of empathy and understanding, despite painful memories. She offered a poignant example: "You know, when I go to her house, there are pictures of their kids' birthday parties. They are lovely photos, and I don't say, 'Gee, I sure wish I could have been there.' You have to move on, let it go, and be happy for what you do have."

Polly, therefore, considered her options clearly and rationally, and decided that ending the estrangement was worth compromising her positions and acquiescing to her daughter's conditions. She told me:

> All I can say, if there's any chance of reconciliation with a child, I don't see putting stipulations down. As the parent, you have to take the high road, in my opinion. And I don't know a nice way to put it: You may have to eat dirt in order to move forward. I know a lot of people refuse to give in. "I will not apologize; I will not do this or that." But you've got to give in to get ahead, if that's what you really want.

Polly agreed to whatever her daughter required. She provided an example:

> She laid down some rules, and I agreed to her stipulations. One big one was that she did not want her children to interact with my husband. And I said, "Okay, fine, whatever." And my husband was like, "Whatever." She also didn't ever want me to talk at all about her father, and I said, "Okay, fine." She needed to feel that she was in control, and I agreed to all her stipulations.

Polly described an experience common to a number of the reconcilers. Accepting the relationship on the relative's terms was a "foot in the door" to a renewed relationship. As time went on, the terms were relaxed as trust was built. Polly shook her head and laughed:

> And you know what? All these stipulations? They all fizzled. All went up in smoke and everything turned out fine. My husband now has a nice relationship with my grandkids. When I babysit, my daughter and her husband come home to a clean house, cooked food, and so how can you complain? The children are happy, they tell my daughter they love being with their grandma, so the original rules just went away.

Polly found that despite giving up some things during the reconciliation, the payoff was well worth it. She recommends that to overcome a long-term estrangement, consider carefully the least you are willing to accept. Polly gave up the need for an apology, agreed to have a relationship with her grandchildren that did not include her second husband, and contributed a considerable amount of time to assisting her daughter's family. She is unambiguous that it was a highly satisfactory transaction: "It was a win-win. Yeah, it was worth it, because now I have her forever, hopefully, or at least until I leave this earth."

YOU CAN GO HOME AGAIN

Nearly a century ago, the author Thomas Wolfe wrote a novel, the title of which became an iconic phrase that sums up inevitable change over the course of life: *You Can't Go Home Again*. That phrase rang frequently in my mind as I listened to estranged family members describe re-entering a relationship after a long separation. After many conversations with them, I came to modify the sentiment to "You *can* go home again— but it won't be the same 'home.'"

Individuals in the midst of a family rift frequently express a sense of longing, of nostalgia for a past in which family relationships, if not smooth, at least provided a comforting base of security and attachment. They described a yearning to have things "return to normal." I learned from my interviews that many people imagine a reconciliation not unlike that of the Prodigal Son. But what happens when the dream doesn't come true?

You are probably familiar with that famous parable from the New Testament (Luke 15:11–32). A father has two sons, one of whom does not want to wait for his inheritance. His father divides his property and gives half to each son. The younger of the two goes off, and as might be predicted, "squandered his wealth in wild living." Broke, starving, and exhausted, he comes back home and declares: "Father, I have sinned against heaven and against you. I am no longer worthy to be called your son." His father not only forgives him, but also orders a feast to celebrate the return. His older son, who has been working the farm diligently at home and has never been given a party, is infuriated. His father tries to reassure him that he is loved too.

It is a wonderful story of love and forgiveness. But what we never hear is, What happened next? The younger son is unlikely to become a model farmworker, nor will his older brother cease to simmer over the injustice. As occurs in many estrangements, we can imagine a tense and difficult future for this family, one that will require many expectations to be dropped. In real life, for relationships to continue, everyone must adjust and readjust their expectations over time.

The Greek philosopher Heraclitus famously offered this maxim: "A person never steps in the same stream twice." Like that proverbial stream, family life during the time of estrangement has continued to flow and change. The prior roles in the family system have shifted. Through becoming aware of the power of expectations, and exploring which ones you are willing to change, the path to reconciliation can become clear. Although we cannot change our relatives, we can change what we expect and demand of them, allowing a new relationship to begin.

CHAPTER 10:

SETTING BOUNDARIES

My mother had anger problems, and I experienced emotional abuse as a child. The issues between us only got worse when I was in college. She was demanding of my time and could never get enough of my attention. I finally couldn't handle my anxiety about being absorbed into this relationship. I moved away and did not speak to my parents for over ten years. After my father died, I decided I wanted to reconcile with my mother. To do so, I had to psychologically prepare myself and protect myself.

I made specific plans for how I would handle the stressful side of the relationship, like limiting the time I spent with her. She was happy that I would visit after years of not being around, and we would do things together. But I always kept a little distance, a protective barrier between her and me. I needed the buffer, and I was never going to allow myself to get sucked in. My advice to others would be to carefully establish their own boundaries. I would tell them that a boundary is like a fence around you. It protects you; it's a sacred place where you can be you. And you will not let the person come in and violate that space.

—ANTONIA LEWIS

When it comes to estrangement and reconciliation, most people experience conflicting positive and negative emotions; in other words, they feel ambivalent. It's what people describe as feeling "torn in two directions," or as a struggle between whether to "follow their head or their heart." Research has shown that we humans find ambivalence to be highly aversive, and we try to resolve it as quickly as we can. But for many people, there is no easy answer to the ambivalence over cutting off a close relative. That's where setting boundaries comes in: By consciously protecting themselves from the upset and anxiety that led to the rift, the reconcilers felt able to reconnect.

My research revealed the internal struggle people undergo in a family rift. Those who initiate an estrangement believe they have very good reasons for doing so. Frequently, at the beginning of an interview, they would assert that they made the right decision and had no choice but to end the relationship. As the interview progressed, however, it would become clear that the estrangement decision was not so clear-cut.

It is hard to avoid guilt when confronted with the relative's obvious pain, or worry about missing the chance to reconcile before the other person dies. In the midst of a long rift, most people also find themselves curious about what a renewed relationship would feel like. Even those who felt fully justified had some degree of ambivalence when confronted with requests for contact from a family member. What stops such individuals from taking the first step toward reconciliation? The answer surprised me—and it shows why boundaries are so important.

ESTRANGEMENT AND ANXIETY

When people explain why a family member has cut them off, they often attribute it to the relative's anger, hostility, selfishness, or other negative attributes. But my interviews uncovered a more important reason why people remain in an estrangement for years: *They are anxious about what it would take to reconcile.* They are afraid to make themselves vulnerable again to unwanted demands, fights, criticism, and disapproval. The anxiety of reconnecting permeated many of the conversations I had with estranged individuals.

Irina Mosley cut off her sister after many angry and upsetting interactions, and she declared that she was relieved to have done so. But when asked to reflect on the rift, she told me:

> I want family gatherings to be better. Families should have happy memories together. I still want to go to family gatherings, because it's my family and I want to see them. I just get too anxious about it, and that stops me from trying. It's awful if my sister is there, and she is vying for everybody's attention and throwing jabs at me. So then I feel I'm right that I should not go to any more to family events. That's kind of sad, but at the same time, without all of that drama in my life, I don't have the stress. I go back and forth between wanting to have all of them and wanting to have none of them.

I was particularly struck by respondents who began the interview by claiming that the estrangement didn't matter. As we sat down, they would begin, "I'm happy to talk to you about this, but I should tell you that it doesn't bother me." But I learned to expect a change among people who initially declared that the rift was inconsequential. As our conversation continued, a more anxious and ambivalent picture would emerge.

Wesley Austin was someone I did not expect to express ambivalence about his estrangement from his brother. Wesley is the strong, silent type. A former military man, he does not express emotions easily, explaining: "Men, in general, don't open up. And the way we were raised in my family, we open up even less." For much of our interview, Wesley was clear about his dislike for his brother, Ike.

Wesley became estranged from Ike when they were in their thirties. Wesley and Ike had always competed intensively; physical fights between the two were common when they were children. Wesley described his brother as smug and intolerant. As adults, they had negative interactions around the care of their parents and the division of the inheritance after they died. Wesley stayed in touch with Ike to please his mother, but after she died became totally cut off from him.

Wesley did not mince words, and in the initial phase of our interview, no one sounded more certain of the choice to stay estranged:

> Growing up, we never got along. He was very hotheaded, and he had an arrogance about him. And I think that's why he and I didn't get along too well. But he didn't get along with many people. At one point, I told him: "I don't trust you, and I have no reason to trust you." He blew up at that. He isn't interested in my family. He's insensitive. So I just shut it off. It's a total cutoff. As for the future, we're not going to reconcile, and it's not going to be any skin off my back.

But later in the interview, when asked about the impact of the estrangement on other family members, Wesley's words and tone shifted. There was an unexpected catch in his voice when he said:

> Okay, I wish my children had an uncle. I'm upset that they didn't have an uncle. I know what family should be, but you know wishes don't make it what it should be. I think family should be close, I think family should be there for each other. I wish I had a family, I wish it wasn't estrangement. I don't even know how to create that web of family. We have friends who have all their relatives come to their house for holidays, and we kind of get adopted into that family. And I see that it's nice to have family, and I wish we had it. I'm just afraid of getting drawn back into his meanness and craziness.

A family-systems approach supports the idea that anxiety drives many estrangements. In Chapter 4, I shared the insights I received through engagement with one such approach: Bowen theory. This perspective is unique in the degree to which it specifically focuses on cutoff in families. A key insight of Bowen theory is that people cut off a relative not because they no longer care but because they may care too much. When the emotional intensity of a relationship becomes too high, cutting it off serves as an escape valve.

This idea, in particular, resonates throughout my studies of estrangement. Bowen theory asserts that family life embodies a fundamental conflict between togetherness, which is referred to as "fusion," and individuality, or "differentiation." When the push toward fusion with family members is too great, anxiety ensues. It is at that point when an either/or decision becomes attractive to a family member. As Peter Titelman, an expert on Bowen theory, puts it, cutting off a relationship "functions to control and reduce anxiety generated by intense contact—stuck-together fusion—with the family of origin." As I uncovered in my interviews, estrangement provides an escape from chronic anxiety about the relationship.

Geraldine Holloway's description of her internal conflict was typical. She was raised in a chaotic and neglectful household by parents who lived on the margins of the law. She was estranged for over two decades, but after the death of her father, her ailing mother began to request help. Although she felt pressured to assist and guilty about failing to do so, her fear of being absorbed by the family stands in the way. She told me:

> I can't reconnect because I can't prevent myself from being triggered, from getting depressed from these interactions, from feeling the lack of love I never got. When I am with her, I can't keep from feeling like the scared, lonely child that I was. I cannot prevent that. When I talk to her, I tighten my body, I can't breathe very deeply, I get angry at everything and everyone around me. This is the nugget of the whole thing. People like me feel conflicted and don't know what to do. Despite ourselves, we feel love and concern for our parents, and yet we know that the parents are going to be the same, and we are terrified of any real contact.

When experts write about difficult family relationships, it is common to raise the issue of "boundaries." Relationship guidance typically frames boundaries as determining where one person ends and the other person begins. The general idea is to set reasonable limitations or rules that respect personality differences and personal preferences, without imposing those of one person on the other. In "The Tool Kit," we examine three strategies to make boundaries work to end a rift.

THE TOOL KIT

For many of the reconcilers, setting boundaries was not a vague, amorphous process. When it came to bringing about a successful reconnection, they realized that the limits needed to be clear and concrete. The reconcilers propose a strategy of setting specific terms for the renewed relationship. Their second strategy involves taking the long view, understanding that it is likely to be a process of setting terms, having them violated, and trying again. Finally, they strongly suggest seeking professional counseling for help in sticking to the terms of the renewed relationship.

THE FIRST STRATEGY: SET CLEAR TERMS

In my interviews with estranged people, I heard a common refrain from both those who initiated the rift and those who were cut off. The two groups made comments that were mirror images of each other, and shared the same fundamental weakness. On one side, those asking to be let back in declared their willingness to "do anything" the relative wanted. The initiators, on their part, claimed that they had already provided many chances and that the relative failed at them (reinforcing the idea of "I'm done!"). From the viewpoint of the reconcilers, however, neither party has followed the path that makes reconnecting work. Whether you are offering or requesting one more chance, their advice is to *make the terms of the reconciliation as specific as possible.*

Here's the difference between that idea—offering a chance based on performing (or avoiding) concrete behaviors—and what often happens when people try to reconnect. A daughter may say to her mother, "I'm willing to try again if you will start treating my husband with respect." Although that boundary seems clear to the daughter, her mother may interpret the directive very differently. Whereas to the daughter "respect" means avoiding any comments about her husband, Mom sees her honesty as respectful—after all, her friends look to her as the one person who will "tell it like it is." Similarly, when a father tells his son that he should tolerate Dad's political beliefs, the son may not see expressing his own opinions as intolerant. Dad, however, views the arguments as assaults on his basic values and wants them to stop entirely.

I learned from the reconcilers that boundaries work best when the conditions under which you will try again are specifically and clearly laid out. The goal is to move beyond old grievances and patterns of behavior, offering the conditions for reconciliation in an unambiguous way. Harriet Dugan did just that with her estranged son, Merrill. Here's how she set clear terms for reengagement, and it worked. She began:

> My son from my first marriage was estranged from me for a number of years. He then lost his job in his late twenties and had mental health problems. He came to me asking for help. He was living in marginal circumstances, and my husband and I said, "We want you to be safe. Come out and stay with us." Things were okay at the beginning but went south after about a year. He attached himself to friends who were having problems with the law, he was lying, he was abusing drugs.

The relationship reached the point where Harriet and her husband said: "You need to move out and start your new life. We're going to be here if you need us, but we're not going to be engaged with you while you're doing these things wrong." Merrill moved and continued to have problems with substance abuse. As difficult as the separation was, Harriet and her husband were afraid to be drawn into the maelstrom of their son's problems. They refused to engage with Merrill or to assist him unless his lifestyle changed.

As might have been predicted, Merrill was arrested and hit rock bottom. At that point, he asked for another try at a relationship with Harriet and her husband. After all he had put them through, they were understandably reluctant and debated about maintaining the estrangement.

Harriet told me that things had to be very different: "We knew that otherwise we would not have a relationship with him, because we could not handle it anymore."

However, they found that their son had, in fact, changed. Through his experiences, Merrill had taken responsibility for his situation and no longer blamed Harriet and her husband:

> He told us that the problems that were happening were not caused by others. He understood that we weren't being mean, or mad, or bad by not being willing to give him everything he wanted when we didn't think that it was right. He said he did a lot of crying in therapy about this anger at himself. He has a job now and a better set of friends. So we came back in and helped him build a reasonable life. Our relationship has reopened.

Harriet was clear about the boundaries she established around her relationship to her son. It was critical that Merrill explain to them clearly that he understood how his own actions had led to his difficult situation. He needed to acknowledge that supporting him had put his parents into financial debt. Harriet was definitive that additional legal problems would lead to a breaking point in the relationship: "We would not go back into the terrible time of wondering when is the next court hearing going to be."

I asked Harriet how she offered these boundaries to Merrill, and she provided a specific description of what she told him:

> We said, "You have to make reasonable choices. If you make those poor life choices, choosing to be with those damaging people, then we will say, 'We don't need that in our lives. We are hoping that we can help you, but we won't stay engaged with that.'" We were clear that we wouldn't feed that behavior when it is going to be just allowing him to continue to make bad decisions. He believed me when I said, "I just can't do this anymore," and that I would step away if this didn't work out. Making the terms very clear made it easier to think less

emotionally and more rationally about the situation. Otherwise, it's hard to break that emotional bond to do rational thinking.

Harriet recommends setting the terms in the form of a distinct plan to renew the relationship and to talk openly with the relative:

> You should be able to say, "Okay, here's the plan." Give yourself some time away from the craziness to be able to make a plan. Then you can go, "Okay, I can live with this plan. It might still hurt, but I can live with this plan." No plan you're going to make is going to be without pain or cost, but for us it had to be done. And it worked out. We are now in touch with our son regularly, we visit him and his girlfriend, and he has not overstepped the boundaries we set.

People pushing for a reconciliation should keep this principle in mind: State clearly what you are willing to change. As we have seen in Chapter 8, individuals who have been cut off frequently take a two-pronged stance: professing to have no idea why the rift occurred while simultaneously expressing a willingness to "apologize for whatever I may have done." Such an offer is not likely to appeal to a relative who has found interaction so difficult that he or she has cut it off entirely. Indeed, a willingness to "apologize for anything" is not much of an apology at all, as it implies that there is nothing reasonable for which to apologize.

A tip, therefore, for those asking for a chance to reconcile is to be as specific as possible in requesting it. Look back over past conflicts, go over the emails and texts, take that long letter off the shelf and reread it. Follow carefully the steps outlined in Chapter 8 about discovering your own role in the rift. Then be prepared to state what specific terms you will accept to make the relationship work.

In some cases, it can be as simple as a promise not to bring up a topic again or not to criticize a relative, an in-law, or a lifestyle choice. Only you can decide what your offer of terms should be. I can assure you, however, that an offer to apologize "for whatever it is that is bothering you" is among the most unlikely reconciliation bids you can make. Identifying specific changes that you can stick to is a much more attractive offer.

THE SECOND STRATEGY: BE PERSISTENT IN SETTING LIMITS

Sanjay Haldar experienced periods of contact with his father interrupted by periods of estrangement. During his interview, I came to admire Sanjay for his determined attempts to work on the relationship with his parents over two decades. His feelings toward his father were a study in ambivalence. The importance of family was a core part of his value system, and abandoning his parents would have led to guilt and sadness. In addition, his father was a complex mix of good and bad: a loving grandfather who desired contact with Sanjay and his family, and an unpredictable, opinionated, harsh critic of those around him.

For Sanjay, reconciliation was achieved through a slow, deliberate process of understanding his own limits and setting boundaries. I learned that the same is true for many people who bridge a rift. Because family patterns of interaction have gone on for many years, establishing new rules for the relationship will take time. Boundaries may be established and then tested repeatedly by another family member. Sometimes another period of cutoff occurs, followed by an attempt to redefine and reinforce the boundaries that reduce anxiety and make a relationship possible. Sanjay was unusually articulate and insightful about his situation, but his experience is common to many of the reconcilers.

Sanjay struggled as a young adult with his desire for connection to his parents and his father's difficult behavior. His father was very critical of everyone in the family, and Sanjay took on the role, as he put it, of "the white knight." His attempts to protect others were unsuccessful. Unable to tolerate the harsh criticism and arguments, Sanjay decided to cut off the relationship. The estrangement produced an immediate sense of relief, although it was also tinged with regret.

After a number of years, Sanjay agreed to a reconciliation, in large part at his mother's prompting. He had moved to within a day's drive of his parents' home in Colorado, which allowed them to visit more frequently. He continued to struggle with his father's criticism: "It always seemed to come down to me. You know: 'Oh, you should have done this. Oh, why didn't you do that?' It always seems to fall on me how things go between us."

When Sanjay was in his thirties, another breaking point was reached because of the mounting tension with his father:

> We were seeing one another, but there were strange interactions with my father. One day he was at my house and he took one of my power tools. I told him, "If you just ask me, I would be happy to give it to you, but you can't just come in here and take something." This blew up into a huge fight, with things spiraling out of control. The last straw occurred when he called me a few days later, and without interruption he lambasted me. He said awful, mean things that he knew would hurt me. I didn't respond, I just let him run out of steam. Then I didn't say it out loud, but in my head, I said, "This is going to be the last time that I speak to him."

Again, Sanjay experienced a sense of relief at cutting his parents out of his life. However, as time went on, he missed the contact and was concerned that his children were losing out on the intergenerational family connection:

> You know, he's a wonderful grandparent. With the kids, that's like the bright, shining star. My dad is the grandpa who will get down on the floor and play games, you know? Which, for me, is all I want: I don't want anything from you; I just want you to play with my kids, just color with them, whatever. They love him; he loves them. I also want to model good behavior for my kids about not cutting off parents, and it's good for them to see that.

Sanjay desired an extended family that included his parents, and his mother often asked him to patch up the differences with his father. Sanjay resolved to try again, but this time he vowed that things would be different. Through careful reflection and the help of a therapist, he achieved a powerful insight that reconfigured his relationship with his parents. Sanjay decided that he would reconcile, but this time with clear limits.

The first step in Sanjay's boundary-setting process was to change his expectations. In particular, he accepted the fact that his father would provoke him. Rather than trying to change his father, he determined to alter his own emotional reactivity to the provocation:

> I realized that we run through the old scripts where my dad says awful
> things, I get upset, and my dad and I get in a fight. Then I'm the jerk
> for getting in a fight, never mind the horrible comments that started it.
> I realized that it's similar to a chronic health issue. For example, I have a
> back problem. I've learned that it's not like one day my back is going to
> get better. My back is always going to be trouble, I just need to stretch
> it and exercise and do those kinds of things. So it is with my father. He
> is always going to have to push my little switches and mental triggers. I
> realized I needed to learn steps to manage them better.

Once Sanjay achieved that insight, he moved to a more realistic view of his father and was able to begin to set meaningful boundaries. Sanjay took one concrete step that greatly reduced his anxiety about a reconciliation:

> I made a rule that we would visit my parents, but that we wouldn't stay
> in their house anymore. I was happy to visit with them, but I definitely
> won't stay with them. That provides an escape valve when things get
> tense. That upsets them, because I had now set a limit. I'd said, "This
> isn't going to happen anymore." I let them back into my life, but now
> we're doing it my way.

To Sanjay's surprise, the new rules worked. His parents have not fully accepted the state of affairs, however. Sanjay explained: "There's this idea in their head that one day it'll be okay, and I'll get over it. They believe it's a problem with me, and not a problem with my father and his behavior. In my recent visits, I have arranged for them to stay in a nearby bed-and-breakfast. It worked well." Sanjay has remained strong in his resolve to keep spatial separation when his parents visit.

Sanjay and his wife also decided which kinds of behavior they would tolerate and which were off-limits:

> First, my expectations needed to be set correctly. And then that led into me setting appropriate boundaries. Now if my father starts going on about a topic that I don't want to talk about, I'll either leave the room or ask him to stop. Generally, I'll just leave the room, because asking him to stop doesn't help. It's working. For example, my dad criticizes how I relate to my kids; he thinks I should be more of a disciplinarian. Recently, I said: "Okay, Dad, are you going to be able to not criticize my childrearing and just let me be the parent? Or would you rather we leave?" It was amazing that I was able to muster those words myself, but lo and behold I did, and he toned it down.

From Sanjay's perspective, the situation, although imperfect, is a good-enough compromise to allow the relationship to continue. He is able to show family loyalty, and his children enjoy a fulfilling relationship with their grandparents. The family also benefits from concrete assistance the grandparents provide, such as child care when needed. Vigilance is necessary, however. Sanjay told me: "I can tell he now tries more of the time to be on his best behavior, although he will probably keep boundary-testing forever." At the moment, the balance works, and Sanjay feels rewarded for the effort he has invested in the relationship. For most of the reconcilers, the process of setting limits involved this same kind of trial and error, determination, and patience.

THE THIRD STRATEGY: GET COUNSELING

I deliberately chose a directive subheading here, because that is exactly what many of the reconcilers told me. The impact of an objective profes-

sional was transformative when it came to setting and sticking to boundaries. Most saw a therapist on their own, since family members often
resisted joint counseling sessions. They worked on themselves, determining what they wanted out of the relationship and aligning their expectations to reality.

Often, they developed a stronger sense of self, allowing them to be better
differentiated from their relative. Paradoxically, some people learned that
they could live without the relationship, which made it easier for them to
reenter it without fear. Sean Fitzpatrick credits therapy for his ability to set
limits with his parents after reconciling:

> I've seen a psychologist, and it's been hugely helpful. Therapy really
> opened my mind. It was through counseling that I came to understand
> not to take everything personally. If someone's having a bad day and
> acting out, they're maybe not acting out because of you; they're acting
> out because of them. I also learned that I'm an active participant in
> some of the problems as well. It is very helpful to have an uninvolved
> third party as a sounding board.

Many of the therapists I spoke to described the potential benefits of
individual counseling. Even if the relative is not available, it's possible to
develop strengths and insights that can facilitate reconciliation. Anne
McKnight of the Bowen Center pointed out how counseling can set the
stage for a reconciliation attempt:

> In cutoff, the anxiety makes the person unconfident in how they
> can hold their ground and manage themselves. We try to help
> the person to be a more solid self in a relationship system, so that
> they are less sensitive and emotionally reactive to it, and more
> knowledgeable about what goes on in that system. Before bringing
> two estranged people together, it can work better to spend time
> helping one of them step back to understand what the reactivity
> is about. Because the emotions, in general, will be retriggered the

minute they get in the room together. They feel they will be overwhelmed.

The idea of becoming "a more solid self" prior to a reconciliation resonated with many of my respondents. Graciela Juarez struggled with her volatile and sometimes emotionally abusive mother. After an estrangement, Graciela wanted to attempt a reconciliation but was deeply frightened of falling back into the negative interactions that stressed and depressed her. Before she could attempt it, she found a therapist who helped her create a stronger sense of self. She told me:

> Talk therapy really saved me. I was able to talk about everything, and learn coping skills, and learn how to set boundaries with people. The biggest thing I learned was that I had the power to say no. I've learned from therapy that you've got to help yourself, and you've got to make sure that you're healthy before you can deal with anybody else's drama.
>
> What I liked is that he let me come to conclusions. He would guide me. I got the strength so that when I felt my mother was abusive, I would just not speak to her. I would just not argue and not engage, and if necessary, I would leave. Eventually she would come back to me and say, "I'm really sorry for what I said, or what I did, and I really miss you."

When both family members are willing to go to counseling together, it can be especially effective. To appreciate how this works, let's take a closer look at how counseling helped one estranged pair surmount the anxiety and ambivalence around reconciliation. Anita Bernal divorced her husband when her daughter, Tory, was in high school. Tory sided with her father and was upset when Anita remarried shortly after the divorce was final. Living on opposite sides of the country, the two were estranged for over a decade.

When Tory, then in her early thirties, took a job near where Anita lived, the idea occurred to both of them that a reconciliation might be possible.

Tory wanted her son to have a relationship with his grandmother, something Anita also desired. Both their lives had changed, but some of the mutual resentment and anger remained. There was another obstacle as well: Other relatives had taken sides and were hindering the reconciliation.

Because there was a history of unpleasant interactions and disappointment, both Anita and Tory were wary of making a first move. They wanted connection, but they needed protection to make the attempt. That's where a talented counselor came in. Anita told me:

> I talked to a therapist in town and told her I would like to have a session with Tory. It was amazing. Our therapist was superb. We were able to cut through many years of family drama in just a few sessions. Our situation was complicated by other family members, who were invested in either my side or my ex-husband's, and they spread rumors and caused trouble. Our therapist helped us to have our own relationship, and we let the rest of the family members know that. As adults, we learned to make our own decisions about the relationship that we want to have. Everybody else in the family can either like it or not like it.

Tory chimed in:

> My mom and I, for lack of better words, put eighteen years of crap behind us in those therapy sessions. I thought, "My gosh, why didn't we do this ten years ago?" But I guess that's the hindsight of growing up. As we talked in the counseling sessions, I started thinking, "I don't really know anything that my mother did to me specifically. I don't think I did anything to her specifically." It was mostly resentment at the remarriage, which is very common.

Anita took up the story:

> I felt the same way. I got to thinking: "What is this thing? What is this big old boulder in the middle of us?" The intent of the sessions was to

talk about what were the issues. We both realized that there basically weren't any. At this point, we realized we would really like to put all this behind us. Even after the first session, we left the therapist's office and hit the ground running.

The therapist played a major role in protecting both Anita and Tory, allowing them to maintain their own boundaries while they discussed reconciliation. She offered to contact Tory because, as Anita told me: "She didn't want me to be disappointed if it did take a bad bounce and Tory refused. She said, 'I can write to Tory and say that Anita would like to meet, and see if we three can talk about positive change.'" Tory was willing, and they made an appointment. As Anita summed it up, "We went in, and it worked!"

Both Anita and Tory agree that the therapist's intervention was critical. Anita reported:

> I think a therapeutic intervention is absolutely needed and vital, because we couldn't do it on our own. I was able to tell Tory that I was afraid of reaching out, afraid of being rejected. She was able to tell me the stories that other family members were telling about me that weren't true. We could not have had that conversation if we sat at the kitchen table, but we could in our therapist's office.

As the person who initiated the estrangement, Tory is especially grateful for the counseling they received:

> I still get emotional about it, getting the email that said, "Anita wants to talk." I'm thinking, "Oh my God, this is fantastic!" There are so many times that I've wanted to reach out to her, but I was always fearful that I would get so much backlash for what had happened. But this was my mom saying she wants to sit down with me. I thought, if she can do this, I can do this. We didn't rehash the past. We were able just to say, "Let's move on from here." The estrangement takes root and

directs your life, but we discovered that there was nothing to it. It's like a ghost that disappeared in the light.

Some estranged people avoid counseling because they believe it must be a long, drawn-out process that will require dredging up painful material from the past. However, many of the reconcilers found that short-term counseling was helpful, allowing them to clarify their feelings, understand the situation, and view it in a more objective and less emotionally reactive way. With the counselor, one has access to regular, reliable support for changing the rift from someone who stands outside the family dynamic.

Sophie Dixon spoke for many in her assessment of counseling's role in reconciling with her father:

> A short time in therapy helped me get stronger so that I wasn't so dependent on my parents' approval, which I was never going to get. It allowed me to change in such a way that I could look elsewhere, provide some of that stuff for myself, and start building my own life. And because I understood myself better, it allowed me to reconnect with my dad.
>
> It takes a lot of strength, a lot of trying, a lot of perseverance, and a lot of guidance to do what Dad and I finally did. Having mental health help let me drop the goal of relying on this unreliable person. From therapy, I learned that there are ways and methods of dealing with your family and setting boundaries. I don't think that someone in my circumstance can necessarily do it for themselves, by themselves. They need guidance, they need strength, they need help.

The overall message of the reconcilers is clear: Discussions, even over the short term, with a counselor who specializes in family issues will help you understand your own boundaries and clarify the specific limits you will accept in the renewed relationship. Many people feel highly anxious when they begin a reconciliation, and a counselor can help you prepare your reconciliation strategy. Find someone who will listen nonjudgmentally and help you clarify your own feelings. In Chapter 1, I told you that "you are not alone." The assistance of professional supporters can make you really feel that way.

GOOD FENCES

In this chapter, we have seen that some people were able to overcome the anxiety of reconciliation by gaining a sense of where they end and the other person begins. Through a better understanding of their own needs and a stronger sense of self, they learned to set necessary limits. In family life, there is always a struggle between contradictory impulses: the desire to be fused with the family and an equally strong desire for independence. People who overcome estrangement discover a protected space in which they can balance these opposing forces, neither becoming absorbed nor cutting themselves off.

Sometimes, a poet is better than a social scientist in explaining a fundamental human process. Therefore, I turn for insight to Robert Frost, whose famous poem "Mending Wall" is all about boundaries. In the poem, Frost's farmer neighbor tells him that they must replace the stones in the boundary wall between their properties. When Frost suggests that it may not be necessary (neither of them owns wandering livestock), the farmer disagrees with the classic line "Good fences make good neighbors." Frost has his doubts, noting: "Something there is that doesn't love a wall." He goes on: "Before I built a wall I'd ask to know / What I was walling in or walling out." This is the journey that people undergo on the path to reconciliation: understanding what needs to be walled in or walled out—and where protective boundaries can be taken down to allow a restored connection.

CHAPTER 11:

ONE LAST CHANCE

My family was devoutly religious, but in high school I pulled away from it. As a young adult, I converted to a different faith. I didn't tell my parents, but I told my brother in confidence—who then went and told them. They sent me a letter telling me that because I had converted, I'm no longer part of the family. So I ended up getting married and had kids, and my family stayed totally away. I was just excluded from their lives, and my brother went along with it.

After many years, my brother couldn't stand the guilt he was feeling. I got an email from him saying, "I'm really, really sorry, and I really want to be a part of your life." And I gave him one last chance. I asked for a meeting, and I made him listen to me: "How could you walk away from me, when we were very close, just because I had different beliefs?" So he had to earn his way in. It took him a long time of showing me. After what I went through, I was clear to him that if our relationship is going to enhance my life, then you're back in. If it's not, then no. And that last chance worked. Our relationship is better than it was before.

—ROSLYN HOCH

I am one of those people who, when the rare fit of inspiration hits, likes to write well into the night. Now, I should admit that I am typically in bed by 9:00 p.m., so this by no means happens every day (or even every month). But a few times a year, I will find myself so immersed in working on a project that I'm wide awake at my computer at 2:00 a.m. I savor those occasional events, when the late-night calm and quiet envelop me and spin my thoughts in unusual directions.

One such night, I had spent the day reading and rereading my interviews with estranged mothers and fathers, sons and daughters, cousins, grandparents, and grandchildren. I'm fortunate to have a study with a fireplace, and rubbing my eyes, I swiveled my chair to face it. Staring into the flames in a sleepy state, I imagined I could hear the thoughts of estranged family members across the country as they lay awake that night, staring up at the ceiling and wondering, "What do I do next?" For thousands—indeed, millions—of people, this question nags at them daily. They find themselves asking: "Is it right to live in a rift?" "Should I reach out now?" "What do I risk by trying to reconcile?" "Should I try again?"

Many of my interviewees were in such a place when I spoke with them. Cutting someone off may have brought immediate relief from conflict and negativity, but most people longed for a return to the relationship and felt that the rift stood in the way of achieving a life well-lived. The dilemma is clear: Do I stay in this estrangement that, although unhappy, is stable and a known quantity? Or do I go forward with a reconciliation attempt that may result in stress but also rewards? In this final chapter, I will share a simple but profound solution from the reconcilers that can help you take the next step.

ARE YOU REALLY "DONE"?

We saw in Chapter 2 that many estrangements begin with the words "I am done." The person who declares—sometimes for good reason—that he or she is "done" sees the rift as an insurmountable barrier. People usually have struggled long and hard with the relationship before one of them decides to cut it off. They initially experience relief from the stress of conflicts, and as the estrangement continues, it becomes a "new normal." The "I'm done" position is both protective and satisfying for an individual who feels wronged and for whom continued connection is a source of anxiety. As years go by, the idea of reconciling feels momentous and life-changing. As one person told me, "The longer this has gone on— fifteen years now—getting back together has become a really big deal!"

This state of affairs leads to a polarization of options: I can either remain entirely cut off, or I must reenter the relationship exactly as it was with its accompanying stresses, fights, and disappointments. As we saw in Chapter 10, estranged people fear being pulled back into old unfulfilling roles, negative interactions, criticism, and unfulfilled expectations. When you're deep in a rift, the very idea of restoring the relationship seems as unattainable as getting to the other side of a deep, unbridged chasm.

What is it like when people say, "I'm done"? Let's look at three examples that illustrate this situation.

Melody Lowe cut off all contact with her father:

> My father was a very harsh, abusive person, and he was an alcoholic. He was very inappropriate. It was really hard growing up with him. When I left the house, I determined that I would have no relationship with my father again. I went to college and never mentioned my father; I let my friends think he was dead. Once he drove up in front of the house with a gift and I would not speak to him. I saw him throw my gift out the window down the street because he was so angry. My oldest brother was on okay terms with my father and asked me if I would talk to him and give him a chance. I told him I would never, never speak to my father again.

Similarly, Carla Frank decided she was done with her brother:

> My brother had emotional problems, and it got worse when we reached our twenties. He started to get really impulsive and angered very easily. The last straw was after my daughter was born. Something I said set him off, and he threw a cup at me when I was holding the baby. And I just thought, "Wow, you know what, I can't be around him." He was irrational and not thinking straight. So I wasn't going to

reach out to him, and he really wanted nothing to do with me. I said: "Okay, you're not in my life, you don't want to be in my life, I don't want you in my life. I can't do this."

Ron Ruiz disliked his daughter-in-law. One day he lost control in an argument and told her in no uncertain terms his opinion of her, which infuriated his son:

> So, the you-know-what hit the fan. My son called me, and he read me the riot act. He called me a lot of different names and was extremely angry. He said I ruined his life and that I would never hear from him again. He told me I was destroying his one chance at happiness. There was nothing for me to do. I didn't know how to react. Then a couple of days later, I heard from my daughter-in-law. She sent a note and said, "Please do not try to contact us again." And so I had no choice. It was over.

"I'm done," "It's over," and similar statements sound like an uncompromising end. But does *done* always mean done forever? The answer to that question is more hopeful than I had anticipated: a resounding no. Here's why:

Melody, Carla, and Ron are all reconcilers.

Their relationships were declared over and done with, and there was no way forward. In each case, however, a pathway to reconciliation revealed itself. Each of these individuals moved from a position of total cutoff to reconnection, and they are glad they did.

I have long been fascinated by the movie *Sliding Doors*. As a sociologist who has studied aging, I am keenly aware of how taking or missing one opportunity can shape the course of a life. In the film, we see the consequences of a seemingly minor event: rushing to catch a train. In one scenario, the main character, Helen, makes the train and returns home to find her boyfriend in bed with another woman. In the other, she misses the train—and the other woman—with very different consequences.

Unfortunately, life usually does not offer this kind of a "control group" for decisions we make. We can only imagine how things might have turned out differently. For people in long-standing rifts, however, there is in fact a way to test the alternative scenario. One of the most powerful insights of the reconcilers is that you can experiment with reconnection, under low-risk, protected circumstances.

I interviewed dozens of estranged individuals who decided to build a single bridge over the rift. They were afraid that a host of family problems would come stampeding across, so they created the bridge under very specific and protected conditions. Most important, they made it a unique, time-limited offer. In the words of these reconcilers, they decided to offer *one last chance*. This final chance allowed for a "test-drive" of a rebooted relationship without long-term commitment and under highly controlled conditions.

The reconcilers believe that you are not confronted with the stark choice of continued estrangement or full reentry into the same old patterns that led to the rift. Instead, you can restore the relationship on a trial basis by offering one last chance. Before making the decision that you are really and truly done, they suggest that you provide one final opportunity for change. If you are a reader who has cut someone off, I can hear you saying: "But that's what I've already done! I gave chance after chance, and it always failed and I came away hurting." I ask you to read on, however, because I am willing to bet that you did not offer *this kind of chance*.

Some very long estrangements ended through a simple action: accepting the other person's offer to "do anything" in order to reconcile and offering a last chance to make the relationship work. Even people who had severed ties because of intolerable behaviors were able to create clear take-it-or-leave-it conditions for one final try. To a degree more common in the workplace than in family relationships, the terms for the "probationary period" were clearly specified, with the explicit understanding that the estrangement would begin again if terms were violated.

Why bother? Because making the "one more chance" effort has several benefits, as we saw in Chapter 5. It fulfills what some would see as a moral obligation. Estrangements cause great suffering to those who are cut off; offering a chance to relieve a person's psychological distress serves a humanitarian purpose. In addition, many people who initiate an estrangement have second thoughts about whether they have done the right thing. Offering one more chance allows an opportunity for confidence that this extreme choice was in fact the correct one.

But here's the best reason to try one more time: *What if it works?* Offering a single opportunity to reset the relationship has relatively few costs. If it is successful, the payoff is the rewards of reconciliation we have seen in many of the stories in this book. If not, you gain peace of mind from having tried. Let's look at how giving one last chance worked for two people in very different ways.

A TALE OF TWO LAST CHANCES

Lisbeth Tobias married right after college and moved away from her hometown with her husband. A relative died, and Lisbeth's mother asked her to drive back for the funeral. After the service, Lisbeth and her mother decided to have lunch together. As Lisbeth recounted the volcanic event that occurred, it was clear that the memory was extraordinarily vivid:

> It was a lovely restaurant. We were sitting having a nice conversation, glass of wine, seafood. Then my mother, who was very moralistic, started going on about "these people who live together before they're married." She used an expression: "A man won't buy the cow when he can get the milk for free." She had said those kinds of things many times before, but this time I spoke up and disagreed. I said: "In my experience, I know several people who have lived together, and they get along just fine. Most of them end up married."
>
> She blew up at me in the restaurant, screaming her head off, calling me every obscenity under the sun, and blaming me. Then she stormed out of the restaurant and left me to pay the bill. I was twenty-three years old and barely had enough money. The waitress came over and

said, "I'm so sorry." I just said, "That's what she's like." I paid the bill. Then I was stuck getting in the car with her. I did not speak to her. She drove me to the bus station. As I got out of the car I said, "I'm done. I never want to see you or speak to you again." Boom. I won't put up with this anymore.

When Lisbeth said, "I'm done," she really meant it. Underpinning this sudden eruption was a legacy of harsh discipline, parental favoritism, and controlling behavior. Left unexpressed for years, the underlying tension spilled out in one volcanic incident. She told me, "It was one event, but the estrangement dates back my entire life." Her mother would not accept the rift. Lisbeth recounted: "After this happened, she would call me regularly, and I would just hang up on her. She got my brother to call and tell me, 'You've got to apologize to Mom.' I said, 'I will never apologize to her, and I don't want to see her or speak to her again.'"

One can imagine a sad end to this story: the relationship atrophies and Lisbeth's mother dies without a reconciliation. That is not, however, the way things turned out. Because after years of separation, Lisbeth offered her mother one last chance. Life events intervened that changed the dynamics of the relationship. She told me:

Two things happened. First, I called my brother to tell him I was pregnant. He said, "You have to call Mom and apologize." I said, "I'm not going to do that." I did not call her to tell her. Not long after, he called me and told me: "Mom has cancer. You have to call her and apologize." I said, "I'm not going to."

What happened next was entirely unexpected:

Soon after those conversations, my mother called me and apologized. She had never before been sorry for anything. But this time, she said she was sorry, that it wouldn't happen again. It was a sincere apology— that is what was remarkable.

Lisbeth now had to make one of the most difficult decisions of her life. The cutoff had brought genuine relief and little regret. However, she was aware of her mother's health problems. The prospect of never reconciling before her death was a disquieting one. In addition, now pregnant, she believed her child should have at least a tenuous connection to her grandmother. Lisbeth took a mental deep breath and told her mother:

> "I will give you another chance, but this is the last chance." When I said, "This is your last chance," she realized that I meant it and that the only way she would get to see her grandchild would be if she really meant the apology. I held to what I said about the last chance, and my mother knew it, and she changed her behavior. The interactions became reasonable, or at least as reasonable as you could be with her.

Lisbeth set very clear conditions for the last-chance opportunity: "I told her, 'Here's what it would take. These are the things I'm not going to tolerate.' I think that it's a good idea to give somebody one more opportunity not to be the way they were. What was really interesting was that she never yelled at me again."

I asked Lisbeth for an example of how her mother's behavior was different after the last-chance ultimatum:

> Okay, here's a small example of how she changed. She had this thing that she did, which was acting like anything that wasn't perfect would be the end of the world. Shortly after we reconciled, she found out that we were going to name our daughter Margaret and nickname her Peggy, which I thought was a very nice name. So, my mother called me on the phone. "Oh, Lisbeth, please don't call her Peggy. You'll ruin her life. Kids will tease her on the playground. They'll call her Piggy. Kids can be so cruel. It will be awful." I said: "Thank you, but actually that's the name it's going to be." And I held my breath.
>
> And she never yelled at me about it. If she had been her old self, she would have screamed at me for disagreeing with her. Somehow the

dynamics shifted—they had reset. In the past with something like this, she would start to go off. But now I could see her stopping herself, because she could sense that there was this change in me. I had said, "I will give you one last chance," and she believed it. What that taught me was that she could control herself and for the first twenty-three years of my life had chosen not to.

Lisbeth swears by the "one last chance" approach. Rather than reject an apology, why not take up the offer for a "reset"? The investment is low and the relationship can be cut off again if the experiment does not work. Lisbeth explained:

I enjoy reading the advice columns in the paper, and so many are about dysfunctional families and estrangement. One of the things that I notice when I read those examples is that people keep putting themselves back into a situation and nothing ever changes. I don't know if I believed my mother could change, but I insisted on it, and I was willing to see if it worked.

In her own version of *Sliding Doors*, Lisbeth has compared in her imagination the path not taken: continued estrangement. In her view, the last-chance experiment paid off richly in contrast to that alternative:

I never regretted giving her one more chance. I'm glad that we reconciled, because in her final years, she got to see her first grandchild. She did get to know Peggy and spend some time with her as a baby and as a toddler. Peggy has very fond memories of her. If I had never spoken to her again and she had died, I don't know that I would have regretted that, but I might have. At the time it felt right to offer her the chance. I guess I did have some need to feel like my mother loved me and wasn't just crazy. I got that. She was just a very difficult person. I don't miss her, but I'm never angry or upset about her anymore. It's just, well, that's what it was, and we go on.

What about the risk that the last chance will fail? I learned that even in that case, people who offered the chance did not regret doing so. They, too, received an enormous benefit: greater peace of mind. If a relative was unable to change even after begging for one more chance, they felt relieved of guilt and more certain about their choice to be estranged.

Karen Huang experienced this kind of relief after enduring the ups and downs of a very difficult relationship with her sister, May. Karen told me:

> My parents divorced when I was young, so I grew up with my mom and my sister. As a child, I didn't feel like I fit in with my family, and I didn't feel like I had anybody I could relate to, anybody on my side. I would see my friends who are super connected to their family, and I'd be like, "Oh, I wonder what that's like."

As an adult, Karen tried to have a relationship with May but found it difficult. "My sister has a volatile personality, and she holds grudges, and she's very excitable and is emotionally kind of on edge." An estrangement occurred after a specific event:

> We were having a phone conversation, and I said the wrong thing about a guy she was dating, and she was very upset with me and offended. So she got angry with me, and I thought she was being unreasonable, and I just stopped talking to her. It was for a period of a couple of years. It was pretty much by mutual agreement.

Then Karen's sister reached out and suggested that they reconcile. Holidays were approaching; her sister wanted to resolve things so that the family could get together harmoniously. In addition, there was pressure from her mother: "She's always expressed her desire and wish for us to be closer. She'll say, 'Oh, I wish you girls could get along better.'"

Karen was not entirely enthusiastic about rekindling the relationship, based on past history, but she felt it deserved one last chance. The sisters decided to see a counselor to help resolve the issues. "We were in therapy for a while and the therapist got us to make some agreements about how we were going to treat each other. We set down some boundaries about behaviors and made agreements about how we were going to talk to each other."

In this case, however, the last chance turned out to be a well-meaning attempt that was not successful. Karen described the outcome:

> Neither my sister nor I could adhere to the agreements after we stopped going to therapy. We just went back to our old ways. And so I was just like, "I'm not going to try to maintain this relationship. It's not doing me any good at all." It was interesting, because the estrangement led to a desire on both of our parts to try to be better sisters, to be closer together. And then when that wasn't successful, that was okay with both of us, you know? We had said, "Let's just give this one more try." And it was one that didn't work out, and it was fine. We learned that it is not a healthy relationship for either of us and it's better not to be connected.

Karen has no regrets about offering the last chance. Rather than being saddled with a lifetime of wondering if she made the right decision, she feels also resolved in knowing she made the effort: "It helped me accept that it would never be anything closer or better." As Lisbeth and Karen show, giving someone a last chance offers an opportunity for reconciliation or for acceptance of the estrangement, at relatively little cost.

THE TOOL KIT

Offering one last chance is a strategy that can be productively attempted by most people who are holding on to an estrangement. It sounds simple: a carefully considered offer to try one last time. What can you do, however, to increase the chances that the one last chance works? It may indeed be the last chance that is offered, so maximizing its effectiveness is a good idea. The reconcilers' strategies include renegotiating the relationship after the estrangement and taking steps to limit the risk of reconciling. I conclude with a strategy that emerged from all my research: to see reconciliation as a unique engine for personal growth.

THE FIRST STRATEGY: USE THE NEW LEVERAGE IN THE RELATIONSHIP

Even after years of difficult interactions, most people experience a final, nonnegotiable cutoff as a shock. Despite warning signs, becoming totally estranged represents a turn of events most people (and especially parents) had not imagined possible. Although I do not recommend entering into an estrangement for this reason, one of the strongest lessons I learned from the reconcilers is this: The shock of estrangement often leads to a radical reevaluation of the relationship.

As we saw in Chapter 9, people take for granted the assumption that families "always stick together and iron out their differences" despite conflict, negativity, and unmet expectations. When the other person does not hold to such norms and cuts off the relationship, those rejected are forced to reorder their worldview regarding the relationship. Therefore, when people claim "Things will be different now" and "I'm willing to change" after a cutoff event, they may actually mean it.

Paradoxically, the shock of the cutoff is precisely why the last-chance approach often succeeds. One person's realization that the relationship can end may lead to dramatic compromises about standards for acceptable behavior in the relationship. Sybil Okafor's journey through a painful estrangement and reconciliation provides a good example. Her relationship with her mother was always difficult and made more complicated by cultural issues. She told me:

> My mother has always been such that there are no boundaries with what she'll say. She feels that with her children she can say anything to us without regard to how it makes us feel or if it's offensive or not. When I was in my twenties, I had a breakdown and was hospitalized. My mother, instead of being sympathetic and concerned, believed I

was just being selfish and immature. She actually came to the hospital and told me: "This is the stupidest thing I've ever heard. You're faking! You're stupid!" I just started screaming at her and saying, "I hate you. I'm this messed up because of you." I did not speak to her for several years. I wouldn't return her phone calls.

Sybil faced family pressure, because cutting off her mother violated strong cultural norms:

My family are Nigerian immigrants, so it was difficult because of the cultural issues. My extended family is extremely close. We all came to this country together, and we all depended on each other for survival. Cutting my mother off was so unusual, and so against our cultural norms, that my extended family was stunned. My uncles and aunts called me and they said, "You need to talk to your mother." I wouldn't do it. I came to the conclusion that it was the best way to approach my mother. I would just not argue with her and not engage her.

Sybil eventually relented and offered her mother one more chance. She made sure that her mother clearly understood that this was a onetime opportunity and that the estrangement would begin again if her behavior reverted to meanness and verbal abuse. The result was a striking change:

After a few years, I decided I would give the relationship one last chance. We began talking again and the estrangement was over. It ended because she understood I had set a hard line about what was going to be acceptable and what was not going to be acceptable for her to say to me. And she saw that I was willing to stick to that. The estrangement scared her and showed her that I was willing to end the relationship.

After the estrangement we had a pretty good relationship, because if she ever said anything offensive to me, I would just walk away. I would just say, "I'm going to hang up the phone now." Or, "I'm leaving now."

I had no problem doing it, and I felt empowered. I could maintain boundaries with her because I had shown I would act if I needed to. So the estrangement really changed our relationship for the better.

Many people who chose the route of one last chance discovered this same dynamic: The relative had learned the value of the relationship through the estrangement and was ready to make concrete behavioral changes. The family member's assertion of "I will do anything if we can try to make this work again" was genuine and not simply a rhetorical device. Rather than believing that all actions are acceptable because "we're family," the relatives changed their behavior to avoid another painful rift.

THE SECOND STRATEGY: LIMIT THE RISK

We have seen in earlier chapters that a major reason that rifts endure is anxiety. People considering reconciliation worry about being over-whelmed by demands, criticism, requests for support, stressful interactions, and falling back into unwanted family roles. There is a fear of being reabsorbed into a maelstrom of family problems. The last-chance alternative can serve as a powerful method of self-protection—and as a way out, if need be.

Maya Schweitzer used this strategy to balance feelings of obligation and guilt with the need, as she put it, "to not go down with the ship." Her father has proved untrustworthy over the years and has lived a very dis-organized life, skirting the edge of bankruptcy a number of times—to the point of being evicted from an apartment and nearly becoming homeless. Maya was very much afraid of being dragged into the drama of her father's life. She told me: "He has major personality flaws, so he would keep losing jobs and we'd have to move all the time. I think he's a narcissist or a sociopath—he has these kinds of issues. I don't have the emotional bandwidth to deal with someone like that."

Maya decided she needed to have a small amount of contact with her father, if only to be reassured that he was not in some kind of life-threatening circumstance. The last-chance concept worked for her, because it has allowed her to keep a minimal amount of communication with him while protecting herself and her family from disruption and unwanted financial obligations. She told me:

> He has money issues, and I worried that if I started engaging with him more, he might want to come here where we live. So I reconnected, but I am completely clear what the limits are. My main fear is going down with the ship and to have my family go down with the ship. So if it ever gets to that point, he knows I'll cut off contact again if that's what has to happen. Because I don't need him. If I can minimally engage with him and no one is harmed from that, that's okay, but if he gets crazier, I won't bring him into my life anymore.
>
> I offered him the chance for limited contact, and he took it, but my motto is still "Don't go down with the ship," especially your own family and your own life. Focus on that and try to preserve your own well-being. It's not going to be very fulfilling, but I feel like I can tell myself I did my best. It's not the way I would've chosen it to be, but I think even at the end, I'll feel like I did the best I could in a difficult situation.

Such a balance is not always easily achieved. Bobbie Vaughn provides an excellent metaphor for the balancing act required: "navigating the edge." She has gone through several estrangements and reconciliations with her deeply troubled brother, and is engaged in what she sees as the last chance she will offer to "hang in there" with him. But she simultaneously stresses self-protection:

> You have to take care of yourself. Don't burn yourself out completely trying to help someone. If someone's in a crisis, and they're accepting help, then you do everything you can for your family. But if they're not putting anything into it, then I would say don't give too much, don't burn yourself out. You have to value your own personal health and

well-being at a certain point. Give one more chance, but know that navigating that edge can be challenging.

Despite the need to carefully monitor the relationship during the last-chance period, most people thought that it was a worthwhile experience. Maya, Bobbie, and many others found that their alternatives were not limited to acceptance of a full relationship and a total cutoff. Offering one more chance on their own terms allowed the relationship to continue, alleviated guilt, eliminated anticipated regret, and relieved anxiety.

THE FINAL STRATEGY: TAKE THE CHANCE TO GROW

At the beginning of this book, I told you that *Fault Lines* is based on social science, informed as it is with data from more than 1,600 people. But I also disclosed that this book represents my search to understand family rifts and that you would sometimes hear my own, admittedly subjective, viewpoint. After wrestling with the problem of estrangement for over five years, a core principle emerged that I offer as my heartfelt advice to you:

If you have a relative desperate to reconnect, offer one last chance; if you are offered one last chance, take it.

You may be one of those people whose child, parent, sibling, cousin, or grandparent has been begging you to end the rift. You have unfollowed them on social media; you refuse all cards, emails, letters, and gifts. And still they reach out, telling you they don't understand why the cutoff occurred, and can you at least sit down over coffee to discuss the situation? They may offer to enter counseling with you. It has become easier for you to say no, as time has passed and inertia has set in. Perhaps you have moved and are no longer forced to interact with your family; you may be harboring a grudge about past behavior; you may have tried before and believe nothing will change.

I urge you to reconsider. You have nothing to lose by offering one last chance *under specific conditions*. Your relative, after the estrangement, may be more amenable to a different relationship; further, he or she may have changed. Most important, however, is this: The suffering experienced by many people who have been cut off is barely imaginable to someone who has not experienced it. As we have seen in Chapter 3, some individuals view the rift as more painful than bereavement. It becomes a source of chronic stress, exacerbated by repeatedly running full force into the brick wall of estrangement despite how painful it is.

Thus, because there is a chance that the relationship might work out on a limited basis, under conditions you specify, it is almost always worth a try. Reaching out to the relative with a clear plan is a protected way of experimenting with contact. If the dynamics are unchanged and cause you pain and anxiety, there is a simple and logical path: closing the relationship off again. I have learned that many people drift out of a relationship without a single, clear opportunity to try again, and thereby lose a sense of resolution at having made an honest attempt to reconnect. I can provide no better evidence than the stories you have read in this chapter. They offer you the peace of mind that comes from giving a final opportunity for reconciliation, whatever the outcome.

When I began my exploration of the landscape of estrangement and reconciliation, I had no idea what I would find. Along the way, I shared some of the despair and helplessness people in rifts experience. Unexpectedly, I also discovered many people who, with courage and determination, found a way to reconnect. Their renewed relationships may not be perfect, but these reconcilers were overwhelmingly grateful that they made the effort. Reconciliation brought them back into a network of kin. We have seen that, for some, the restored ties provided support and resources for them and their families.

But there is another reason to give an estranged relative one last chance that may come as a surprise to you. After spending years talking with people who reconciled after estrangement, I will leave you with this discovery: *Reconciliation can be a powerful engine for personal growth.* In Chapter 5, we saw that most of the reconcilers reconnected not out of altruism, but for themselves. A weight dropped from their shoulders, and they were freed from guilt and obsessive thinking about the estrangement.

I learned that something else goes on when people reconcile. They grow through the powerful experience of surmounting a challenge, engaging with their fears, exploring their own actions, and, in some cases, forgiving. Many reconcilers told me that the process of reconnecting, although difficult and even painful, taught them lessons about themselves they could not have learned in any other way. Not only was the reconnection itself beneficial, but also the process had changed them for the better.

Because this book's journey began with Tricia Stewart, it is appropriate to enlist her wisdom at its close. Tricia described how she reconnected with her father and mother after a nightmarish upbringing and a long estrangement. She found that reconciling with her admittedly difficult parents allowed her to live out her values and helped her son understand the importance of intergenerational connections.

There was an even more powerful result for Tricia (and, I learned, for many others). Reflecting on decades of stormy family drama, she told me that moving from estrangement to reconnection led to an enhanced sense of self. Achieving the reconciliation taught her critically important lessons about how to meet her own needs while accepting differences and showing compassion to others. She would not be the person she is, she told me, had she not worked to repair the relationship. She explained:

> I learned how to take what I experienced and translate that into what not to do. You don't have to be a product of your circumstances. You and your brain at some point can make a decision: "I don't choose to do that." Boundaries exist with my parents. I get to choose.

Tricia believes that the growth she achieved after a horrible childhood resulted from restoring her parents to her life, rather than from keeping them out:

> I needed to reconnect with them to understand their impact on me and to deal with what had gone on. I couldn't do that if I cut them off for the rest of my life. I now have space to still be in a relationship with

them and not own whatever they have going on. I have preserved some of what family life is supposed to be like, and that includes the grandparents of my child. Working through things with them has helped me be comfortable with who I am and owning the choices that I've made.

Tricia's message echoes the major insights I received over the course of this research. She learned she was not alone in being estranged. She enlisted the help of friends and professionals in creating a successful reconnection. She explored her past history and present needs, forming a stronger and more resilient sense of self. Most important, she went from a position of weakness and vulnerability to one of control. She gained power: the power to shape the relationship and the ultimate power to leave again if it became intolerable. Along the way, she gained confidence and self-esteem.

As I listened to the reconcilers, I had a revelation: They are not talking about a single event, but rather of reconciliation as a *discipline*. You may recognize that term, because it is used in fields from spiritual development to business management. It has nothing to do with the idea of punishment—in fact, it is the opposite. A discipline is a developmental pathway in which one improves at something through self-exploration, risk, and determined practice.

It's important to remember that practicing a discipline is a long-term process; you do not arrive suddenly at success and then stop working at it. Instead, you are continually striving to master the discipline. Whether it is training for a cycling race, learning to play the guitar, or becoming expert in a martial art, all disciplines require short-term sacrifice to reap long-term rewards. When the reconcilers talk about their experiences, it is this kind of discipline they have in mind: not giving up, working out compromises, persevering, finding creative solutions for problems, and seeking help when necessary. Failure is not a possibility, because setbacks are critical learning experiences that guide the next steps.

We live in a world that too many people feel is increasingly polarized.

Divisions have deepened between political viewpoints, socioeconomic classes, ethnic groups, and generations. Most of us have little direct influence on these national and global divisions. Instead we watch them with growing alarm. We do, however, have the power to overcome divisions in our own immediate spheres. St. Augustine wisely said, "Peace in society depends on peace in the family." Practicing the discipline of reconciliation is a small step we can take to create harmony in our own families while growing as human beings. If you agree, then it's probably time to take a chance.

ACKNOWLEDGMENTS

Throughout this project I have received invaluable support and encouragement from a large number of individuals. It is a pleasure to acknowledge them here.

My heartfelt thanks goes to my interviewees, who donated their time and stories freely and openly. I admire them greatly for their efforts to understand and improve their family lives and for making their experiences useful to others in similar situations. I am unable to repay them for their investment in this book. I can only hope that I have conveyed their thoughts and advice as they would have wished.

I am deeply grateful to individuals who assisted in collecting the data. Catherine Johnson's skills as project interviewer helped me obtain the detailed responses that enrich the book. Rebecca Schillenback and Marie Cope Nicholson also ably conducted interviews. Gregory Chen joined the project as an undergraduate at Cornell and was responsible for recruiting and interviewing several dozen college students, allowing me to include the viewpoints of estranged emerging adults. Invaluable assistance was provided by the Yasamin Miller Group in conducting the national survey. Yasamin has helped me with data collection on all three of my books and is a joy to work with.

I was assisted immensely by members of my research team. I owe a particular debt of gratitude to Marie Tillema Cope, who carried out many complex management tasks, including coordinating the interviews and coding, and making sure the data were organized and easy to use. I also benefited from her considerable editorial skills and the insights of her social work training. Leslie Schultz supported the research activities and provided feedback on study findings. Nora Burrows worked diligently to code the responses.

I owe a special debt to Amy Dickinson, the nationally syndicated "Ask Amy" columnist. Long before I began this study, I was impressed by the wise advice for estranged family members in her column. Her assistance in recruiting reconciled family members helped make that component of the study possible.

Conversations over the years with colleagues on topics related to this book have been very helpful. In this regard, I would like to acknowledge J. Jill Suitor, Mark S. Lachs, Megan Gilligan, Risa Breckman, Cary Reid, Rhoda Meador, Daniel Lichter, Sharon Sassler, Karen Fingerman, and Merril Silverstein. I also appreciate the interest of individuals affiliated with the Bowen Center, several of whom were interviewed for this project. I am especially grateful to Dr. Anne McKnight, director of the Bowen Center during the time of this project. Although I could not convey in depth the complex insights of Bowen theory in this book, I hope I have inspired some readers to learn more about it.

Two people provided invaluable help by reviewing the manuscript. As she has for my previous books, Sheri Hall reviewed and edited the chapters throughout the writing process. I am also grateful to Sheri for convening members of her highly astute book group to review a draft of the manuscript. It is a joy to be able to rely on the writing advice of Peter Wolk for my books. In addition, Peter graciously opened his home in Gardiner, New York, for our writing retreats. I wrote the first and the last words of this manuscript in that lovely setting.

I am fortunate to have the best agent ever, Janis Donnaud. I consider her an invaluable partner in creating my books, and I would be lost without her assistance. I would also like to acknowledge Caroline Sutton, editor in chief at Avery, for her support of and belief in this book.

I owe thanks as well to the Trappist monks of the Abbey of the Genesee in Piffard, New York. If you, like me, struggle with distractions, there is no better place to write than a retreat house run by monks who take a vow of silence. It is open to men and women of all faiths, and time spent in that serene, rural setting (with no TV, Wi-Fi, or conversation) was my secret weapon for overcoming the occasional bout of writer's block.

I received extensive support from family members in writing this book. I am in the unusual position of having a wide range of expertise available from my relatives. My wife, Clare McMillan, provided her stellar editorial skills and her enthusiastic support, as well as came up with the book's title. My sister-in-law Jane Pillemer carefully reviewed the manuscript from the perspective of a marriage and family therapist. My daughter Sarah Pillemer not only provided a careful review based on her expertise as a clinical psychologist but also benefited the family by adding my new son-in-law, Richard Weiner. My daughter Hannah Pillemer and her husband, Michael Civille, also offered support. Even more important, during the project they created (objectively and scientifically speaking) the two most adorable grandchildren in the world, Clare and Thomas.

Finally, I cannot leave a book on estrangement without mention of my own family of origin: my brothers David, Stephen, and Eric Pillemer and spouses Jane Pillemer, Helen Rasmussen, and Wendy Pillemer. In a world where families are challenging for so many, it is a blessing to be a part of one that includes them and their children.

APPENDIX:

HOW THE STUDY WAS CONDUCTED

This book is based on information collected from approximately 1,600 people using several different methods. For the sake of convenience, I will refer to these data-collection activities as the Cornell Family Reconciliation Project (CFRP). Aspects of CFRP and this book follow standard methods of sociological research. In my scientific work, I have conducted many such studies and published the results in academic journals.

For this book, however, the ways that I interpret the results and present the findings differ at some points from the standard social scientific approach. Because this is a book for everyone, rather than just other social scientists, I engage in more interpretation and personal reflection than I do in research articles. My goal was to provide a deep understanding of the landscape of estrangement and reconciliation from the standpoint of people who experienced them and to convey their advice in rich and nuanced detail.

In this Appendix, I provide background on the methods used to collect the data on which this book is based. When I became interested in the topic of family rifts, I first searched existing literature on the topic. Although much has been written in scientific journals about factors that predict the quality of family relationships, I was surprised to find that very little research had been conducted specifically on estrangement, and almost none on reconciliation. Following accepted social science research methods when little guidance exists from past research, I carried out the following set of research activities. A word of warning: Unlike in the rest of this book, you will find more technical discussion here. For the professional or amateur social scientists among you, happy reading!

In-Depth Interview Study

SAMPLE RECRUITMENT

In this component of the project, my goal was to obtain detailed descriptions of the processes of estrangement and reconciliation from a large group of individuals who had experienced them. As you can imagine, there is no national database of people in family rifts, so I knew that recruitment of a sizable sample would be challenging. Conducting a representative national survey involving in-depth interviews would have been economically unfeasible. I therefore used a combination of convenience sampling and snowball sampling for this component of the study.

Convenience sampling is a method of non-probability sampling that is appropriate for research goals like mine. I was not trying to achieve accurate sampling to be able to describe a clearly defined population. Instead, I needed to recruit a large sample of people who had experienced the problem I was interested in. Convenience sampling is a lot like it sounds: One begins by asking people who are more or less easily accessible. In this case, my research team and I created large lists of individuals in our personal and professional acquaintance and sent them a standard email describing the study. Individuals who responded were then invited for interviews.

Snowball sampling is another non-probability sampling technique. The term comes from the image of a snowball rolling downhill, getting bigger as it descends. The individuals we contacted were also asked if there were people who had experienced family rifts among their acquaintances. They provided family members, friends, and others with the study information, and some of those people contacted us.

The recruitment email provided the following criteria for being in the study:

> In this study, estrangement is defined broadly as a situation in which an individual has ceased to have contact with a family member, or has only minimal contact (less than once a year). In particular, we are interested in talking with people who consider themselves estranged from a parent, child, sibling, grandparent, grandchild, or another relative who is significant to them. Further, we are interested in speaking with individuals who have lost or ceased contact with a family member regardless of the reason.

As described in the Introduction, as the project progressed, I became increasingly interested in locating individuals who had reconciled. A small number of reconcilers were already in the sample, but I needed substantially more interviewees to be able to share advice on the reconciliation process. I received invaluable assistance from the nationally syndicated advice columnist Amy Dickinson ("Ask Amy"), who publicized the reconciliation interviews in her column. The combined recruitment activities resulted in 270 in-depth interviews. I had reached the point of "saturation," where no new themes or ideas were emerging, so data collection was ended.

Of these interviews, 100 individuals had reconciled, and 170 were still in family rifts. In terms of demographic characteristics, the in-depth interview sample was disproportionately female (78 percent) and predominately white (86 percent). Of the remainder of the sample, 7 percent were Asian American,

4 percent were Hispanic, and 3 percent were African American. In terms of age, 21 percent were ages 18–24; 6 percent were 25–34; 7 percent were 35–44; 10 percent were 45–54; 24 percent were 55–64; and 32 percent were 65 or over.

Individuals who expressed interest in the study were contacted by the research team and provided with additional information. An interview was then scheduled. Because this was a national sample, most interviews were conducted by telephone, with a small number conducted in person. The interviews were recorded and transcribed. Interviews averaged around 45 minutes, with some lasting an hour or more. We were able to conduct follow-up interviews approximately one year after the initial interview with 49 sample members.

The interview began with the opportunity for the respondents to tell the story of the estrangement in their own words. They were told: "I'd like to begin by asking you to describe the situation in your family. Please tell me the story however you would like to. If you thought of the experience like a book, what are the main chapters? We would like to learn about how the issues began, what happened, and where things stand today." Follow-up questions were asked to make sure we had information on the respondents' views about what they believe caused the estrangement and how it progressed to the present day. The interview continued with questions covering the impact of the estrangement on them and other family members and how it might have been prevented. Individuals who had reconciled were asked in detail about the process and experience of reconnecting.

A substantial portion of the interviews was devoted to the respondents' advice for others. We asked what concrete steps they took to deal with the estrangement and to overcome it, sources of help they found useful, and specific tips or strategies for reconciliation. Almost all respondents found the interview to be interesting and a positive experience. When asked if we could speak with them again, only four individuals declined.

HUMAN SUBJECTS

Like all university-based social science studies, this project was reviewed and approved at Cornell for what is called "Protection of Human Subjects." This means that certain procedures had to be followed regarding how the data were collected. It's worth noting that unlike those in some surveys, respondents in this project were not guaranteed total confidentiality. They were promised anonymity—that's why all names of those interviewed in this book are pseudonyms, created by a random-names generator. But they were informed that I intended to use their direct quotes and that it was possible that they could be identified by the details in the quotations.

No one refused after being given that warning; indeed, a few wished they could have had their real names next to their stories. To offer additional protection, however, I followed procedures to further anonymize some of the interviews, including changing details in the interview that might make a person identifiable. The sense and meaning of the quotes and case studies, however, remain unchanged.

ANALYSIS

Coding of the interviews was carried out using the software program Dedoose. These data are what I rely on when I say things like "one of the most frequently mentioned issues . . ." However, I did not employ statistical techniques and quantitative analyses in analyzing the data. Instead, I followed the widely accepted sociological approach of qualitative and narrative analysis. I read the entire interviews and the coded excerpts dozens of times, identifying major themes and the examples and case studies that illustrated these themes.

National Random-Sample Survey

As described in Chapter 1, I wanted to shed light on the prevalence of estrangement, asking how frequently it occurs in the general population and how it is distributed among several subgroups. With the assistance of the Yasamin Miller Group, I surveyed a national sample of people age 18 and older in the United States. One way to accomplish this task would be to conduct a national survey by face-to-face or telephone interviews. Conducting enough in-person interviews from a random sample of the general U.S. population would be extremely expensive, and so it was ruled out. Telephone surveys are also very costly, and with declining response rates, there is debate about how representative random-digit-dial telephone interviews actually are and whether these probability-based approaches are indeed still probability-based. Further, they are now difficult to conduct because so few people have landlines and so many are unwilling to answer cell phone calls from unrecognized numbers.

To deal with these issues, social scientists are increasingly conducting "web-based panel" (or "online internet panel") studies, which have been found to be effective ways of approximating survey results from a true random sample. In this method, a database is assembled of potential respondents who declare that they will participate in surveys if invited. Such online surveys are faster, more efficient, and less expensive than conventional survey approaches, such as telephone, face-to-face, and mail interviews. Drawbacks have also been identified in the literature—in particular, possible bias created by self-selection into a web panel.

A number of providers offer panels of possible survey respondents who fit the needs of a specific study. For the national survey I conducted, a Qualtrics research panel of U.S. adults ages 18 years and older was used for recruitment. To exclude duplication and ensure validity, Qualtrics checks every IP address and uses a sophisticated digital fingerprinting technology. Qualtrics randomly selects respondents for surveys in which respondents are highly likely to qualify. Each sample from the panel base is proportioned to the general population and then randomized before the survey is deployed. Qualtrics works to guarantee that the population surveyed meets the requirements of the specific survey as defined by the investigator.

Potential respondents are sent an email invitation informing them that the survey is for research purposes only, how long the survey is expected to take, and what incentives are available. To avoid self-selection bias, the survey invitation does not include specific details about the content of the survey. In total, 8,203 panel members were eligible to participate, and 1,340 completed the survey (a 16 percent completion rate). As shown in the table, the final composition of the sample is nearly identical to that of the U.S. population.

Table 1: Comparison of Family Estrangement National Survey (FENS) respondents with U.S. population (adults ages 18 and over)

Age	FENS	USA
18–24	13%	12%
25–34	18%	18%
35–44	17%	17%
45–54	18%	18%
55–64	17%	17%
65+	17%	18%

Gender	FENS	USA
Female	53%	52%
Male	47%	48%

Race	FENS	USA
White or Caucasian	61%	60%
Black or African American	12%	12%

Race	FENS	USA
Asian	6%	5%
Hispanic	16%	18%
Other/Multiracial	5%	5%

Education	FENS	USA
Some College or College Degree	48 %	44 %

Geographical Region	FENS	USA
Midwest	22%	21%
Northeast	19%	18%
South	39%	37%
West	20%	23%

All respondents in the national survey were asked the question, "Do you have any family members (i.e., parents, grandparents, siblings, children, uncles, aunts, cousins, or other relatives) from whom you are currently estranged, meaning you have no contact with the family member(s) at the present time?" Individuals who answered yes to this question were asked a set of additional questions, including the degree of upset over the estrangement, how long it had gone on, and the demographic characteristics that are used in Chapter 1.

SUPPLEMENTAL RESEARCH EFFORTS

In addition to these two main research activities, I also gathered information from several other sources that informed the book. First, for the reconciliation component of the in-depth interview study, a website was created where individuals could submit their reconciliation stories. A number of these individuals (approximately 75) provided a written story but did not wish to be interviewed. These stories helped flesh out the advice for reconciliation. Second, in my interviews with hundreds of older people in the Cornell Legacy Project, a number of individuals had experienced estrangement and helped my understanding of family rifts in later life. Finally, I interviewed 10 marriage and family therapists who work with estranged families, and their insights are reflected at various points in the book.

How This Book Differs from a Social Science Study

The data-collection procedures for these studies followed standard social science practice. I balanced purposive samples of individuals who were specifically interested in the topic with a representative national sample of people selected at random. However, this is of course a popular book for general audiences. Therefore, some ways I have presented the information are different from what I would do if I were publishing the data in a scientific journal.

I have edited the quotations to make them more readable, cutting out the use of "um" and "ah" and standardizing grammar. I have not indicated missing segments of quotations, and I think readers will be grateful to be spared sentences like "Well, um, I guess . . . the problem was, hmm, I'm not sure . . . probably something like . . ." However, the quotations used in this book all capture the spirit of the recorded interviews. I have kept the tone and expressiveness intact so that readers can get the full flavor of the respondents' viewpoints.

I took another liberty in this book in the interest of readability. The in-depth interview component of this project involved 270 interviews, all of which I could not have personally conducted. However, I designed all the questions that were asked, I carefully trained the interviewers, and I met with them for supervision. I ensured that all questions were asked just the way I intended and went over the taped and transcribed interviews countless times. I also conducted many interviews personally. For this reason, I use the first-person pronoun in this book for all the interviews that were conducted. Again, I believe readers will thank me for not repeating: "Interviewer 2 asked . . ." and for going instead with the clearer "I." I feel this is justified given my intensive involvement in all aspects of the data-collection process.

Finally, more than in a scientific study, I have inserted myself into the interpretation and presentation of the information. I include my reactions and personal experiences at various points in the book. Further, I made decisions regarding the selection of the main themes and specific advice in part based on my own reaction to and interpretation of the interviewees' responses. As noted earlier, the themes did not emerge from quantitative analysis, such that some received more "votes" than others. This book is the product of my interaction with the interview material, both as a social scientist and as a member of an extended family trying to apply the insights to my own life.

NOTES

Introduction

1 He became estranged from his father: Maria Carter, "Why the Real Christopher Robin Hated 'Pooh,'" *Country Living*, July 31, 2018, https://www.countryliving.com/life/entertainment/a43801/real-christopher-robin-hated-winnie-the-pooh/.

5 article for my blog: https://legacyproject.human.cornell.edu/2013/03/06/children-who-break-your-heart-a-reader-asks-for-your-advice/.

5 The monumental *Handbook of Family Therapy*: Thomas L. Sexton and Jay Lebow, *Handbook of Family Therapy* (New York: Routledge, 2016).

15 our family relationships can affect us: Karen L. Fingerman et al., "The Baby Boomers' Intergenerational Relationships," *Gerontologist* 52, no. 2 (2012): 199–209, https://doi.org/10.1093/geront/gnr139.

Chapter 1: You Are Not Alone

21 "a haven in a heartless world": Christopher Lasch, *Haven in a Heartless World: The Family Besieged* (New York: Basic Books, 1977).

21 We present our family lives: Oren Gil-Or, Yossi Levi-Belz, and Ofir Turel, "The Facebook-Self": Characteristics and Psychological Predictors of False Self-Presentation on Facebook," *Frontiers in Psychology* 6, no. 99 (2015), https://doi.org/10.3389/fpsyg.2015.00099.

21 makes other people value them less: Carol T. Miller and Brenda Major, "Coping with Stigma and Prejudice," in *The Social Psychology of Stigma*, ed. Todd F. Heatherton, Robert E. Kleck, Michelle R. Hebl, and Jay G. Hull (New York: Guilford Press, 2000), 243–72.

22 Some researchers believe that estrangement: Lucy Blake, "Parents and Children Who Are Estranged in Adulthood: A Review and Discussion of the Literature," *Journal of Family Theory and Review* 9, no. 4 (2017): 521–36, https://doi.org/10.1111/jftr.12216.

24 estrangement is a "silent epidemic": Lisa Flam, "Parental Estrangement: A 'Silent Epidemic' of Cut-off Kids," *Today*, April 1, 2013, https://www.today.com/parents/parental-estrangement-silent-epidemic-cut-kids-1C9163139.

28 The playwright Anton Chekov: Anton Chekhov, "Gooseberries," in *Anton Chekhov's Short Stories*, ed. Ralph E. Matlaw (New York: W. W. Norton, 1979), 192.

28 **psychologist Alexander Jordan has pointed out:** Alexander H. Jordan et al., "Misery Has More Company Than People Think: Underestimating the Prevalence of Others' Negative Emotions," *Personality and Social Psychology Bulletin* 37, no. 1 (2011): 120–35, https://doi.org/10.1177/0146167210390822.

Chapter 2: Pathways to Estrangement

31 **Qualitative research like mine:** Bren Neale, *What Is Qualitative Longitudinal Research?* (London: Bloomsbury Academic, 2018).

35 **They may feel that their former spouse:** Matthijs Kalmijn, "Relationships Between Fathers and Adult Children: The Cumulative Effects of Divorce and Repartnering," *Journal of Family Issues* 36, no. 6 (2015): 737–59, https://doi.org/10.1177/0192513X13495398; James R. Dudley, "Increasing Our Understanding of Divorced Fathers Who Have Infrequent Contact with Their Children," *Family Relations* 40, no. 3 (1991): 279–85, https://doi.org/10.2307/585012.

38 **This worry is not an irrational one:** Chalandra M. Bryant, Rand D. Conger, and Jennifer M. Meehan, "The Influence of In-Laws on Change in Marital Success," *Journal of Marriage and Family* 63, no. 3 (2001): 614–26, https://doi.org/10.1111/j.1741-3737.2001.00614.x.

41 **As the sociologist Jacqueline Angel points out:** Jacqueline L. Angel, *Inheritance in Contemporary America: The Social Dimensions of Giving Across Generations* (Baltimore: Johns Hopkins University Press, 2008).

41 **a will may specify:** Marlene S. Stum, "Families and Inheritance Decisions: Examining Non-titled Property Transfers," *Journal of Family and Economic Issues* 21, no. 2 (2000): 177–202, https://doi.org/10.1023/A:1009478019537.

47 **In a series of studies:** J. Jill Suitor et al., "Intergenerational Relations in Later-Life Families," in *Handbook of Sociology of Aging*, ed. Richard A. Settersten and Jacqueline L. Angel (New York: Springer, 2011), 161–78.

47 **We specifically studied estrangement:** Megan Gilligan, J. Jill Suitor, and Karl Pillemer, "Estrangement Between Mothers and Adult Children: The Role of Norms and Values," *Journal of Marriage and Family* 77, no. 4 (2015): 908–20, https://doi.org/10.1111/jomf.12207.

50 **The psychologist John Gottman:** John M. Gottman and Nan Silver, *The Seven Principles for Making Marriage Work: A Practical Guide from the Country's Foremost Relationship Expert* (New York: Harmony, 2015).

53 **Our narratives, in turn, help guide:** Robyn Fivush, *Family Narratives and the Development of an Autobiographical Self: Social and Cultural Perspectives on Autobiographical Memory* (New York: Routledge, 2019).

Chapter 3: "It Never Stops Hurting": Living in a Rift

55 **We hear reports that traditional family bonds:** Timothy P. Carney, "Failing Families," *Washington Examiner*, June 26, 2018, https://www.washingtonexaminer.com/opinion/american-culture-is-moving-into-a-post-family-era.

56 **Researchers at the respected Pew Memorial Trust:** "Parenting in America," Pew Research Center, last modified December 17, 2015, https://www.pewsocialtrends.org/2015/12/17/1-the-american-family-today/.

57 **As the neuroscientist Matthew Lieberman puts it:** Jill Suttie, "Why Are We So Wired to Connect?," review of "Social: Why Our Brains Are Wired to Connect," by Matthew D. Lieberman, *Greater Good Magazine*, December 2, 2013, https://greatergood.berkeley.edu/article/item/why_are_we_so_wired_to_connect.

58 **It occurs in situations where demands are unrelenting:** "Stress: The Different Kinds of Stress," American Psychological Association, accessed February 5, 2020, https://www.apa.org/helpcenter/stress-kinds.

62 **When people to whom they are attached:** R. Chris Fraley, "Adult Attachment Theory and Research: A Brief Overview," University of Illinois, last modified 2018, http://labs.psychology.illinois.edu/~rcfraley/attachment.htm.

62-3 **Attachment figures who play these roles:** Victor G. Cicirelli, "Attachment Theory in Old Age: Protection of the Attached Figure," in *Parent-Child Relations Throughout Life*, ed. Karl Pillemer and Kathleen McCartney (Hillsdale, NJ: Erlbaum Associates, 1991), 49–66.

65 **when people lose an attached figure:** John Bowlby and Colin Murray Parkes, "Separation and Loss Within the Family," in *The Child in His Family*, ed. E. James Anthony and Cyrille Koupernik (New York: Wiley, 1970), 197–216.

66 **The psychologist George Slavich has studied:** George M. Slavich et al., "Black Sheep Get the Blues: A Psychobiological Model of Social Rejection and Depression," *Neuroscience and Biobehavioral Reviews* 35, no. 1 (2010): 39–45, https://doi.org/10.1016/j.neubiorev.2010.01.003.

66 **The intentional, active severing of personal ties:** George M. Slavich et al., "Targeted Rejection Predicts Hastened Onset of Major Depression," *Journal of Social and Clinical Psychology* 28, no. 2 (2009): 223–43, https://doi.org/10.1521/jscp.2009.28.2.223.

68 **rejection highlights our isolation:** Guy Winch, "10 Surprising Facts About Rejection," *Psychology Today*, last modified July 3, 2013, https://www.psychologytoday.com/us/blog/the-squeaky-wheel/201307/10-surprising-facts-about-rejection.

69 **stress of ambiguous loss:** Pauline Boss, "Ambiguous Loss Theory: Challenges for Scholars and Practitioners," *Family Relations* 56, no. 2 (2007): 105–10, https://doi.org/10.1111/j.1741-3729.2007.00444.x.

73-4 these lines from the poem "For Grief" by John O'Donohue: John O'Donohue, "For Grief," in *To Bless the Space Between Us: A Book of Blessings* (New York: Doubleday, 2008), 117–19.

Chapter 4: Collateral Damage

83 Studies have also found that negative themes persist: Daniel S. Hubler et al., "The Intergenerational Transmission of Financial Stress and Relationship Outcomes," *Marriage and Family Review* 52, no. 4 (2016): 373–91, https://doi .or/10.1080/01494929.2015.1100695.

84 Murray Bowen, a psychiatrist, conducted: "About Murray Bowen," Bowen Center for the Study of the Family, accessed February 5, 2020, https://thebowen center.org/theory/murray-bowen/.

84 As Victoria Harrison: "The Family Diagram and Family Research," Center for the Study of Natural Systems and the Family, accessed February 5, 2020, https:// www.csnsf.org/the-family-diagram-family-research/.

91 Research shows that the closer we are to someone: Cameron Anderson, Dachner Keltner, and Oliver P. John, "Emotional Convergence Between People over Time," *Journal of Personality and Social Psychology* 84, no. 5 (2003): 1054–68, https://doi.org/10.1037/0022-3514.84.5.1054.

91 Studies demonstrate that we experience emotional contagion: Joan K. Monin and Richard Schulz, "Interpersonal Effects of Suffering in Older Adult Caregiving Relationships," *Psychology and Aging* 24, no. 3 (2009): 681–95, https://doi.org /10.1037/a0016355.

Chapter 5: Why Reconcile?

108 Usually, we think of regret: Kin Fai Ellick Wong and Jessica Y. Y. Kwong, "The Role of Anticipated Regret in Escalation of Commitment," *Journal of Applied Psychology* 92, no. 2 (2007): 545–54, https://doi.org/10.1037/0021-9010.92.2.545.

108 "teach us to number our days": 1 Psalms 90:12 (NIV).

118 "transtheoretical model" of behavior change: James O. Prochaska and Wayne F. Velicer, "The Transtheoretical Model of Health Behavior Change," *American Journal of Health Promotion* 12, no. 1 (1997): 38–48, https://doi.org/10.4278 /0890-1171-12.1.38.

Chapter 6: Volcanic Events

126 Colleen Harmeling and her colleagues: Colleen M. Harmeling et al., "Transformational Relationship Events," *Journal of Marketing* 79, no. 5 (2015): 39–62, https://doi.org/10.1509/jm.15.0105.

127 negative relationship events have a particularly powerful impact: Leslie A. Baxter and Lauren-Ashley Buchanan, "Relational Turning Points," in *The International Encyclopedia of Interpersonal Communication*, ed. Charles R. Berger and Michael E. Roloff (Malden, MA: Wiley Blackwell, 2016), https://doi.org /10.1002/9781118540190.wbeic018.

127 because estrangement events are strongly emotional: Dorthe Berntsen and David C. Rubin, "When a Trauma Becomes a Key to Identity: Enhanced Integration of Trauma Memories Predicts Posttraumatic Stress Disorder Symptoms," *Applied Cognitive Psychology* 21, no. 4 (2007): 417–31, https://doi.org/10.1002/acp.1290.

127 They define "angry rumination" as: Thomas F. Denson, "The Multiple Systems Model of Angry Rumination," *Personality and Social Psychology Review* 17, no. 2 (2013): 103–23, https://doi.org/10.1177/1088868312467086.

132 In a large interview study: Karl Pillemer, *30 Lessons for Living: Tried and True Advice from the Wisest Americans* (New York: Hudson Street Press, 2012).

135 offer short-term mediation: Justin R. Corbett and Wendy E. H. Corbett, *The State of Community Mediation* (Kentucky: National Association for Community Mediation, 2011), https://www.researchgate.net/profile/Justin_Corbett /publication/256016882_The_State_of_Community_Mediation_2011/links /5d795002299bf1cb8099724f/The-State-of-Community-Mediation-2011.pdf

138 rethink the narrative of the volcanic event: William Borden, "Narrative Perspectives in Psychosocial Intervention Following Adverse Life Events," *Social Work* 37, no. 2 (1992): 135–41, https://doi.org/10.1093/sw/37.2.135.

138 going beyond just remembering an event: Nic M. Weststrate et al., "'It Was the Best Worst Day of My Life': Narrative Content, Structure, and Process in Wisdom-Fostering Life Event Memories," *Journals of Gerontology: Series B: Psychological Sciences and Social Sciences* 73, no. 8 (2018): 1359–73, https://doi .org/10.1093/geronb/gby005.

Chapter 7: Let Go of the Past

141 The past is never dead: William Faulkner, *Requiem for a Nun* (New York: Vintage, 2012), 73.

148 psychologist Robyn Fivush puts it succinctly: Robyn Fivush and Natalie Merrill, "An Ecological Systems Approach to Family Narratives," *Memory Studies* 9, no. 3 (2016): 305–14, https://doi.org/10.1177/1750698016645264.

Chapter 8: Taking Responsibility

164 "taking on the role of the other": Mitchell Aboulafia, "George Herbert Mead," *The Stanford Encyclopedia of Philosophy*, ed. Edward N. Zalta, (Stanford, CA: Stanford University, 2020), https://plato.stanford.edu/archives/fall2016/entries/mead/.

166 **Research suggests that we possess a mental system:** Robert A. Josephs et al., "Protecting the Self from the Negative Consequences of Risky Decisions," *Journal of Personality and Social Psychology* 62, no. 1 (1992): 26–37, https://doi.org /10.1037/0022-3514.62.1.26.

167 **Instead of actually confronting the problem:** A. David Nussbaum and Carol S. Dweck, "Defensiveness Versus Remediation: Self-Theories and Modes of Self-Esteem Maintenance," *Personality and Social Psychology Bulletin* 34, no. 5 (2008): 599–612, https://doi.org/10.1177/0146167207312960.

176 **Empathy is also a cognitive skill:** Chun Bun Lam, Anna R. Solmeyer, and Susan M. McHale, "Sibling Relationships and Empathy Across the Transition to Adolescence," *Journal of Youth and Adolescence* 41, no. 12 (2012): 1657–70, https://doi.org/10.1007/s10964-012-9781-8.

176 **conflicts occur because each person:** Céline Hinnekens et al., "Empathic Accuracy and Observed Demand Behavior in Couples," *Frontiers in Psychology* vii (2016): 1370, https://doi.org/10.3389/fpsyg.2016.01370.

176 **In any intimate relationship, conflicts occur:** Nicholas Epley and Eugene M. Caruso, "Perspective Taking: Misstepping into Others' Shoes," in *Handbook of Imagination and Mental Simulation*, ed. Keith D. Markman, William M. P. Klein, and Julie A. Suhr (New York: Psychology Press, 2008), 297–311.

180 **"step back to move forward":** Jiyoung Park, Özlem Ayduk, and Ethan Kross, "Stepping Back to Move Forward: Expressive Writing Promotes Self-distancing," *Emotion* 16, no. 3 (2016): 349–64, https://doi.org/10.1037/emo0000121.

180 **Eli Finkel and his colleagues:** Eli J. Finkel et al. "A Brief Intervention to Promote Conflict Reappraisal Preserves Marital Quality Over Time." *Psychological Science* 24, no. 8 (2013): 1595–1601.

181 **seek out people who are very much like them:** Peggy A. Thoits, "Mechanisms Linking Social Ties and Support to Physical and Mental Health," *Journal of Health and Social Behavior* 52, no. 2 (2011): 145–61.

Chapter 9: Changing Expectations

189 **The author Brené Brown states:** Brené Brown, *Rising Strong* (New York: Random House, 2015), p. 139.

192 **strive for independence and autonomy:** Yijung K. Kim and Jeffrey E. Stokes, "Intergenerational Stake," in *Encyclopedia of Gerontology and Population Aging (Living Edition)*, ed. Danan Gu and Matthew E. Dupre (Springer, 2019), https:// link.springer.com/referenceworkentry/10.1007%2F978-3-319-69892-2_894-1; Kira S. Birditt et al., "Extending the Intergenerational Stake Hypothesis: Evidence of an Intra-individual Stake and Implications for Well-Being," *Journal of Marriage and Family* 77, no. 4 (2015): 877–88, https://doi.org/10.1111/jomf.12203.

201 They often become happier: Laura L. Carstensen, Derek M. Isaacowitz, and Susan T. Charles, "Taking Time Seriously: A Theory of Socioemotional Selectivity," *American Psychologist* 54, no. 3 (1999): 165–81, https://doi.org/10.1037/0003-066X.54.3.165.

Chapter 10: Setting Boundaries

211 humans find ambivalence to be highly aversive: Karl Pillemer and J. Jill Suitor. "Explaining Mothers' Ambivalence Toward Their Adult Children," *Journal of Marriage and Family* 64, no. 3 (2002): 602–13.

214 As Peter Titelman: Peter Titelman, *Emotional Cutoff: Bowen Family Systems Theory Perspectives* (London: Routledge, 2014), 23.

228 I turn for insight to Robert Frost: Robert Frost, *Selected Poems* (New York: Holt, Rinehart and Winston, 1963), 23.

Chapter 11: One Last Chance

247 A discipline is a developmental pathway: Peter Senge, *The Fifth Discipline* (New York: Doubleday, 2006).

Appendix: How the Study Was Conducted

254 nationally syndicated advice columnist Amy Dickinson: Amy Dickinson, "Ask Amy: Woman's Partner Hates Her Family," *Chicago Tribune*, October 18, 2018, https://www.chicagotribune.com/lifestyles/ask-amy/ct-ask-amy-ae-1018-story.html.

256 Such online surveys are faster: Miliaikeala S. J. Heen, Joel D. Lieberman, and Terance D. Miethe, *A Comparison of Different Online Sampling Approaches for Generating National Samples* (Center for Crime and Justice Policy at University of Nevada, Las Vegas, 2014), https://www.unlv.edu/sites/default/files/page_files/27/ComparisonDifferentOnlineSampling.pdf.

256 possible bias created by self-selection: Ron D. Hays, Honghu Liu, and Arie Kapteyn, "Use of Internet Panels to Conduct Surveys," *Behavior Research Methods* 47, no. 3 (2015): 685–90, https://doi.org/10.3758/s13428-015-0617-9.

INDEX